Bureaucracy and democracy

Also by Eva Etzioni-Halevy

Political Manipulation and Administrative Power
Social Change: The Advent and Maturation of Modern Society
Political Culture in Israel (with Rina Shapira)

Bureaucracy and democracy

A political dilemma

Eva Etzioni-Halevy

Routledge & Kegan Paul
London, Boston, Melbourne and Henley

First published in 1983
by Routledge & Kegan Paul plc
39 Store Street, London WC1E 7DD,
9 Park Street, Boston, Mass. 02108, USA,
296 Beaconsfield Parade, Middle Park,
Melbourne, 3206, Australia, and
Broadway House, Newtown Road,
Henley-on-Thames, Oxon RG9 1EN
Set in Press Roman 10/12 by Columns, Reading
and printed in Great Britain by
Hartnoll Print, Bodmin, Cornwall

Library of Congress Cataloging in Publication Data

Etzioni-Halevy, Eva.

Bureaucracy and democracy.
Bibliography: p.
Includes index.
1. Bureaucracy. 2. Democracy. I. Title.
JF1411.E89 1983   306.2   83-9498

ISBN 0-7100-9573-2

To my daughter Tamar,
with love

Contents

Preface

This book presents a general overview of the relationship between bureaucracy and the politics of democracy intended primarily for students of sociology, political science and public administration. It is designed to help guide students as painlessly as possible through the maze of classical and modern theories on this topic, to give them some basic information on the historical developments in this area, and to present them with case studies on the actual relationship between bureaucrats and politicians in democratic societies.

While it is an overview, the book also presents my own views. I therefore hope that it may be worth a glimpse by scholars in the field as well, if only for the purpose of stimulating some of the critique and controversy on which the social sciences so evidently thrive. I further hope that journalists, bureaucrats and members of the general public who take an interest in bureaucracy may also find it helpful.

The intent to reach such a diverse audience entails a diversity of obligations. A well-known observer of bureaucracy, Brian Chapman (1961, p. 20),[1] once wrote: 'Bureaucracy is like sin: we all know something about it, but only those who practise it enjoy it.' In this book I hope to fulfil some of the obligations towards the audience by showing that not only the *practice* but also the *study* of bureaucracy can be enjoyable. Or at least, that it need not be unenjoyable.

In the first place, I have set myself the task of showing that the study of bureaucracy need not be unduly difficult. To this purpose I have made special efforts to minimize professional jargon and to express all ideas as simply and concisely as possible. I have worked on the assumption that ideas that cannot be expressed clearly are themselves muddled and therefore are not worth expressing at all.

Secondly, I have set myself the task of showing that the study of bureaucracy need not be confusing. It has been claimed that theories of organization are in a state of disarray; that, in fact, 'organization theory is rather like a flying saucer — never seen in the same place twice' (Parker *et al*. 1972, p. 89). In this book, which deals with state bureaucracy only, I hope to show that, in that more limited area at least, it is possible to introduce into the multitude of theories a certain pleasing order.

Finally, I have set myself the task of showing that the study of bureaucracy need not be tedious. The common image of bureaucracy may well be one of uncommon boredom. But in this book I hope to show that reality is quite different: that indeed the relations among bureaucrats themselves and between bureaucrats and politicians are rather intriguing, and therefore that case studies illustrating such relations will be quite colourful.

I can only conclude with the well-worn but ever-applicable phrase that it must be left to the reader to decide to what extent I have been successful.

Acknowledgments

The work of the social sciences thrives on critique and controversy, and this book is no exception. It has profited greatly from the critical comments of Mr W.G. Craven, Ms Desley Deacon, Dr John Higley, Mr Jim Kitay, Mr Richard Lipscombe, Dr William D. Rubinstein, Dr Marian Sawer, Mr Mark Shadur and Professor W.E. Willmott, to all of whom I am deeply grateful. My special thanks go to Mr Fergus J. Gibbons, Dr John Hart, and again to Mr Jim Kitay and Dr Marian Sawer for providing material and information vital to the creation of this book. I am also greatly indebted to my colleagues in the Department of Sociology, The Faculties, The Australian National University, and especially to the Head of Department, Dr Robert G. Cushing, for their professional and personal support.

Finally, I would like to express my gratitude to Ms Harriet H. Halliday for her excellent work in editing several of the book's chapters, to Mrs Ann Illy for her most helpful and unfailingly cheerful research assistance, to Mrs Julie Myers, Mrs Zeta Hall and Mrs Sandra Kruck for their skilful typing of the (all-too-frequently-illegible) manuscript and to Mrs Herta Smith for her kind help in co-ordinating the effort.

E. Etzioni-Halevy
Canberra

Introduction

Are Western democracies[1] in crisis? This question is being asked with increasing frequency by social scientists and other observers. Those who believe a crisis is imminent attribute it to anything from the rise in oil prices, inflation and unemployment to the internal contradictions of capitalism. Those who oppose the idea point to the growing affluence and extensive welfare systems of Western democracies. They add that democracy has had a turbulent history from its very inception and that the claim of an oncoming crisis could have been made with greater validity, say, a hundred and fifty or even fifty years ago.

Of course, the term 'crisis' is rather vague, and this controversy raises (but does not answer) the question: when does a mere 'problem' turn into an ominous 'crisis'? Against the background of this general debate, this book addresses itself to the more modest question of whether Western democracies are faced, if not with a crisis, at least with some formidable problems through internal contradictions in the democratic political structure itself, especially those created by the role of bureaucracy in it.

As has been observed, ours is an administered society and the state bureaucracy in charge of this administration has become one of modern society's most prominent institutions. Some observers have argued that by now bureaucracy has passed its peak. An increasing rate of change and a more uncertain environment have made bureaucratic structures obsolete. They are therefore about to give way to other, more flexible types of organization. Thus, Warren Bennis wrote an article in which he predicted the coming death of bureaucracy (1968).[2] Just two years later, though, he wrote another article entitled 'A funny thing happened on the way to the future' (1970), in which he substantially revised his previous forecast.

Sociologists should know by now that funny things always happen

1

on the way to the future. However, as far as one can make out at present, there is no doubt that bureaucracy is still very much with us, and that far from approaching its coming death, it has become even more pervasive in recent years. The question is, therefore, whether this growing pervasiveness poses a threat to democracy and, if so, whether the threat has recently increased.

Various theorists have addressed themselves to these issues either directly or by implication. Some (e.g. the pluralists) have argued that bureaucracy's growing pervasiveness has made it more vulnerable rather than more powerful. Others (e.g. the 'technocrats' and some Marxists) have argued that bureaucracy's power has in fact grown, and this is the view adopted in this book as well. Most pluralists maintain (by implication) that bureaucratic power has not jeopardized democracy while the technocrats and the Marxists maintain that it has.[3] But none of them has suggested that the growing power of bureaucracy has actually favoured democracy or is, at any rate, indispensable for it. That, in part, is the argument presented in this book.

This argument holds that bureaucracy generates a dilemma for democracy: a powerful, independent, non-politicized bureaucracy poses a threat for democracy, and yet is also indispensable for it. By the same token, democracy generates a dilemma for bureaucracy: under the present, rather inconsistent democratic rules, bureaucracy is expected to be both independent and subservient, both politicized and non-politicized at one and the same time. There is thus an uneasy, though symbiotic, co-existence between bureaucracy and democracy, or even a paradoxical or self-contradictory relationship between the two: bureaucracy is necessary for democracy, yet is also a constant source of tension, friction and conflict in it. Indeed, it seems that the strains bureaucracy creates for democracy grow more salient the more powerful bureaucracy becomes.

In the past, bureaucratic power has grown through increased state intervention. This intervention was in part a response to an evolving conception among the public which increasingly saw the state as responsible for its (the public's) welfare and in part a response to the rising expectations for ever-higher levels of such welfare. It has also been a response to various downturns of the capitalist economy, which have from time to time jeopardized that welfare (the New Deal of the 1930s in the United States would be a prime example). Hence, the recent difficulties in Western economies, where relatively high unemployment and inflation have been combined with relatively low economic growth, would seem to indicate a growing gap between the public's expectations from the system and what the system is actually able to offer. This points to greater public demand for even greater bureaucratic intervention to close these gaps.

Ostensibly, there has recently been a reversal in the trend of public opinion. People now seem to balk at big government and the ever-increasing taxation it entails. In several countries anti-statist movements have gained influence. In the United States, both Presidents Carter and Reagan were aided in their election campaigns by promising their electors cuts in government spending, and similar promises were made by the Prime Ministers of Britain and Australia. However, when the crunch comes, it is doubtful that the public would be willing to pay the price for such cuts in terms of reduced government services. Thus it seems more likely than not that in the long run bureaucracies will continue to swell and further increase their power and, with it, the problems they pose for democracy.

In recent years there has been an attempt to countervail this growth of bureaucracy's power by more effective restraints designed to curb its possible maltreatment of individuals. These restraints have taken the form of various types of legislation (e.g. for freedom of information on bureaucratic action), parliamentary committees, administrative tribunals and ombudsmen. These mechanisms have indeed filled important functions in protecting the individual from the bureaucracy. However, they have acted as restraint only on the *abuse* of bureaucratic power not on the *use* of bureaucratic power as such nor on the continuous growth of that power.

Thus the problems that the growth of bureaucratic power poses for democracy are not amenable to a ready-made solution. The present analysis can do no more than indicate the need to search for one.

It is customary for social scientists to label each other by trying to fit one another's work neatly into some 'school of thought'. To facilitate this task for the reader of this book, I declare that the perspective adopted herein is not Marxist. I have found many Marxist ideas of great value; others, however, are arguable. For instance, Marxists have asked if ownership is the source of power in society and have answered in the affirmative. As Lindblom (1977, p. 201) put it, however, this is a 'good question but poor answer'. For ownership, or the control of assets, is itself dependent on political power and, implicitly, on coercion. Hence I have adopted Weber's insights and a modified elitist perspective as guidelines for the present analysis. In accordance with these guidelines I consider political power as crucial in its own right rather than as an offshoot of ownership or economic power and I view political and bureaucratic elites who wield such power as basically serving their own interests rather than those of property-holding classes.

It seems strange that Marxist analyses, concerned with economic power, are widely considered progressive and radical, while elitist analyses, concerned with political power, are usually considered conservative. Contrary to this view, I suggest that political-bureaucratic domination may be no less exploitative than economic domination and, hence, that exposing manipulation by state elites is no less avant-garde than uncovering the expropriation of surplus value. It is true that Marxists set as their goal the elimination of economic (class) exploitation while elitists do not hold the parallel goal of the elimination of political (elite) domination and indeed do not believe in the possibility of such an elimination. But I suggest that curbing elite power and making it subject to publicly monitored democratic regulation is a no-less-progressive goal.

It may be argued, from a Marxist viewpoint, that the details of how political-bureaucratic elites exert their power are not really important. In any case these elites promote or preserve inequality and further the advantages of the advantaged or, in Marxist terms, the ruling class. In contrast, the assumption guiding the present discussion is that the manner in which political and bureaucratic elites exert their power is of the first order of importance for the preservation and promotion of democracy. And democracy, in turn, is worth preserving and promoting as it is the most effective framework for decreasing political inequalities and enhancing political freedom. Democracy is also worth preserving as the most effective framework in which the struggle for decreasing *economic* inequalities can take place. Certainly, many of the political struggles since the emergence of Western democracies have revolved precisely on this issue.

The guidelines for bureaucratic action in relation to politics and those of political action in relation to bureaucracy are thus highly significant for, as US Supreme Court Justice Felix Frankfurter has said,[4] 'the history of American freedom is, in no small measure, the history of procedure', and this holds no less for other Western countries. Hence the fact that bureaucratic-political procedures are subject to strains and incompatibilities, that bureaucracy itself is a constant source of strain for democracy, is highly significant as well.

It has been argued (Dye and Zeigler, 1975) that the best safeguard for democracy is to be found in the values of elites, in their willingness to adhere to democratic rules of the game, in the normative and procedural restraint that they are willing to put on their own power. At the same time, democracies are exceedingly fragile, beset by internal strains and contradictory requirements, of which the dilemmas posed by bureaucracy are prominent examples. These inconsistencies present both political and bureaucratic elites with the constant temptation of slipping into less regulated ways of wielding power, of becoming less democratic as they go along. The task is therefore to preserve the regulation of elite power already achieved and to press for the further curbing of that power. This must be done by making the democratic rules for elite action clearer and more consistent and by making the elites' closer adherence to such rules pay off as part of their struggle for power. This will not bring about the utopia of an eliteless or a classless society. But a brief glance towards certain societies (which shall remain unnamed) in which such regulation is totally or partially absent shows that it is exceedingly important in making life in an elite-dominated society more tolerable. This is the perspective that permeates the present analysis.

Plan of the book

This book is designed so as to furnish a general overview of the relationship between bureaucracy and the politics of democracy, and at the same time develop the above mentioned argument from an elitist-democratic perspective. Accordingly, the first part of the book presents a critical survey of the major classical and contemporary theories on the relationship between bureaucracy and the politics of democracy (chapters 1-6). It concludes with the development of the aforementioned argument in the context of its theoretical antecedents (chapter 7).

The second part of the book marshals support for this argument by presenting an overview of the development of bureaucracies in Western democratic societies and of their relationship with politics (chapters 8-12). It then furnishes a series of case studies on the relationship between bureaucracy and the politics of democracy and the strains and conflicts emerging out of these relations (chapter 13). Finally, in the Conclusion, the threads of argument are drawn together, the problems that bureaucracy poses for democracy are summarized, and some possible solutions are critically examined.

Part I
Theoretical perspectives

This part of the book presents an overview of classical theories (chapters 1-2) and modern theories (chapters 3-6) on the relationship between bureaucracy and politics. The overview is designed to serve several purposes: firstly, to supply students with some basic knowledge, help guide them through this field, and make them privy to the intellectual debates going on in it. Secondly, it is designed to make students aware of the significance, contribution as well as shortcomings of each school of thought or theory, and thus stimulate them to take sides in the intellectual debate. Finally, the overview is meant to provide the theoretical background and lead up to the theses developed in the last chapter (chapter 7) of this part of the book.

Chapter 1

Classical theories: Marx, Michels, Mosca[1]

Interest in bureaucracy and its relation to democracy predates the advent of sociology as a discipline. The term bureaucracy itself is usually attributed to the physiocrat and political economist Vincent de Gournay, who is said to have coined it in 1745. It was originally used pejoratively for government by officials and for excessive official power. In early nineteenth-century Europe, the bureaucracy was often the target of ridicule for its alleged laziness and inefficiency, for the high-handed manner of its officials and for its tendency to over-regulate social life and abuse power. Much of bureaucracy's work was thought to be self-generated as well as oppressive and debilitating for the rest of society. Honoré de Balzac, for instance, referred to bureaucracy as a gigantic power set in motion by dwarfs; Frédéric Le Play, for his part, saw it as a diseased form of administration, whereby officials are accountable to no one and citizens are turned into children. This derogatory view was also held by Marx, the first among the founding fathers of sociology to make a significant contribution to the analysis of bureaucracy.

The ideas of Karl Marx (1818-83)

Bureaucracy, the state and the ruling class
Marx first developed his ideas on bureaucracy through a critique of Hegel in his essay, *Critique of Hegel's 'Philosophy of Right'* (written in 1843). For Hegel, the state represented the general interest as against civil society, a collection of groups, corporations and estates, which represented particular and clashing interests. The role of bureaucracy was to mediate between the two. Marx accepted Hegel's distinction between the state and civil society but modified its content. For him,

the state did not represent the general interest any more than civil society did, and this held for bureaucracy as part of the state as well. The bureaucracy purports to advance the common welfare, but under the cloak of universality it actually furthers its own. Its apparent idealism is but a cloak for its materialist ends. The bureaucracy can mask its true role through the secrecy that shrouds its actions and through the creation of special myths which sanctify them. These, moreover, are applied not only to outsiders but to insiders as well. In this manner, bureaucracy manipulates the world as well as its own members:

> The bureaucracy has the being of the state . . . in its possession; it
> is its private property. The general spirit of the bureaucracy is the
> secret, the mystery, preserved inwardly by means of the hierarchy
> and externally as a closed corporation. . . . But at the very heart of
> the bureaucracy, this spiritualism turns into a crass materialism. . . .
> As far as the individual bureaucrat is concerned, the end of the state
> becomes his private end: a pursuit of higher posts, the building of a
> career. (1970, p. 47)

By 1845 Marx's theory, generally known as historical materialism, had been fully developed and his ideas on the state, especially the capitalist state, had been more clearly crystallized. In *The German Ideology* (written in 1845-6), Marx came to regard the state as 'nothing more than the form of organization which the bourgeois necessarily adopt . . . for the mutual guarantee of their property and interests' (1969c, p. 77).

At that stage he thought that the state may have a certain independence, but only where the traditional estates still exist, where they have not been superseded by modern classes, and where no one section of the population can therefore achieve dominance over any other. This situation prevailed in Germany at the time, but only for a transitional period. Once the transitional stage is passed and the bourgeoisie has established itself as the ruling class the state loses its independence and becomes nothing more than that class's representative, or as Marx put it most concisely in the *Manifesto of the Communist Party* (written in 1848): 'The executive of the modern State is but a committee for managing the common affairs of the whole bourgeoisie' (Marx and Engels, 1969, pp. 110-11).

The *coup d'état* of Napoleon III in 1851 in France challenged these assertions, for through it the political power of the French bourgeoisie was clearly eroded, while the power of the state – a dictatorship based on a bureaucratic machine – was clearly overwhelming. In *The Eighteenth Brumaire of Louis Bonaparte* (written in 1852) Marx tried to reconcile this reality with his conception of the state.

Under the absolute monarchy, during the French revolution, and under Napoleon I, Marx argued, the bureaucracy had been the means of preparing for the class rule of the bourgeoisie; under the Restoration and under the parliamentary republic, it has become the instrument of this rule. Only under the second Bonaparte (Napoleon III) did the state seem to gain independence of the bourgeoisie. The bourgeoisie had built up the power of the state in order to enhance its own power. It now seemed as if the servant had turned against the master. This had taken place because the bourgeoisie's economic interests had to be secured by a strong state, but subsequently the bourgeoisie was too weak to control the state it had strengthened.

This state of affairs, however, was merely an apparent contradiction to Marx's basic conception. For the bourgeoisie only gave up political power to secure its economic powers; it only gave up its crown to serve its purse. Bonaparte's own power rested on the fact that he had broken the political power of the bourgeoisie while protecting its material power. 'But by protecting its material power, he generates its political power anew' (1969d, pp. 484-5).

While the Bonapartist regime, and the bureaucracy by which it ruled, protected the bourgeoisie, they were based to a large extent on the small-holding peasantry, the most numerous class in France. This class comprised people who were isolated from each other and so were unable to organize. They were therefore easily dominated, providing the ideal basis for bureaucratic power. By representing different classes, Bonaparte's government thus set itself contradictory tasks, which explains 'the confused groping about which seeks now to win, now to humiliate first one class and then another . . .' (1969d, p. 485). In any case, Bonapartism and its bureaucracy were merely a transitional response to a crisis. Soon the small-holding peasantry would be undermined and the bureaucracy based on it would collapse as well.

In *The Civil War in France* (written in 1871) Marx developed some of these ideas somewhat further. As he now saw it, the French bourgeoisie had attempted to augment its power through the parliamentary republic, with Louis Napoleon as its president. At that time, they had used the state power mercilessly 'as the national war engine of capital against labour' (1969a, p. 219). To do so, however, they were bound not only to invest the executive with increased powers of repression but also to divest their own power stronghold – the National Assembly – of its means of defence against the executive. This made possible the transition to the Second Empire of Napoleon III, and with it the erosion of the bourgeoisie's political power. But once the bourgeoisie was freed from political care it attained unprecedented economic prosperity; this led, eventually, to the recapture of its political power as well.

In sum, then, Marx did not see the state (which included the bureaucracy) as a passive tool of the ruling class. For certain, limited periods, the state even seemed to gain autonomy from it. This was so, especially under the dictatorial regime of the Second Bonaparte, when the state and its bureaucracy accummulated considerable power over all classes. But even then, the state still promoted the interests of the ruling class.

Bureaucracy and democracy

Marx's analysis of the Second Empire in France shows that he recognized different forms of the modern state, especially the difference between dictatorship and what came to be known as 'bourgeois democracy'. Marx was not enthusiastic about such democracy, and in *The Class Struggles in France* (written in 1848-50) he denounced the democratic republic of 1848 as nothing but a purely developed form of bourgeois rule. Nevertheless, he thought, it had some advantages because it deprived the bourgeoisie of absolute power and of the absolute assurance of its power:

> The classes whose social slavery the constitution is to perpetuate, proletariat, peasantry, petty bourgeoisie, it puts in possession of political power through universal suffrage. And from the class whose old social power it sanctions, the bourgeoisie, it withdraws the political guarantees of that power. It forces the political rule of the bourgeoisie into democratic conditions, which at every moment help the hostile classes to victory, and jeopardise the very foundations of bourgeois society. (1969b, pp. 235-6)

The virtues of democracy are evident especially in comparison to authoritarian regimes such as that of the Bonapartist state. In *The Eighteenth Brumaire of Louis Bonaparte*, Marx noted that this regime was distinguished by an extreme concentration of executive power, by an overwhelming military organization and by an immense bureaucracy that stifled the life of civil society. All parts of civil society were now made the object of bureaucratic intrusion. The bureaucracy had become an 'appalling parasitic body, which enmeshes the body of French society like a net and chokes all its pores' (1969d, p. 477). Thus, in Marx's view, democracy was valuable not only because it was inversely related to bourgeois power but also because it was inversely related to the concentration of state power, and with it to the concentration (or over-concentration) of power in the bureaucracy.

However, the bourgeoisie cannot afford to let democracy prevail in the long run, as it would eventually destroy the bourgeoisie's rule. Whenever that rule is really threatened, the bourgeoisie does not hesitate to repudiate universal suffrage. This is precisely what made possible the *coup d'état* of the Second Bonaparte. For this reason, Marx was rather sceptical about the possibility of achieving socialism by democratic means. He thought it conceivable that this would occur in some cases, but he did not expect it to be the common pattern. In most cases, socialism could come about only through a revolution.

After the revolution

It is only after the revolution, and with the advent of a communist society, that true democracy can develop. For only in this society would there be true individual freedom, the abolition of classes, and with it the abolition of the ruling class, which had prevented the realization of democracy in capitalist society. Also, it is only in this post-revolutionary society that the state that represents the interests of the ruling class would wither away, and with it, oppressive bureaucracy would wither away as well.

Marx never clarified what this 'withering away' would entail. 'He did not express himself any more clearly about the dismantling of bureaucracy in the socialist state than about the withering away of the state in general' (Eisenstadt and Von Beyme, 1972, p. 332). Apparently, what he had in mind was that bureaucracy, like the state in general, would lose its coercive and exploitative character, and that its functions would gradually be absorbed into society at large. The administration of public affairs would not disappear, but it would now be carried out in a democratic manner: administrative tasks would be everyone's concern; all citizens would be administered and administrators at one and the same time. This would all be part of the general transformation in communist society, in which the division of labour would wither away as well, and in which each person would be free to do one thing today and another thing tomorrow.[2]

The ideas of Gaetano Mosca (1858-1941)

Marx dealt with the problems of bureaucracy mainly to the extent that they coincided or overlapped with other problems, such as those of class exploitation, which was his primary concern. In contrast, Mosca treated bureaucracy as a central topic of inquiry in its own right and viewed the bureaucratic order as a distinct type of political organization. Also, Marx integrated his thoughts on bureaucracy with a theory of an *economically* dominant (ruling) class. In contrast, Mosca developed his ideas on bureaucracy as part of a theory on a *politically* dominant (ruling) class.

The nature of the ruling class
In his book *The Ruling Class* (written in 1895, with some later additions) Mosca argues that in all societies — from the simplest to the most advanced — two classes of people appear: a class that rules and a class that is ruled. The first monopolizes political power and enjoys the advantages that power brings, while the second is controlled by the first. The ruling class may be a group of warriors, a group of religious functionaries, a landholding aristocracy, a wealth-holding or a knowledge-holding class, or some combination of these. In any case it is its political power that sets it apart from the rest of society.

The ruling class is always less numerous than the class which it rules. According to democratic theory majorities rule minorities. In fact, however (writes Mosca), minorities rule majorities. Because they are minorities they have the ability to organize themselves, while the masses remain unorganized. The political domination of an organized minority over an unorganized majority is inevitable. When a ruling class is deposed, there will be another one to take its place. Indeed, the whole history of civilization comes down to the struggle between existing ruling classes and their contenders.

Ruling classes never rule merely by brute force; they justify their rule by political formulas, i.e. by abstract principles (such as 'divine right' or 'the sovereignty of the people') which frequently are accepted by those they rule. When ruling classes are vigorous in their capacity to impose their political formulae, to manage society and render a service to it, when they are open to the more talented and ambitious people among the ruled, gradual rejuvenation of the ruling class itself and gradual change and progress in society will take place. But when ruling classes lose their vigour, when they cease to find scope for their capacities, when they can no longer render their previously rendered services or when they become closed to talented and competent outsiders, violent upheavals are likely to take place. These frequently result in the total replacement of the ruling classes. There usually follows a period of rapid innovation in which people from the bottom of the social ladder can easily force their way up. This, in turn, is often followed by a period of crystallization of the new ruling class, which also spells a period of social stability. Thus, the character and structure of the ruling class is of major importance in determining the rate of change and progress in society. It is also important in determining a society's political regime.

The ruling class in the bureaucratic state

There are a few major types of such regimes into which all political entities may be classified — most important among them are the feudal and the bureaucratic. The feudal system is one in which the same members of the ruling class exercise all the governmental functions: the economic, the judicial, the administrative, and the military. In this system too, the state itself is made up of small social aggregates, each of which possesses all the organs required for self-sufficiency. Europe of the Middle Ages offers the most familiar example of such a regime, but there are many others in the past or contemporary history of other people.

The bureaucratic regime is one where there is a greater specialization within the ruling class. There, the various governmental functions have become separated from each other and have become the exclusive domain of distinctive sections of the ruling class. Among these sections are the bureaucracy and the military establishment. Under this type of regime the government conscripts a considerable portion of the social wealth by taxation and uses it to maintain an extensive number of public services and military forces, both of which are manned by large numbers of salaried personnel.

In a bureaucratic state the ruling class exerts more power over those it rules than it does in a feudal state, but the power it wields is less personal. Society is less under the control of an individual personality, more under that of the ruling class as a whole. Egypt and the Roman Empire furnish examples of highly bureaucratized states in antiquity. Later on, with the close of the Middle Ages, feudalism gradually evolved into absolute bureaucratic monarchies in Europe, and this is one of the processes that has most profoundly affected world history.

Bureaucracy and democracy

The absolute bureaucratic state may be regarded as fully and permanently established in Europe in the seventeenth century. In less than a century and a half, however, it was transformed into the modern representative, parliamentary state.

The representative regime does not spell the sovereignty of the people, government by consent of the governed and majority rule as democratic theory would have it. 'What happens in other forms of government — namely, that an organized minority imposes its will on the disorganised majority — happens also and to perfection, whatever the appearance to the contrary, under the representative system' (1939, p. 154). This happens because the only candidates who have any chance of succeeding in elections are those who are championed by organized minorities.

Moreover, the representative system on its own does not even provide adequate curbs on ruling-class power. Elected representatives and assemblies tend to concentrate excessive power in their own hands, in which case the whole government machinery falls prey to their irresponsible tyranny. Government control goes astray under personal and partisan electoral ambitions. The ability of elected representatives to govern well is distorted by their tendency to pursue their own interests, especially those of getting themselves elected, and their tendency to pursue the interests of the party which backs their election. This leads to improper interference of elected representatives in court procedures, in public administration and generally in the distribution of wealth that accrues to the state through taxes and levies. In its more extreme form it leads to the transformation of administrative departments into electioneering agencies and thus to the improper interference of bureaucracies in elections. 'All this gives rise to a shameful and hypocritical traffic in reciprocal indulgences and mutual favors, which is a veritable running sore in most European countries' (1939, pp. 265-6).

Herbert Spencer wrote that the divine right of kings was the great superstition of past ages, and that the divine right of elected assemblies was the great superstition of the present age. According to Mosca, this idea is not wholly mistaken but does not exhaust all aspects of the question, for a representative system has a few things to recommend it as well. Political forces which in an absolute state would remain inert become organized in a representative system and so exert an influence on government. In addition, there are advantages in a system in which all government acts are subject to public discussion. Parliamentary, individual and press liberties serve to call attention to abuses of power.

This forces the ruling classes to take account of mass sentiments and public discontent.

The importance of elected assemblies themselves is that they check and balance the power of those that govern, in particular the bureaucracy, and thus prevent them from becoming omnipotent. The development of the modern representative state from the absolutist state has divided the political class, or the ruling class, into two distinct branches — the one, derived from popular suffrage and the other, from bureaucratic appointment. This has made it possible to distribute political power, and that distribution constitutes the chief contribution of the representative system to the bureaucratic state. In this manner, power limits power, thereby restraining the arbitrariness of the rulers and increasing the liberty of the ruled.

The absolute predominance of any single principle of political organization makes it difficult for diverse social forces to participate in the political process and to counterbalance each other. It therefore leads to despotism. It makes little difference whether this despotism is based on divine right or on ostensible popular sovereignty; in any case it leads to unlimited power and to the abuse of power. The political regime that provides the most liberty is a mixed regime, where different forces curb each other.

It follows that the defects of parliamentary assemblies and the evil effects of their control of power, are mere trifles compared to the harm that would result from abolishing them. The downfall of the democratic system would lead to the violations of justice and liberty 'and those violations would be far more pernicious than any that can be laid to the charge of even the most dishonest of parliamentary governments.' (1939, p. 257). It would inevitably be followed by a bureaucratic, absolute regime. Its chief characteristics would be to eliminate from public life all forces and values except the ones represented in the bureaucracy or to subordinate such forces and values to bureaucratic power. In view of the great perfection of the modern state machine, bureaucracy would shatter all individual and public resistance and not be subject to any restraint whatsoever. The result would be a more powerful and unbearably oppressive despotism than had ever been seen before.

Such a regime would in fact come into being under collectivist socialism or communism. Under this regime, the multiplicity and counterbalancing of political forces would be destroyed, as would private enterprise and individual independence.

Under collectivism, everyone will have to kowtow to the men in the government. They alone can dispense favor, bread, the joy or sorrow of life. One single crushing, all-embracing, all-engrossing tyranny will weigh upon all. The great of the earth will be absolute masters of everything, and the independent word of the man who fears nothing and expects nothing from them will no longer be there to curb their extravagances. . . . The heads of a communist or collectivist republic would control the will of others more tyranically than ever; and since they would be able to distribute privations or favors as they choose, they would have the means to enjoy, perhaps more hypocritically but in no less abundance, all the material pleasures . . . which are now perquisites of the powerful and wealthy. Like these, and even more than these, they would be in a position to degrade the dignity of other men. (1939, pp. 285-6)

The ideas of Robert Michels (1878-1936)

Michels's ideas bring us back from what was, at the time, a hypothetical future to existent reality. He too, was concerned with socialism. His concern, however, revolved not around a future socialist regime but rather around present-day (his own present-day) socialist parties. In addition, he had some (though lesser) interest in the present-day modern state. These two interests were combined in his analysis of bureaucracy and oligarchy.

Bureaucracy in the modern state

According to Michels, bureaucracy is necessary for the existence of the modern state. In his book *Political Parties* (written in 1911) he explains that the modern state needs a large bureaucracy because through it the politically dominant classes secure their domination. For this purpose the state attaches to itself the greatest possible number of interests. It does so by creating numerous positions for officials, i.e. for persons directly dependent on it. Among the citizens there is great demand for such positions. They — especially the better educated middle class whose material existence is insecure — endeavour to find safe positions in it for their offspring. In this manner they hope to shelter them from the play of economic forces. State employment, with the important pension rights attached to it, seems created especially for their needs.

Those middle-class intellectuals who have succeeded in obtaining bureaucratic positions are always ready to undertake the defence of the state that provides them with their livelihood. Those who have not obtained such positions tend to become its sworn enemies. For this reason the state is forced from time to time to open its doors to thousands of new candidates and thus to transform them 'from dangerous adversaries to zealous defenders and partisans' (1915, p. 197). Even so, the state bureaucracy cannot expand as rapidly as the potentially discontented elements of the middle class; the demand for bureaucratic positions is always greater than the supply. In this manner an antagonistic 'intellectual proletariat' is created. In part, its members also assume the leadership of the revolutionary parties of the real proletariat.

While the bureaucracy is necessary for the stability of the state, it is at the same time becoming less and less compatible with the welfare of the public. For bureaucrats, especially lower ranking ones, are the sworn enemy of individual liberty and initiative. Their dependence on superior authorities suppresses individuality, corrupts character and engenders moral poverty.

In every bureaucracy we may observe place-hunting, a mania for promotion, and obsequiousness towards those upon whom promotion depends; there is arrogance towards inferiors and servility towards superiors . . . the more conspicuously a bureaucracy is distinguished by its zeal, by its sense of duty, and by its devotion, the more also will it show itself to be petty, narrow, rigid and illiberal. (1915, p. 200)

The bureaucracy is thus a source of power for the politically dominant class, a source of security for a large part of the middle class, but a source of oppression for the rest of society.

All this holds mainly, but not solely, for the state bureaucracy. The modern political party possesses many of these traits in common with the state. Like the modern state, it too, endeavours to give its own organization the widest possible base and to attach to itself in financial bonds the largest possible number of people.

Bureaucracy, oligarchy and democracy
This leads us to the topic with which Michels was most extensively concerned, the structure of political parties and trade unions. Drawing his material from European socialist-democratic parties and unions around the turn of the century, Michels showed that even organizations whose principles were democratic come to be organized

in an oligarchic manner.

The democratic principle calls for guaranteeing to all equal participation and influence in regulating the affairs of the organization; it calls
for self-government according to decisions of popular assemblies and
for free elections in which all are electors and all are eligible for election.
In fact, however, every organization becomes divided into a minority of
directors, or leaders, and a majority of directed, or led. The leaders
exert almost unlimited authority and power over the rank and file who
usually accept this situation and defer to their leaders in every possible
way. The leaders who at first are merely the executive organs of the
collective become independent of its control and instead gain control
over it. The external forms of democracy are maintained, but underneath it oligarchy becomes more and more pronounced. Significantly,
what Michels characterizes as oligarchy is closely akin to what he (and
Weber too) characterizes are bureaucracy (see chapter 2) — namely a
hierarchical organization where power is concentrated at the top and
where control descends from the top to the bottom.

But why did such oligarchic bureaucratic structures develop? State
bureaucracy is necessary because it preserves the advantages of the
advantaged classes. But why have bureaucratic or oligarchic tendencies
developed in the socialist parties that were aimed precisely at abolishing
the advantages of these classes? As Michels put it: 'The concentration
of power in those parties which preach the Marxist doctrine is more
conspicuous than the concentration of capital predicted by Marx . . .'
(1915, p. 137). Why is this so? The principal aim of socialist-democratic
parties is the struggle against inequality and oligarchy. How then is one
to explain the development in such parties of the very tendencies they
were established to eradicate? Michels explains this development
through the following interrelated set of reasons.

Size The democratic principle calls for all to participate in decision-
making. The large size of the modern political party makes this practically impossible. Even if it were feasible to assemble the multitude of
members in a given place at a given time, the assembled masses would
not be able to work out intelligent decisions in common.

Complexity Hand in hand with the increase in size goes the increase in
complexity. As the problems facing the organization become more
complex, they become less comprehensible to the rank and file. Hence
the need for delegation. Once leaders have been elected, they tend to

concentrate more and more decision-making power in their own hands, once more, for several reasons:

The need for quick decisions For the organization to run effectively, decisions have to be made speedily. Democratic procedures invariably cause delays, hence the constant temptation for leaders to forgo these procedures so as to get things going.

The need for expertise Because of the growing size and complexity of modern political parties, their decision-making processes require expertise. Leaders have the advantages of education and training — hence their technical superiority as against the technical incompetence of the masses. Many leaders become salaried officials and thus become specialists in various areas of organizational activities. This makes the leaders indispensable, and with their indispensability their independence from the rank and file increases as well.

Information and communication Inside information on what is going on in the organization is also monopolized by leaders and administrators, as are the means of communication by which such information may or may not be disseminated. The internal press is in the hands of the leaders and out of reach of the rank and file. Leaders attempt to control the freedom of speech of their potential opponents by suppressing any independent press, and they are quite frequently successful in this attempt. This makes it possible for leaders to manipulate and distort information to the detriment of their potential rivals — the contenders for leadership positions. It is thus almost impossible for an effective opposition to be established, and the leaders' position becomes almost impregnable.

Political and leadership skills Through their continued experience leaders acquire not only technical skills but also leadership and political skills (e.g. oratory skills, bargaining abilities) which no one else in the organization possesses. This, too, makes them almost irreplaceable.

The need for continuity To be effective, organizations — including parties and unions — must have continuity. Frequent changes in leadership would cause confusion and disorder. Members are usually aware of this and hence prefer to maintain the same people in office rather than rock the boat.

Apathy This, in turn, is connected with the fact that most members prefer not to become involved in party or union affairs themselves. The number of those who have a lively interest in such affairs is minimal; most display profound indifference. Most, moreover, voluntarily renounce their right to decision-making. They are quite happy to be left alone and let others run the show. In fact, they are grateful to those others who are willing to do so. This gratitude is displayed in these people's frequent re-election to leadership positions.

Vested interest in power The apathy of the masses has its counterpart in the natural greed for power among the potential leaders. And once they have attained power, leaders have a vested interest in maintaining it and a marked reluctance in relinquishing it. This stems from the rewards of power and from power itself as a reward. The rewards of power include fame and financial advantages. Whoever has once obtained such fame will not readily return to a former obscure position and will not readily endure the financial setbacks this would entail. Hence, the liberal payment of party officials nourishes their dictatorial appetites.

In short, the needs and characteristics of both the rank and file and the leaders, as well as those of the organization itself, lead to oligarchy. So much so that leaders usually manage to monopolize positions for long time-spans, and, in due course, even succeed in selecting their own successors. Even if the leaders are finally replaced, the new ones will once more perpetuate oligarchy.

In view of all this, Michels formulated his famous iron law of oligarchy: 'who says organization says oligarchy' (1915, p. 418) and the more developed the organization, the stronger the oligarchy. Since oligarchy overlaps with bureaucracy, this may be regarded as the iron law of bureaucracy as well. Michels considered the possibility of countering this tendency through referenda, syndicalism[3] or anarchy, but concluded that none of these could withstand the iron law of oligarchy.

Oligarchy, of course, comes close to being the antithesis of democracy. This is so not only because in it leadership is self-perpetuating and exceedingly powerful, leaving members little or no say, but also because once in office, the leaders no longer represent the interests of the members who elected them. They become detached from those interests because by rising to power they undergo a profound metamorphosis − they have now become part of the elite. Their own interest now is no longer to promote the radical-socialist aims of the organization but rather to maintain the organization on which their elite position depends. From a means the organization's machinery turns into an end. Henceforth, the leaders' sole preoccupation is to avoid anything that may clog this machinery.

But not only the leaders' interests change; their mentalities change as well. In this context it has been remarked that once a person obtains a position that entitles him to a large office, carpet and secretary, the urgent problems he was appointed to solve lose much of their urgency unless, of course, they concern that very office, carpet and secretary. This remark certainly fits the mentality of the socialist parties and union leaders, as Michels saw them. All this explains why parties that set out as radical become more conservative as they go along. It thus forms what Michels saw as the conservative basis of the organization.

The officials of state bureaucracies and the leaders of socialist parties thus have much in common: they are both intent on preserving their own positions and the rewards accruing from them, and, by so doing, they strengthen the bureaucratic and/or oligarchic, non-democratic character of the organizations of which they form a part.

Critique and evaluation

Of the three theories reviewed in this chapter, the earliest, the most widely known and the most momentous in its impact is that of Marx. Indeed, no classical social thinker has been as influential (or as controversial) in the social sciences as Marx. Not only has he fathered a school of thought that has sustained itself from his times to ours and whose influence has been growing in recent years, but much of non-Marxist social science has developed out of a controversy with Marx, as either a revision or a refutation of his framework.

In the area of bureaucracy, one of Marx's most essential contributions lies in his conception of that establishment (and the bureaucrats who staff it) as promoting certain interests, a conception that is inexplicably missing from Weber's model (as will be seen below). Since Marx saw bureaucracy as promoting certain interests, he also saw it as entangled in various power struggles, and thus as part and parcel of the modern state's political arena – a conception that (once again) does not come through in Weber's model. Consequently, Marx also saw bureaucrats as much more human, as creatures of real flesh and blood, rather than as the rational and automatic executors of instructions that emerge out of Weber's model. Marx was also more aware than many later social theorists of the dominating and potentially repressive nature of bureaucracy. Moreover, by pointing to the importance of the bureaucratic secret (that is, bureaucratic monopolization of knowledge) in safeguarding its domination, Marx has pre-empted one of the most central ideas of one of the most modern central schools of thought — the technocratic school (to be dealt with in chapter 4).

However, while in his earliest writings Marx saw bureaucracy and bureaucrats as furthering their own interests, he soon shifted to the idea that the state (including the bureaucracy) merely serves to advance the interests of the capitalist ruling class. Perhaps this shift is partly responsible for the fact that Marx never made bureaucracy his central concern. To do so would have been inconsistent with his newly developed view that however powerful bureaucracy may become under certain circumstances, it can gain only limited independence from the ruling class. From this view it follows that the ruling class as it relates to other classes and to the state, rather than the bureaucracy as part of the state, merits to become the main focus of attention. The same holds for bourgeois democracy. Since this institution, too, is seen merely as an instrument of class rule (albeit a vulnerable and self-contradictory one) it does not deserve to hold centre stage either. For this reason, Marx never developed a full-fledged theory of bureaucracy, of democracy and of the relationship between the two.

Marx's central idea that the state, and with it the bureaucracy, safeguards the interests of the ruling class has served as the cornerstone for the contemporary Marxist theory of the state. At the same time it has been attacked on the ground that the wealth-holding class serves the interests of the state no less than the latter serves the interests of the former. Since Marx never developed an elaborate analysis of this topic, he did not furnish his followers with the ammunition with which to counter this attack.

A similar observation may be made about Michels. He, too, treated bureaucracy only incidentally. His idea that blocked mobility into the bureaucracy creates an 'intellectual proletariat' that militantly opposes the state and supplies the potential leadership for protest movements is an important one; it certainly deserves further elaboration and follow-up through empirical research. But his main focus was on oligarchy vs. democracy. It is here that he made his most memorable contribution, and it is for this contribution that he is chiefly remembered today. While this topic overlaps with that of bureaucracy vs. democracy, it is not identical with it, and its application to state bureaucracy in particular (which is our main concern here) would be exceedingly problematic.

Of the three theories reviewed in this chapter, the most extensive contribution on the relationship between bureaucracy and democracy is that made by Mosca. The originality of his theory has sometimes been disputed. Mosca apparently developed his theory of the ruling class at the same time at which Vilfredo Pareto developed his theory of the elite, and there is no reason to believe that Mosca copied Pareto's ideas. However, the observation that minorities rule majorities, had certainly been made before.[4]

On this, Arthur Livingstone, in his introduction to Mosca's *The Ruling Class* made the following observation: 'The maxim that there is nothing new under the sun is a very true maxim; that is to say, it covers about half the truth, which is a great deal of truth for a maxim to cover' (Mosca, 1939, p. X). Many have mentioned Mosca's main ideas before, proceeds Livingstone, but no one has made these ideas the central basis of a theory. Mosca's main originality lies not in the idea of the ruling class as such, but in the manner in which he has utilized and elaborated it.

With regard to bureaucracy and democracy, the most significant of Mosca's contributions is the idea that the application of one single political principle leads to the abuse of power by the ruling class, while a mixed political regime leads to mutual checks and balances between various parts of the ruling class and hence to the curbing of its power. Importantly, he emphasized that when the democratic principle alone reigns supreme, this gives rise to the excessive power of elected politicians and hence to abuses in the forms of mutual favours and indulgences; that a purely bureaucratic regime would bring about the most oppressive ruling class despotism that history has ever known, and that a mix between democracy and bureaucracy is optimal as far as the curbing of ruling class power is concerned. Finally, there certainly was something prophetic in Mosca's pronouncement that a communist regime would come close to being purely bureaucratic; that in it the administration, by being in control of all resources, would make all individuals totally dependent on it. In any case this prediction was certainly more realistic by far than Marx's prognosis on the withering away of bureaucracy in the communist state.

Marx worked on the assumption that bureaucracy represented ruling-class interests and on the further assumption that in communist society all classes would be abolished. Hence he inevitably had to reach the conclusion that in such a society, bureaucracy would wither away as well. Mosca, on the other hand, worked on the assumption that the bureaucracy was itself part of the (political) ruling class and served basically its own interests of preserving and augmenting its power. This led him to the conclusion that in communist society where other power centres (such as private enterprise) would be abolished, the bureaucracy would gain even more power than it had before. Since actual developments show Mosca's conclusion to be more to the point, one must deduce that his assumption, too, was the more realistic one. In general, Marx's theory is undoubtedly the more highly regarded and the more influential today but as far as bureaucracy is concerned, it was Mosca rather than Marx who made the more substantial contribution.

Chapter 2

Classical theories:
the Weberian framework[1]

For Marx the issue of bureaucracy was marginal, while Mosca and Michels are themselves (rightly or wrongly) considered marginal as far the contemporary analysis of bureaucracy is concerned. The theorist who made bureaucracy one of his central concerns and whose conception is considered central to the contemporary analysis of bureaucracy is Max Weber (1864-1920).

Power, authority and bureaucracy

The framework for Weber's conception of bureaucracy is to be sought in his ideas on power, domination and authority. For Weber, power is 'the probability that one actor within a social relationship will be in a position to carry out his own will despite resistance . . .' (1947,[2] p. 152). Domination (or imperative control) is power in a hierarchy; it is 'the probability that a command . . . will be obeyed by a given group of persons' (1947, p. 152). Authority exists whenever obedience is based on a belief in the command's legitimacy. Thus, legitimacy turns power and domination into authority.

Three types of authority may be distinguished on the basis of their claim to legitimacy:

— traditional authority: legitimated by time, by its existence in the past, that is, by the sanctity of tradition;
— charismatic authority: legitimated by outstanding personal leadership characteristics of the bearer;
— legal-rational authority: legitimated by being in accordance with formally correct rules and by the right of those in authority — under such rules — to issue commands.

This typology of authority provided Weber with the basis of classifying organizations. Traditional authority forms the basis of traditionalist organizations (such as a patriarchal kinship unit or a monarchy). Charismatic authority forms the basis of charismatic movements (such as early Christianity under the charismatic leadership of Jesus). Legal-rational authority forms the basis of bureaucracy (1947, pp. 130-2; 328-63; Gerth and Mills, 1958,[3] pp. 245-52).

The features of bureaucracy
Drawing on his knowledge of the German (especially the Prussian) and the British bureaucracies, Weber constructed a model of bureaucracy which includes the following main features:

— each office has a well-defined sphere of competence with duties clearly marked off from those of other offices;
— offices are ordered in a hierarchy; each lower office is under the supervision and responsibility of a higher one;
— authority is restricted to official duties; beyond these, sub-ordinates are not subject to their superiors; there is a complete segregation of official activity from private life;
— officials hold office by appointment (rather than by election), and on the basis of a contractual relationship between themselves and the organization;
— officials are selected on the basis of objective qualifications; these are acquired by training, established by examinations, diplomas or both;
— officials are set for a career: they are protected from arbitrary dismissal and can expect to maintain office permanently; promotion is by seniority, achievement or both;
— officials are entirely separated from the means of administration, hence they cannot appropriate their positions;
— activities are regulated by general, consistent, abstract rules; the generality of these rules requires the categorization of individual cases on the basis of objective criteria;
— official duties are conducted in a spirit of impersonality without hatred but also without affection;
— a bureaucracy frequently has a non-bureaucratic head. While bureaucrats follow rules, he sets them. While bureaucrats are appointed, he usually inherits his position, appropriates it or is elected to it (1947, pp. 328-40; Gerth and Mills, 1958, pp. 196-8).

Because of these features (Weber claims), bureaucracy is, from a purely technical viewpoint, capable of attaining the highest degree of rationality[4] and effectiveness. From this viewpoint the fully developed bureaucratic mechanism compares with other organizations exactly as does the machine with non-mechanical means of production. This is so, since the division of labour minimizes duplication of tasks as well as friction. Hierarchy facilitates central planning and co-ordination as well as control and discipline. Employment on the basis of qualifications makes for a higher level of knowledge and more competent work. Rules save effort by standardization; they obviate the need to find a new solution for each individual problem; therefore they also spell calculability of results. Impersonal detachment promotes objectivity and prevents irrational action as well as such inequitable treatment as favouritism on the one hand or discrimination on the other. Finally, the non-bureaucratic head ensures non-rational commitment to the organization's rationality; personal identification with that individual provides the psychological leverage that reinforces commitment to impersonal rules (1947, pp. 214-16: Gerth and Mills, 1958, p. 337).

This scheme is what Weber referred to as an 'ideal type'. An ideal type (not to be confused with an ideal) is a theoretical construct, combining several features of a phenomenon in their purest and most extreme form. An ideal type as such is never found in actual reality; it is a conceptual tool which simplifies and exaggerates reality for the sake of conceptual clarity. Thus, Weber never claimed that all modern organizations, or even all state administrations, display all the aforementioned features. He merely claimed that there is a general tendency in this direction and that the closer an organization comes to displaying these features, the more rational and effective it is likely to be. When Weber wrote of actual administrations, he referred to them as bureaucracies even when they displayed only in part the characteristics of his ideal type.

The historical development of bureaucracy — an explanation

Bureaucracy appeared in Europe on an increasingly large scale and in an increasingly pure form with the growth of absolutism. Bureaucracy had existed in the past: the ancient Egyptian, Roman and Chinese state administrations (at some stages of their development) are cases in point; the Roman Catholic Church (especially since the end of the thirteenth century) is another. But previously bureaucracies were less purely bureaucratic. Also, they were limited in numbers and confined to state and religion. With modernization, however, bureaucracies became more bureaucratic; in addition, they proliferated and penetrated much wider spheres of social life. Not only state administrations, armies and churches, but universities, economic enterprises and political parties became bureaucratized as well. According to Weber this development was the result of several causes:

1 *The creation of a money economy* – a process which occurred with Europe's emergence from the Middle Ages. This was not an absolute prerequisite: bureaucracies based on compensation in kind had existed, for instance, in Egypt, Rome and China. But payment in kind could not ensure dependable revenues for bureaucrats. Hence the tendency has been to reward them by grants of land and/or the collection of tax revenues from given territories. This, in turn, has tended to lead to the disintegration of bureaucracies into feudal or semi-feudal domains. A money economy, on the other hand, permits payment of secure, regular salaries, which, in turn, creates dependable organizations.

2 *The emergence of a capitalist economy proper*, as happened in Europe, in early modernity. Modern capitalism is distinguished by the rational estimation of risks and the systematic calculation of profits. This requires regular market processes that are not unpredictably disrupted by external forces, such as arbitrary government policies or even robbery. Hence, capitalism requires and encourages strong and orderly governments, which is just another way of saying that capitalism requires and encourages governments based on bureaucratic organizations.

Moreover, the requirements of rationality and calculability – the prime features of capitalism – have led capitalist enterprises themselves to follow bureaucratic principles of organization. Capitalism has stimulated unionization and many unions have come to be bureaucratized as well. Strange as it seems, it is thus the system of free enterprise that has fostered bureaucracy. It did not *cause* bureaucratization in the usual sense of the term, but it created the needs which bureaucratic organization came to satisfy.

3 *The more encompassing trend towards rationality in Western society*. This trend found expression in a general 'disenchantment' or demystification of the world, in a more effective adaptation of means to ends, and a more systematic organization of reality. It was evident, for instance, in the development of the Protestant Ethic, which encouraged hard work and self-discipline. This ethic was the basis of the spirit of capitalism, which called for the rational investment of time and effort

so as to maximize profits and achievements. This spirit, in turn, was one of the preconditions for the development of rational capitalism. The general trend towards rationality is also evident in the development of modern science with its combination of rational theory, mathematical calculation and systematic empirical observation. Protestantism, capitalism, science and bureaucracy are thus all part of one cluster of developments — the process of rationalization.

4 *Democracy*. This political regime has played a part in the development of bureaucracy by opposing and helping to eliminate the traditional rule of notables and by encouraging education and appointment to office on the basis of knowledge.

5 *The growth of the European population*. Population growth multiplies administrative tasks, which must be coped with through larger organizations. Larger organizations, for their part, tend to assume bureaucratic forms.

6 *The emergence of especially complex administrative problems*. In ancient Egypt the complex task of constructing and regulating waterways gave rise to one of the first large-scale bureaucracies in history. In Europe the newly emerged centralized states had to cope with heretofore unknown administrative tasks. Not only did they have to control larger territories and populations but they also had to provide social services of a nature that no previous state had had to procure before. The complexity of these tasks required expertise and effectiveness in organization, that is, bureaucracy.

7 *The modern forms of communication*. These have both required and facilitated a more complex and effective type of administration that is to say, a bureaucratic one (Gerth and Mills, 1958, pp. 204-14; 1958;[5] 1947, esp. p. 338).

Thus, bureaucracy developed, because its rationality and technical superiority made it the most appropriate tool for dealing with the tasks and problems of complex, modern society. Because of this superiority, bureaucracy had to become more pervasive and it is bound to become even more so in the future.

The effects of bureaucracy

Weber was less than enthusiastic about this prospect; indeed he was quite ambivalent about it. For although he regarded bureaucracy as technically superior, he was deeply concerned about its effects both on the individual and on society at large. He saw the impact of bureaucracy on the individual within it, the bureaucrat, as the crippling of his personality. Bureaucracy creates a person who is nothing but a little cog in a big machine, who clings to his position while desperately hoping to become a bigger cog. Together with capitalism, bureaucracy creates technical experts, who replace the previously prevalent cultured persons and who are unjustifiably convinced of their own superiority: 'Specialists without spirit, sensualists without heart; this nullity imagines that it has attained a level of civilization never before achieved' (1958, p. 182).

According to Weber, bureaucracy holds equally grave dangers for society as a whole. In the past, bureaucratization of society (as part of a growing rationality) had a liberating effect on society by destroying oppressive traditions. But Weber saw further bureaucratization as leading to the permeation of bureaucratic values and ways of thought throughout the population, a prospect he did not find heartening.

> This passion for bureaucracy . . . is enough to drive one to despair. It is . . . as if we were deliberately to become men who need 'order' and nothing but order, who become nervous and cowardly if for one moment this order wavers, and helpless if they are torn away from their total incorporation in it. (1976,[6] p. 362)

While at first, then, bureaucracy brought liberation, it is now apt to bring about the opposite: over-organization. The question is, therefore, what we can do to combat this development:

> it is in such an evolution that we are already caught up, and the great question is therefore not how we can promote and hasten it, but what can we oppose to this machinery in order to keep a portion of mankind free from this parceling out of the soul, from this supreme mastery of the bureaucratic way of life. (1976, p. 362)

Bureaucracy and democracy

Weber was also ambivalent about the political implications of bureaucracy, especially in relation to democracy. On the one hand he stressed that bureaucracy developed simultaneously with democracy and that (as noted) democracy promoted the development of bureaucracy among other things by its fight against the rule of traditional notables. He also emphasized that many democratic mass parties were themselves bureaucratically organized. On the other hand he held that, under certain conditions, democracy creates blockages to bureaucratic organization. Wherever possible, democracy opposes bureaucracy as a caste of officials removed from the people by expertise and tenure of office. Democracy strives to shorten the term of office by election and by not binding the candidate to a special expertness. This practice, however, detracts from the organization's rationality and effectiveness. 'Thereby democracy inevitably comes into conflict with the bureaucratic tendencies which, by its fight against notable rule, democracy has produced' (Gerth and Mills, 1958, p. 226).

On the one hand, again, Weber stressed the subordination of bureaucracy to its (political) master, in a democracy, the elected politician. On the other hand, again, he was deeply concerned that those who staffed the bureaucracy would themselves become the masters of the state. As Krygier (1979d, p. 67) put it: 'It was less a fear that we would all become bureaucrats than that we would all come to be *ruled* by bureaucrats.' Weber saw bureaucracy as an instrument of power held by others: 'bureaucracy as such is a precision instrument which can put itself at the disposal of quite varied interests, purely political as well as purely economic ones, or any other sort' (1968,[7] p. 990). In a democracy, it is thus the 'precision instrument' of the elected politician. He also saw the executive staff as bound by obedience to the political power holder, and stated that 'The honor of the civil servant is vested in his ability to execute conscientiously the order of the superior . . . even if the order appears wrong to him . . .' (Gerth and Mills, 1958, p. 95). He added however, that in practice the superior's ability to ensure obedience

> is possible only in a very limited degree to persons who are not
> technical specialists. Generally speaking, the trained permanent
> official is more likely to get his way in the long run than his nominal
> superior, the Cabinet Minister, who is not a specialist. (1947, p. 338)

The official is an expert in relation to whom the political master finds himself in the position of a dilettante. Moreover, in the course of his duties, the official acquires a great deal of concrete information. This information, not always at the disposal of the political superior, is yet another source of the bureaucrat's power. Thus 'bureaucratic administration means fundamentally domination through knowledge' (1968, p. 225).

It follows that the very same superiority that has made bureaucracy so essential to modern society also poses a threat to modern democracy. A further threat has its source in codes of bureaucratic secrecy, in the fact that the most important spheres of bureaucratic action are withdrawn from public scrutiny. 'The concept of the "official secret" is the specific invention of bureaucracy, and nothing is so fanatically defended by the bureaucracy as this attitude . . .' (Gerth and Mills, 1958, p. 233). Formally, citizens may complain to politicians about bureaucratic action, but that action's secrecy makes redress difficult. Bureaucratic domination may be checked to some extent through elected representative bodies. But these checks are limited because bureaucracy maintains secrecy *vis-à-vis* parliament as well and fights every attempt by parliament to gain knowledge. In the final analysis the extent to which bureaucracy may exert power over its political master, and thus endanger democracy, depends to a large extent on that bureaucracy itself. If it chooses to overrule its master, there is nothing to prevent it from doing so. '*against* the bureaucracy, the ruler remains powerless' (1968, p. 993; see also 1958, pp. 232-5).

Weber was also ambivalent with regard to bureaucracy's consequences for social equality. The impersonality of bureaucratic rules leads to impartiality, hence is certainly in line with the democratic ideal of equality before the law. Bureaucracy also brings about a levelling of the governed in opposition to the bureaucratic ruling group. Further, bureaucracy prevents the development of a closed, hereditary group of officials, in the interest of the broadest possible basis of recruitment. At the same time, bureaucracy does not bring about substantial equality in society or within bureaucracy itself. The training necessary for the bureaucrat's technical qualifications affords a distinct advantage to the wealthy. Weber refers to this phenomenon as 'the tendency to plutocracy growing out of the interest in the greatest possible length of technical training' (1947, p. 340; see also Gerth and Mills, 1958, pp. 221-8).

All in all, then, bureaucracy is rather suspect in its implications for both democracy and equality. But it would be fruitless to try and eliminate it. For one could do so only with the aid of an alternative organization which, in the course of time, would itself become a bureaucracy. Even the possible future abolition of capitalism would not lead to the decline of bureaucracy. Like Mosca and in contrast to Marx, Weber did not believe that under socialism or communism bureaucracy would wither away. On the contrary, it would become even larger and more powerful. The management of the nationalized enterprises would become part of the state bureaucracy, and bureaucratic power would be exclusive. 'For the time being', wrote Weber, 'the dictatorship of the official and not that of the worker is on the march' (1924, p. 508).[8] Thus, as Alvin Gouldner has aptly pointed out, Marx argued that through a socialist revolution workers had nothing to lose, while Weber contended that they had nothing to gain either.

Critique and evaluation

Weber's theory, like Marx's, has attracted widespread and continued criticism, and his conception of bureaucracy has been one of its prime targets. But this is really an indication of the theory's impact. Unimportant theories are usually disregarded and quickly forgotten; only theories that have served as a landmark in the development of the discipline have been singled out for repeated onslaughts. And the more they have been attacked, the more resilient they have become. Weber's theory of bureaucracy is a clear case in point. Innumerable contemporary authors on bureaucracy start out with a critique of his theory. Yet these same authors use it as a point of departure for the exposition of their own views — if only to show how theirs differ from his.

Weber's theory has been criticized from several angles. In the first place it has been commented that his ideal type is far from being ideal as a conceptual tool, for it has led Weber to a lopsided view of bureaucracy. Of the many discrepant and contradictory features of bureaucracy Weber has highlighted one side only, that which fits in with his ideal type. This, in turn, shades over into a second criticism, namely that Weber's conception of bureaucracy has not adequately captured empirical reality. Weber, it has been asserted, regards bureaucracy as having a purely formal structure. In reality it also features an informal one, i.e. one that is not officially recognized. This informal structure, which Page (1946) referred to as 'bureaucracy's other face', includes informal relations, informal norms and values, an informal power hierarchy and informal power struggles — all of which have no place in Weber's model.

Thus, the human relations school[9] has alerted social scientists to the existence in organizations of cohesive social groups and to their importance in shaping members' morale, norms and output. Other observers (e.g. Bensman and Rosenberg, 1969) have called attention to the existence in bureaucracies of *pseudo*-cohesive groups, or cliques, in which warmth and sincerity are feigned and which are used to manipulate social relations so as to support their members in their struggle for advancement. Indeed, such cliques are held to be so important in this respect that officials who unwittingly befriend people from the wrong camp are likely to consign themselves to oblivion. 'In sum: the formation of cliques tends to alter operational bureaucracy to something quite different from its ideal type' (Bensman and Rosenberg, 1969, p. 58).

Further, informal groups (whether truly cohesive or pseudo-cohesive) tend to generate informal leaders. Thus, formal authority bearers are not necessarily the actual power-holders. And the relations between these two, the power struggle that may develop between them or, conversely, the support they may lend to each other, are most important in shaping organizations (including bureaucratic ones) — yet they have been left unexplored by Weber's model.

Weber has pointed to the importance of formal, general and impartial rules as a major feature of bureaucracy. Observers such as Gouldner (1954), however, have shown that the organization's formal rules are frequently used informally, in a manner quite different from that envisaged by Weber. By showing leniency and disregarding the infraction of minor rules by workers, supervisors may gain those workers' loyalty and thus increase their own power; by clamping down and enforcing previously disregarded rules, they can punish disloyal workers, bring recalcitrant workers back into line and thus — once more — enhance their own power. Weber thus disregarded the fact that formal rules may be used as weapons in informal contests of power.

Weber imputed clear spheres of competence to bureaucratic posts — an arrangement that supposedly minimizes duplication and friction. Yet (it is argued) whosoever has had experience in or with bureaucracy knows that it thrives on 'empire building'. As Sir Henry Bland (1975, p. 5) put it:

> It is left to the odd Parkinson to underline the empire building trait, so highly developed among public administrators . . . set about amassing staffs so that they may embark on everything they can conceivably assert to be within their sphere of interest and, in the course, overlap and duplicate the proper functions of other departments.

Moreover, empire building is a practice whereby bureaucrats and bureaucratic agencies not only infringe on each other's spheres of competence, but indeed attempt to swallow up each other's domains, in their unceasing struggle for power.

By disregarding its informal aspects, Weber was thus oblivious (among other things) to bureaucracy's internal power struggles and thus to its 'domestic' politics. By the same token he did not make an out-standing contribution to the analysis of bureaucracy's external politics either. Thus, Weber imputed to bureaucracy appointment and promo-tion of officials by objective qualifications and (as noted) activities in accordance with formal generalized rules. Yet, as will be shown below (chapter 11), many modern bureaucracies have practised appointment and promotion by partisan-political loyalties rather than by objective qualifications and allocation of benefits by partisan criteria rather than by formal generalized rules. Thus, bureaucracies have become involved in party political power struggles; and even where such practices have subsequently declined, this has itself been the result of intense political struggles. Because he did not take this into account, Weber could not explore the type of external politics that bureaucracy may be involved in, and the problem this may create in a modern democratic state.

Patronage appointments and promotions have commonly been made, among other reasons, because they help ensure the loyalty of sub-ordinates to their superiors and thus form another formidable weapon in the bureaucrats' internal struggles for power. By failing to take systematic notice of this, Weber thus also failed to explore the connec-tion between the bureaucracy's external and internal politics. In short, Weber has not sufficiently emphasized the fact that bureaucracy (like man in Aristotle's view) is a political animal and has failed to analyse the social implications of this basic fact.

All this is not to imply that Weber was unaware of the informal aspects of bureaucracy and of the power struggles in which bureau-cracies are internally and externally embattled. For instance, Weber was well aware of the widespread existence of patronage appointments and political 'booty' in his own time (see Gerth and Mills, 1958, pp. 86-8). But apparently he regarded them as incidental or idiosyncratic, not a systematic part of bureaucracy's basic features. Hence he failed to incorporate them into his model. In fact, however, the critics have claimed, not only are the informal aspects of bureaucracy (including its pervasive power struggles) an integral part of bureaucracy, but they are a necessary part of it. Indeed, they are the dynamic aspects of bureau-cracy, and by making bureaucracy more flexible they make it more effective as well.

This, in turn, leads to the next criticism: that (contrary to Weber's view) the features he incorporated into his model of bureaucracy may not really make for maximum effectiveness; they may equally well make for ineffectiveness and strain. Hierarchy, for instance, does encourage central guidance, planning and discipline. But it also encourages timidity and buck-passing; it discourages initiative and stifles the imagination. It thus prevents the full utilization of bureaucracy's human resources. So bureaucracy is faced with a dilemma: lack of hierarchy spells lack of co-ordination; too stiff a hierarchy spells lack of creativeness. Weber has shown no sign of being aware of this dilemma.

Hierarchy has also been said to obviate responsibility, a problem which Weber squarely disregarded. Weber imputes an ethic of responsibility to politicians (see Gerth and Mills, 1958, pp. 115-28) but imputes no such ethic to bureaucrats. The actions of Weber's bureaucrats find their justification solely in the fact that they have been carried out according to rules and instructions from above. As Carl Friedrich (1952) sees it, Weber thus allows his bureaucratic officials to elude all responsibility for their actions.

Some observers go as far as to claim that the inadvertent result of this conception was Nazism – a regime in which officials justified mass murder by orders from above. As Hanna Arendt has emphasized, the peculiar feature of the Nazi regime was not so much the evil it perpetrated as the trivialization of evil through bureaucratic discipline. It is hard to see, however, how the blame for this can be laid at Weber's feet – even indirectly – unless, of course, one assumes that for Weber the ideal type of bureaucracy was also an ideal. This, however, was not the case, and (as was seen before) Weber himself was deeply concerned over the social implications of bureaucracy.

There is somewhat greater justification for another related critique: bureaucracy encourages a compulsive obsession with rules that greatly detracts from its effectiveness – of which Weber was oblivious. According to Merton (1957b) bureaucracy ensures conformity with rules by encouraging strong positive sentiments towards them. This often causes ritualism, that is, the transference of commitment from the organization's goals to its rules. In this situation, rules, which were originally intended as means for the bureaucracy's ends, now turn into ends in their own right. This may be exaggerated to the point where bureaucrats turn into virtuosos of adherence to rules. They may embrace those rules even when they impede the realization of bureaucracy's ends, unnecessarily overload it with tasks, make its operations more cumbersome and thus defeat their own purpose.

An amusing example of such blind adherence is reported by Jacob (1966, p. 47). He tells of an official who used to receive dozens of papers a day, which he read, duly initialled (as per rules, of course) and deposited in his 'out' tray. One day, a report meant for another official found its way to his desk and was dealt with in the usual manner. Two days later the report was returned. Attached was a memorandum which read something like this: 'This document was not intended for you to handle. Please erase your initials and initial your erasure.' Anyone who has ever had dealings with bureaucracy could supplement this example of ritualism with many others. Yet Weber was not sufficiently aware of this phenomenon to incorporate it into his model.

In Weber's defence it has been argued that rules are not always the villain they are made out to be. Perrow (1979), for instance, suggests that a bureaucracy without explicit rules would place officials and clients in intolerably ambiguous situations. For officials this would create anxiety, which would detract much more from their effectiveness than rules ever could. For clients it would create a feeling of being arbitrarily disadvantaged. For both it would cause confusion and frustration. Rules, proceeds Perrow, are a bore and we would all like to be rid of them – or so it seems. Actually, good rules are rarely noticed and may in fact increase the official's autonomy. Only the bad ones are a nuisance. So all really depends on the quality of the rules.

Rules have special importance with regard to the relationship between bureaucracy and the politics of democracy. Weber did not incorporate into his model the notion (developed in some of the following chapters) that rules governing bureaucratic action are sometimes unclear and confusing. Also (as noted) he failed to incorporate into his model the observation that in many Western countries officials have deviated from formal rules and have passed out positions, promotions and benefits by party political criteria. But he was certainly right in his emphasis that when generalized rules *are* clear and adhered to, this obviates both favouritism and discrimination – especially favouritism and discrimination on political grounds. As will be shown below (chapters 11 and 12), the elimination of such political favouritism is a basic prerequisite for fair, competitive electoral procedures and, hence, for democracy. While Weber did not map out these implications himself, it is his model that points the way for such an analysis.

As noted, some of Weber's critics have argued that strict adherence to certain bureaucratic rules may lead to totalitarianism and (under extreme circumstances) to the perpetration of genocide. It is my argument, however, that strict adherence to *other* bureaucratic rules is a prerequisite for democracy, a fact that Weber's critics have disregarded. Other critics have argued that compulsive adherence to bureaucratic rules (or ritualism) may detract from bureaucracy's ability to realize goals. It is my argument, however, that if the goal is that of strengthening democracy, then deviation from pertinent bureaucratic rules may have even greater adverse effects on this ability (see chapter 7).

It has further been argued that bureaucrats' obsession with rules causes an inability to adapt to changing conditions. Thorstein Veblen referred to this phenomenon as 'trained incapacity': when bureaucrats are trained to do things in a certain way, they become incapable of doing them in any other way. As Crozier (1964, p. 187) saw it, in this way bureaucracy becomes a rigid organization that cannot correct its behaviour by learning from its errors.

Hence, it has been added, bureaucracy may well have been effective in Weber's time but it is not really appropriate for the rapidly changing society of recent years. Therefore bureaucracy (including state bureaucracy) is increasingly being replaced by more flexible organizational structures (see, for instance, Bennis, 1968 and Toffler, 1970). This, however, seems to be more of a forecast (and a dubious one at that[10]) than a statement on actual reality. At present, bureaucracy (especially state bureaucracy) is still alive and well, as is Weber's model for its analysis. Frequently this model is used in order to show how actual bureaucracy differs from it and the problems that are thereby created or solved. But this is in itself a way of paying tribute to the model. It is also the way in which the model is being utilized in this book.

Chapter 3

Modern theories: pluralism and government overload

Among modern observers, one group that has made a substantial contribution to our understanding of the state, bureaucracy, and the politics of democracy is the pluralist school of thought. Contrary to Weber, who viewed the modern state and bureaucracy as coherent in structure and effective in the execution of tasks, pluralism views them as disjointed in structure and blundering in performance. Despite Weber's continued eminence, pluralism has been popular for many years especially in the United States in the 1950s and 1960s. As D. Knoke (1979) has pointed out, the more established version of pluralism has recently fallen on hard times. There are, however, some newer versions, concerned primarily with pluralism in the bureaucracy and with governmental 'overload' and 'ungovernability' which have become more widely accepted in recent years.

The pluralist power structure

The older version of pluralism holds that after modernization in the West, and particularly in the twentieth century, political power has come to be increasingly fragmented and diffused. Absolutism marked the growth of centralized state power (without which modernization would have been impossible). The subsequent advent of democracy, however, marked the reversal of this process.

Accordingly, the contemporary Western and notably the American political system is seen as an intricate balance of power amongst overlapping economic, professional, religious, ethnic and other groups or associations. Each group is held to exercise a certain influence on the policy-making process, but none of them is seen as possessing a monopoly or decisive share of power, since the different groups all check and counterbalance each other. Thus no distinct power elite is discernible, and the idea of such an elite is held to be more fiction than reality. The government, to be sure, is vested with power but it is increasingly subject to pressures from the various interest groups. In order to keep itself in office, it must respond to these pressures so as to keep everybody reasonably happy. The *independent* power of the government is therefore minimal.

As Robert Dahl (1967, ch. 1) sees it, one of the most striking characteristics of the American political system is the extent to which authority is divided among a variety of independent actors. Many policy issues are placed in the hands of private or semi-public organizations. And whenever a group of people believes that they are adversely affected by national policies, they have extensive opportunity for presenting their case and for initiating negotiations that may result in more acceptable alternatives. 'In some cases, they may have enough power to delay, to obstruct, and even to veto the attempt to impose policies on them' (p. 23). The United States has thus evolved into a pluralist system where, instead of there being a single centre of sovereign power, there are multiple centres − none of which is wholly sovereign. (See also Dahl, 1971, esp. ch. 7.)

A similar view has been concisely expressed by David Riesman (1961), who wrote:

> There has been in the last fifty years a change in the configuration of power in America, in which a single hierarchy with a ruling class at its head has been replaced by a number of 'veto groups' among which power is dispersed. (p. 206)

> In the amorphous power structures created by the veto groups it is hard to distinguish rulers from the ruled. (p. 214)

> Even those intellectuals . . . who are frightened of those who they think have the power, prefer to be scared by the power structures they conjure up than to face the possibility that the power structure they believe exists has largely evaporated. (p. 223)

Pluralism and the bureaucracy

This thesis refers to the state in general, but a similar thesis has been presented with regard to the bureaucracy in particular. Bureaucrats are unable to rule alone, and yet no one else can rule without them; they cannot always achieve their goals, but they can prevent others from achieving theirs; they are constrained by political elites, but they are influenced by private interests and are constrained by them too; and they, for their part, then constrain others. They are thus but one of several veto groups in a pluralist political system (Rourke, 1976, ch. 7).

In principle, the lifeblood of administration is power. But in the American political system, this power does not flow into the administration exclusively from its top. Indeed, administrative subordinates cannot depend on the formal chain of command to supply enough power to permit them to do their jobs. To fill this void, power must flow into the administration from structures of interests that enclose it. Thus, there is another source of power which competes with that of the formal administrative hierarchy.

Also, political parties that come to power fail to create a political consensus on measures to be carried out. Hence, the relevant bureaucratic agencies must themselves create sufficient consensus to permit policies to be moulded and executed. A bureaucratic agency thus has a large share of responsibility for building and maintaining political support for its own programs, and even for organizing the political basis for its own survival and growth (Long, 1966). In order to survive, any bureaucratic agency must, in the first place, mobilize the support of the legislature. In fact, members of Congress occupying strategic positions (e.g. committee or sub-committee chairpersons) may be able to benefit or damage a bureau more than its departmental head. Hence, bureaucrats may be more sensitive to legislative influence than they are to departmental directives.

Further, any bureaucratic agency must have the support of its clientele and of interest groups or individuals indirectly affected by its programs who can influence the legislature. Finally, the general public through its vote may become a source of support for, or opposition to, administrative agencies. For the party in power may feel that a particular agency is adversely affecting public opinion and therefore must be interfered with. So as to secure support by the public, the bureaucratic agency also needs a sympathetic response from the media. Administrative agencies are thus boxed in by intricately related and opposing interests and in order to survive they have to take into account and be responsive to all politically effective groups who promote those interests and even the public at large (Redford, 1969; Rourke, 1965, p. 187; Simon *et al.*, 1965; Thomson, 1965[1]).

Clearly this system is not conducive to the creation of overall, co-ordinated policies by the political echelon, which the bureaucracy can implement. The advent of Keynesian economics and the erosion of *laissez-faire* have created an intellectual climate for the formulation of overall government policies. But they have not created the political conditions that would make such policies feasible. And because the American political system does not create such overall policies or clear-cut guidelines for the bureaucracy, it does not provide the conditions for even a partial divorce of administration from politics. This is in contrast to Europe, where, because of the conventions of the parliamentary system in combination with security of position, bureaucrats have historically had less reason and less opportunity to engage in direct political activity (Long, 1966; Rourke, 1976).

The political system is pluralist not only in its being subject to a plurality of pressures but also in its very structure. The complexity of the state structure affords interest groups multiple access points at which to exert their influence. State institutions provide arenas for the interplay of contending internal factions, a situation that is fully exploited by interest groups. Within the state institutions, elite persons or groups compete with each other in promoting their own interests, often with the aid of interest groups, and often to the benefit of the latter (see Knoke, 1979).

The bureaucracy is thus part of a pluralist state structure. In addition, it is a pluralist structure in its own right. Contrary to its image, the bureaucracy is not a monolithic hierarchy. Rather, it is a highly fragmented set of agencies that are partly interdependent but are also in fierce competition within and among themselves for survival and primacy. Bureaucratic agencies must not only secure legislative and interest group support and monetary or other facilities but they must also compete with each other for such resources. At the same time, to survive, these fragmented bureaucratic agencies must seek mutual adjustments with each other. Such adjustments are carried out through internal alliances, exchanges of favours, persuasion, threats, manipulation and countless other ways. The fragmentation of bureaucracy and the external and internal adjustments necessitated by it are probably greatest in the United States because of its particular tradition of constitutional checks and balances, but they occur to some extent in all industrialized democracies (Lindblom, 1977, ch. 2; Redford, 1969, ch. 3; Rourke, 1976, ch. 7; Thomson, 1965).

Governmental overload

One version of the pluralist approach has gained special popularity in recent years: the thesis of governmental overload (as propounded by scholars such as D. Bell, M. Crozier, S.P. Huntington, A. King, R. Rose, and others). According to this thesis, there has recently been a growth of pressure on governments to meet an array of newly defined and vastly expanded demands. These demands result from a revolution of entitlements: the involvement of an increasing number of groups in political activity; an increasing expectation on the part of these groups that government is responsible for their needs, and an escalation in what these groups conceive their needs to be (Bell, 1975; Crozier *et al.*, 1975).

Thus, the range of matters for which governments are held responsible has been vastly increasing; just about all grievances now get dumped into the lap of government. Government has come to be regarded as 'a sort of unlimited-liability insurance company, in the business of ensuring all persons at all times against every conceivable risk' (King, 1975, p. 286). 'Once upon a time, then, man looked to God to order the world. Then he looked to the market. Now he looks to Government' (p. 288).

Governments, however, have trouble trying to play God. For just as the range of responsibilities of governments has increased, so their capacity to exercise their responsibilities has declined. This is evidenced by the fact that most government programs do not work well, 'and consist principally of "throwing money at problems" ' (Schultze, 1977, p. 2). It is further expressed in the failure of many policy objectives – for instance, the failure to further a higher rate of economic growth, to curb inflation or to reduce crime. There is thus a combination of increasing demands on governments, and governments' increasing inability to cope with such demands.

With the development of modern society there has been an expansion of the role of governments in the economy and society, and an increasing complexity of the tasks involved. But because of the increasing overload of demands on the decision-making bodies that assume these tasks, the consequence has been – a decrease in their power. It has traditionally been believed that the power of the state depended on the number of decisions it could make. In fact, however, the more decisions the modern state has to handle, the more helpless it becomes. 'Decisions do not only bring power; they also bring vulnerability' (Crozier *et al.*, 1975, p. 13). Or, as King, (1975, p. 286) formulated the idea:

Americans used to write of 'Big Government' as though the State, in becoming all-embracing, would become all powerful. Today our image of government is more that of the sorcerer's apprentice. The waters rise. The apprentice rushes about with his bucket. The waters rise even faster. And none of us knows when, or whether, the magician will come home.

Another result of the escalating demands and responsibilities has been an imbalance between government commitments and government resources. The costs of public policy have been growing at a faster rate than the economy as a whole. In recent years, economic growth has slowed down, yet the costs of public policy have continued to rise as before. The overload of demands has therefore been coupled with a fiscal overload of the system.

Implications for democracy

How do all these processes — the fragmentation of structure, the pluralism of power and governmental overload affect democracy? According to the older version of pluralism its effects are favourable for it leads to the representation of all major interests in policy decisions and therefore to a general, or at least an optimal satisfaction of policy demands. As Dahl (1956, p. 137) asserts: 'all the active and legitimate groups in the population can make themselves heard at some crucial stage in the process of decision'. Moreover, it is the government's task to balance out the various pressures, and hence it cannot act in a partisan fashion and give exclusive support to the interests of the more powerful. Indeed, governments help to countervail the power of the more powerful (e.g. business) interests, by acceding to the demands of opposing and less powerful (e.g. labour) interests. As J.K. Galbraith in one of his earlier writings (1952, p. 141) put it: 'Without the phenomenon itself being fully recognized, the provision of state assistance to the development of countervailing power has become a major function of government — perhaps *the* major domestic function of government.' According to this view, pluralism is also conducive to democracy because it helps tame the power of governments, reduce coercion to a minimum and settle conflicts peacefully (Dahl, 1967, ch. 1).

All this is especially true for the bureaucracy. The bureaucracy has become a forum for the representation of all major popular interests and is recognized as such by interest groups. In democratic theory, policy is determined by counting the votes; the administrative equivalent is the weighing of the relevant pressures (Long, 1966). Moreover, the plurality of pressures tames the power of the bureaucracy and minimizes its threat, for it ensures that bureaucracy cannot gain ascendancy over democratically elected institutions and that no one interest group can gain ascendancy through it. Internal fragmentation of the bureaucracy is desirable as well, for it provides checks and balances within the bureaucracy itself and hence forces negotiation and compromise.

In addition, pluralism is conducive to democracy because it is closely related to the growing impact of the general public on the political arena. As V.O. Key Jr (1958, p. 9) saw it, in this system 'the people may not really govern themselves, but they can stir up a deafening commotion if they dislike the way they are governed'. According to other observers, too, control of non-elites over pluralist elites is considerable. And the chief mechanism of rendering elites accountable to interest groups and non-elites in general is competitive elections. The fear of losing office, the desire for advancing their political careers and the necessity of doing so through elections makes politicians responsive to their voters. The mechanism of selection and replacement of politicians through the polls thus creates an indirect influence of public preferences on policy. 'Aside from casting extremists out beyond the pale, free elections . . . operate to bring governmental policy roughly in line with intense public preferences over a reasonable span of time' (Polsby and Wildavsky, 1968, p. 280[2]; see also Dahl, 1956; Downs, 1957; Knoke, 1979; Redford, 1969; Thomson, 1965).

Many pluralists have thus regarded the perceived situation as eminently desirable. But theoretical pluralism prevails in the pluralist school itself and not all adherents of this school have concurred with this evaluation. Some have even regarded the pluralist system and the power it affords interest groups as excessive and dangerous. McConnell (1966), for one, has held that 'the accessibility to a share in power for almost any coherent and determined group has given American democracy some of its most serious and perplexing problems'. And, further, that 'Some groups have used their opportunity with much greater effectiveness than others, for some, indeed, have been unable to seize the opportunity at all . . . equality of political opportunity has become as much a mockery as equality of economic opportunity' (pp. 26-7).

Furthermore, government deference to interest groups does not eliminate power but transfers it to private hands, thereby making possible the exploitation of public policy for private interests. It therefore verges on corruption. In this manner, too, power has become more arbitrary and despotic. For the remarkable fact about the power of interest groups (such as business and trade unions) is that it is internally oligarchic. It also lacks the limitations, checks, and protective forums against injustice that are inherent in public power, including, among other things, the countervailing power of pressure groups themselves.

The excessive power of interest groups is a result not only of the excessive responsiveness of government but also of excessive splintering, especially of the bureaucracy, since isolated factions in the bureaucracy enter into independent alliances with private interests. This has led to a situation where the governments' 'various fragments . . . are beholden to particular interests' (McConnell, 1966, p. 164), a situation of 'the conquest of pieces of governmental authority by different groups' (p. 7). Rather than leading to government mediation between diverse interests, the excessive power of interest groups has led to government agencies becoming little more than pawns in the hands of private groups, indeed to private power run rampant.

The idea that pluralism has adverse effects on democracy has also been expressed by the scholars concerned with governmental overload. Whereas it was previously thought that the demands of conflicting pressure groups lead to compromise and to optimal satisfaction of needs, these scholars believe that it leads, on the contrary, to universal frustration. 'The essential perversity of the policy milieu is its ability to frustrate nearly everyone at the same time' (Wildavsky, 1973, p. 27). Not least among those frustrated are the politicians themselves: 'Laboratory experiments show that rats who are consistently given contradictory commands become neurotic, if not psychotic. The same phenomenon is readily visible among politicians' (Wildavsky, 1973, p. 25). In addition, the various pressure groups become more and more capable of thwarting each other's purpose. This, in turn, leads to loss of effectiveness of government and to stalemate and paralysis in its policy formation, which is part of a falling away of the democratic process (Moynihan, 1978).

Other observers of this group, for instance Crozier *et al.* (1975), argue that Western democracies are in crisis because they have increasing difficulty mastering their own growing complexity. Beyond a certain degree of complexity, nobody can control the outcome of a system, or even sort out priorities and reach decisions in any coherent manner. Hence, in J. Reston's words,[3] 'The present decision-making "system", if that's the right word, is an incoherent mess.'

All this, in turn, leads to civic indifference. If government does not produce what is expected, citizens are likely to turn away from it, and to withdraw from political life. Such indifference is not likely to bring about revolution or anarchy, but it may well have a negative effect on compliance with laws, willingness to pay taxes and other types of co-operation with government; it may thus have a crippling effect on government authority (Rose, 1979; see also Rose and Peters, 1978; Scharpf, 1977).

Other ramifications of the system's loss of coherence are declining legitimacy of, consent to, and trust in government, as well as rising discontent. Leaders no longer get credit for what is done, and are increasingly subject to attack and personal abuse, while the political system of which they are part is being condemned 'as vicious, immoral and depraved' (Wildavsky, 1973, p. 30). And such '[a] repudiated regime, without effectiveness or consent, can be consigned to the ranks of historical has beens' (Rose, 1979, pp. 354-5). Not surprisingly this situation in its totality leads to ungovernability:

> We demand more of government but we trust it less. Angered and annoyed by evident failures, our reaction is not to reduce our expectations of what government can accomplish but to decrease its ability to meet them. That is how a society becomes ungovernable. (Wildavsky, 1973, p. 26)

An intermediary view has been expressed by C. Lindblom. This author concurs that modern policy-making and decision-making have become exceedingly complex and that comprehensive, rational government decisions, taking into account all possible values, interests, means, exigencies and outcomes are all but impossible. What actually tends to happen in Western democracies, and especially in the United States, is that policy decisions are worked out through a process of mutual adjustments among various interest groups and government agencies. This means that policies frequently happen by 'muddling through' rather than by being actually decided on.

'Muddling through' may not be an ideal way of policy-making. It may be a cumbersome process and, even after considerable time, an agency may be 'still muddling, not yet through'.[4] But it is the optimal procedure that is actually available. Indeed, under the present complex conditions, social problems may often be attacked more comprehensively through interaction than by anyone's attempt to understand the problems. Thus, pluralism is not only a method of curbing government power but it is also one of raising the rationality of decision-making. Certainly the system of mutual adjustments and muddling through does not lead to chaos or to a 'mess'. Rather it expresses the *Intelligence of Democracy*[5] and leads to policy co-ordination that is frequently superior to central co-ordination by the government (if that could be achieved at all, which is doubtful).

This superiority stems, among other things, from the fact that a certain division of labour between various groups and agencies tends to occur, so that each value or interest neglected by one group or agency is the major concern of another. In this manner, every important interest or value has a watchdog, and the system accomplishes an adaptation of policies to a wide range of interests. It is true that not all pressure groups are influential in proportion to the number of citizens for whom they act. Large business corporations clearly take on a privileged role unmatched by other interest groups. In fact, a close, symbiotic relationship has developed between business and government. Hence, the mutual adjustment, or 'muddling through' process, cannot ensure equality. But it certainly leads to a greater degree of equality than central decision-making, which has historically served mainly as an instrument for protecting inherited inequalities (Lindblom, 1959, 1973, 1977, 1979).

Critique and evaluation

The merits of pluralism are manifold. They lie in its bringing interest groups into the orbit of political analysis and in its focusing on the power of such groups as countervailing that of the modern state. They lie in its emphasis that not only governments and political elites but bureaucracies and bureaucratic elites, too, are boxed in between divergent and intricately related interests and pressures which they must placate in order to survive. They lie in its highlighting the increasingly frequent, inextricable entanglement of public with private interests. They lie in bringing into relief the internal complexity and interplay of contending forces within the modern state, including the bureaucracy.

Finally, the merit of pluralism lies in its convincingly making the case that the modern state, including the bureaucracy, is by far not as systematic and rational as (following Weber) it might have widely been thought to be. It thus includes an implicit, and perhaps inadvertent, but largely well taken criticism of Weber's model, together with a shift to a more down to earth image and a more realistic appraisal of the limits of bureaucratic effectiveness.

At the same time pluralism is somewhat one-sided in its approach.

Many of its elements have evidently been geared primarily to the analysis of the American political system; even by the admission of its own proponents it has contributed only in a minor way to the analysis of other Western countries. And if its analyses partially fit some Western European cases (see chapter 9) this is more by chance than by design. While a theory to suit one society only is certainly a legitimate endeavour, it needs to be supplemented by other viewpoints, in the search for an analytical tool that will conceptualize the relationship between bureaucracy and democracy in general.

In addition, this propensity to focus on American society to the near-total exclusion of anything else, reflects a tendency towards ethnocentricity in American social science. This is not to deny that some serious general or comparative analyses have recently been undertaken (see, for example, Huntington, 1968; Putnam, 1976; Aberbach *et al.*, 1981). But in reading some other prominent writings of some other American scholars, one sometimes gains the impression that the authors are only dimly aware that societies other than the United States even exist. Or, if they are aware of their existence, they either do not deem them worthy of analysis or else, they see them as junior relatives of the American system, exhibiting the same characteristics as the American (albeit in a less pronounced manner) or at least as being about to assume these characteristics as they go along. While this avuncular attitude has recently been attenuated with regard to Third World countries, it is still quite evident in some of the pluralist thinking on Western democracies.

It must further be queried whether the pluralist model does, in fact, adequately reflect the American system itself, or whether it is not one-sided in this respect as well. Recently the view has been expressed that American pluralism may well prevail on a superficial level, only to conceal a much more concerted power hierarchy underneath it; that counterbalancing of pressures may well prevail on secondary issues, while the most fundamental issues are decided by much more centralized and one-sided power elites. And, further, that these power elites structure the situation in such a manner that the most basic issues never even come up for decision and therefore are not — at any stage — open to pluralist pressures (see Lindblom, 1977, 1979;[6] Domhoff, 1979, and many others).

Also, it has been pointed out (and indeed admitted by some pluralists themselves) that interest group leaders do not necessarily represent the interests of their rank and file members, while the groups themselves do not usually represent all parts of the population. Various segments of the population differ greatly in their ability to organize and in the pressure they can bring to bear on the bureaucracy. The bureaucracy, in turn, is usually selective in its response to pressures. In Albrow's (1970, p. 118) words: 'The public speaks, yet it is the official who chooses when to listen, to whom, and with what degree of attention.' The bureaucracy displays a distinct tendency to be more responsive to the better established, the more articulate, the more powerful among the interest groups. Those which lack economic, social and political power — the poor, the social and ethnic minorities, in short the underprivileged — are apt to have their pressures disregarded. Thus, as E.E. Schattschneider (1960), has rightly suggested, the flaw in the pluralist heaven is that the heavenly chorus sings with an upper-middle class accent.

Perhaps it is precisely because these views have become more widely accepted that the older version of the pluralist model has recently fallen on hard times, as Knoke (1979) has so aptly pointed out. And possibly it is the lack of awareness of some of the less obvious and less openly observable power centres which has led to the complacency and over-satisfaction of many pluralists with the existent state of affairs. For, as Carole Patemen (1970, p. 16) put it, according to many pluralists 'the system that we ought to have is the very one that we do in fact have'.

However, even those pluralists who are dissatisfied with the existing situation have greatly overstated the dissipation of the power of modern government and, with it, that of modern bureaucracy. This is evident especially in the argument put forward by several eminent scholars on the modern government's inability to cope with its own complexity, its overload of demands, and its consequent helplessness. The idea that complexity and overload lead to political impotence seems to rest on an exaggerated expectation of what power is and what power holders can actually accomplish. Lord Acton is reported to have said that 'Power corrupts; absolute power corrupts absolutely.' While it may be true that power corrupts, it is questionable that absolute power corrupts absolutely, simply because there is no absolute power, except, perhaps under most extreme circumstances, the power of the gun. Certainly, the power of governments and rulers never spells complete control; it is always limited by various constraints such as the biological vulnerability of the rulers themselves,[7] the need for co-operation on part of substantial groups of people — including secondary elites, armies, police forces, tax collectors, and the like — and at least the passive acquiescence of the public at large. Thus, power is always limited by the possibility of passive resistance, sabotage, or riots. Power is by its very essence, therefore, fragile. Complexity and overload only add another aspect to this fragility — they do not obviate power as such, for power exercised in an incoherent manner is still power. A bureaucracy may well be doing no more than 'muddling through' and yet wield considerable power over the public because there are so many who are so greatly dependent on the bureaucracy's 'muddling through' for their livelihood, their health, and sometimes for their very lives. Moreover, if state administrations are muddling today, how much more was this the case at the beginning of modernity and even under 'absolutism'. In those times, administrations and their tasks grew rapidly, yet their structures were still haphazard, and standard operating procedures were only slowly being established. In comparison to those days, then, bureaucracy has clearly become not less but more powerful. This, among other things, will be demonstrated in chapters 8-10.

Chapter 4

Modern theories:
the technocratic view

An antithetical view to that of pluralism has been expressed by what may be referred to as the technocratic school of thought. In France, where the idea of technocracy has been most prominent, this phenomenon has been defined as 'a political system in which the determining influence belongs to technicians of the administration and of the economy'.[1] The technocratic school is that group of thinkers who believe that such a political system has in fact come into existence in modern society.[2]

In some ways, this school is akin to the elitist model which holds that societies are divided into the few who rule and the many who are ruled. The first group (the elites) effectively monopolizes power and is able to enjoy its advantages; it almost invariably gets its way whenever important public decisions are made. The second group (the masses) is invariably in a dependent position, and has no choice but to acquiesce in this arrangement. This model of society was originally developed by Vilfredo Pareto, Gaetano Mosca and Robert Michels.[3] After the Second World War it was further elaborated by C. Wright Mills (1959, 1973). Mills saw modern, and especially American, society as dominated by a power elite which manipulates the masses into accepting its rule. This elite consists of the upper political, military and corporate economic personnel whose power is derived from their key positions in their respective institutional structures. Members of Congress and trade union leaders make up the middle levels of power, and at the bottom are the masses, who are mostly passive and have little influence of their own.

More recently this model has found new proponents such as S. Keller (1963), T.R. Dye and C.H. Zeigler (1975), and G.L. Field and J. Higley (1980), who stress that even in democracies elites continue to rule as exclusively as they ever did before, who proclaim elite rule as a requisite that must be met if society (including democratic society) is to survive, and who stress the elite-determined character of democracy itself.

The technocratic school of thought puts similar emphasis on the power of elites. However, most members of the elitist school are concerned with ruling elites, or power elites, in which the bureaucratic-technocratic elites form only one of several powerful components. The technocratic school, on the other hand, is concerned specifically with the power of the bureaucratic-technocratic elites, and argues that they increasingly replace other elites in determining policy.

The technocratic school also has a theoretical affinity with, and in some ways can be traced back to, James Burnham's thesis in *The Managerial Revolution* (1942). Burnham held that because of the shift of control in economic enterprises from owners to managers and the growing government control of the economy, the bourgeoisie as a ruling class would be replaced by the managerial class, which is already wielding power by virtue of its technical superiority. In the category of managers, Burnham included production managers, administrative engineers, supervisory technicians, and government administrators. He saw no sharp distinction between managers in industry and the state. 'To say that the ruling class is the managers is almost the same as to say that it is the state bureaucracy' (p. 150). In this sense he is certainly a legitimate forerunner of the technocratic school which puts much emphasis on the power of the bureaucracy as derived from its technical expertise. However, Burnham saw managers not merely as powerful but as the forthcoming rulers of society, and he has been severely criticized for this. The contemporary technocratic school does not go so far as to make this claim.

The nature of bureaucratic power

Its central (and somewhat more moderate) thesis is that in Western countries the power of technocrats, and especially of bureaucrats,[4] has recently grown at the expense of elected political bodies, and that this poses a threat to democracy. 'There is an English saying that experts must be "on tap but not on top"; this rule no longer applies today . . .' (Meynaud, 1964, p. 183). Formally, the proponents of this view (including M. Dogan, J. Meynaud, E. Strauss and others) hold, this is still so: bureaucracy is a hierarchy, with an elected minister at the top. The minister makes the political decisions, while the bureaucrats translate them into practice. The minister issues the directives, while the bureaucrats carry them out. In fact, however, the dividing line between policy and administration is by no means clear, and at the top level of the administration they tend to merge. While political leaders do indeed issue directives to the administration, there is both advice and feedback from the administration which limits and guides these directives. Hence, bureaucracy has never been totally under the control of the political leadership, and this control had tended to weaken even further in recent years, while the power of the officials has tended to increase correspondingly. Certainly today the realistic picture is not one of control but of mutual influence between the top administration and the political level. Indeed, they work in such close conjunction that their respective contributions are sometimes hard to distinguish.

Moreover, when the political echelon fails to heed bureaucratic advice, it frequently encounters passive or active opposition. Policies devised by politicians may be invalidated by the method of their execution. Actions thwarting such policies may vary from delaying tactics — such as the amassing of technical difficulties — to outright sabotage. One must not overrate the frequency of such occurrences, but the potential is always there, and this implicit threat acts as a constraint on political decisions.

This does not mean that political leaders can never carry through their own decisions against the active opposition of the bureaucracy. In fact, political leaders can assert their will on any issue if they choose to do so. But each collision with the bureaucracy tends to sap the politicians' energy and erode their power. Hence, they will usually exert their authority over the administration only on a limited number of, to them, most crucial issues.

There obviously is a sphere where the advice of the civil servants is neither solicited nor accepted by the political heads of the government. On the other hand, there are measures of legislation or policy, which are conceived, prepared, and executed by civil servants without the intervention of their political chiefs. The normal run of government policy probably falls between those extremes, with the politicians likely to get their way on measures important to them and the civil servants likely to get their way on many others. In matters deeply affecting the public service, the latter usually has the last word.

In sum, then, although there is an habitual compromise or accommodation between the government and the bureaucracy, this compromise tends more in favour of the public service and at present the civil service is a mammoth organization whose movements are controlled much more effectively by its own chiefs than by political governments. Or as R.D. Putnam (1975, p. 87), reverting to a Burnham-like perspective, put it:

> Can there really be much doubt who governs our complex modern societies? Public bureaucracies, staffed largely by permanent civil servants, are responsible for the vast majority of policy initiatives taken by governments . . . In a literal sense, the modern political system is essentially 'bureaucratic' — characterized by 'the rule of officials'.

The officials so involved usually number no more than a few thousand in each country, the exact number depending on the size of the country. They usually include no more than one per cent of the total personnel in the administration. Of these, there is an even more influential core of a few hundred, or no more than one-tenth of one per cent of the personnel in the administration. The public is not usually aware of this because, unlike politicians, even the most influential officials exert their power behind the scenes. But despite their small numbers and the concealed nature of their activities, and perhaps because of this, these officials wield very real power that has grown substantially in recent years.

Bureaucratic power — an explanation

How can one explain this large and growing power of the top bureaucrats?

1 *Increasing government intervention* One of the main explanations given by the technocratic school lies in the increasing scope and intervention of modern governments in socio-economic life. The growing volume of government activities necessarily leads to the increasing size and power of those who manage those activities — that is, the bureaucracies.

2 *Increasing complexity of government tasks* As their intervention grows, the tasks governments must perform are not only multiplied but become more complex as well. Contrary to pluralists concerned with government overload who believe that greater complexity leads to greater vulnerability (see chapter 3), many observers of the technocratic school believe that it leads instead to greater power of the bureaucracies in charge of these tasks. For, according to this view, it means not only

that larger staffs are required for the execution of tasks but also that these staffs must be more effectively organized, hold a greater measure of discretion, and command more expert knowledge. This in turn, leads to the next explanatory factor.

3 *Expertise* As complexity grows and as technology advances, political decisions are based increasingly on expert technical knowledge. The bureaucracy commands the expertise that political leaders, especially ministers, lack. Devoid of such knowledge, they cannot really control their departments, and they become increasingly dependent on them. Indeed, the technical-expertise of bureaucrats as against the lay status of the politicians has been singled out by this school as the most important factor for the growing power of bureaucracy and it is, of course, this factor that has provided this school of thought with its name. It is, in turn, closely related to yet another explanatory factor.

4 *Information* To make political decisions, political leaders – and especially ministers – must rely on information (or 'briefings') forwarded to them by their departments. These departments are thus in a position to manipulate the information so as to influence decisions. Frequently they do so by screening, timing the release, editing, and even distorting the information in such a manner as to lend support to their own advocated policies.

J. Ellul (1965, p. 259) goes as far as to claim that 'In fact, the politician no longer has any real choice; decision follows automatically from the preparatory technical labors.' Others argue that in many cases, the political leadership may retain the right of making final decisions, but it must choose between alternatives which have usually been mapped out by the administration. Under these circumstances the choice may be more formal than real, because by monopolizing the relevant expertise and by shaping the relevant information, the bureaucrats define the options. In this manner, political leaders are practically compelled to make the choice favoured by their officials.

5 *Time and numbers* Elected politicians have small resources in terms of time and numbers – in contrast to the vast machine of the bureaucracy which they formally control. Hence politicians can pay only sporadic attention to issues on which bureaucrats work for years.

6 *Interest* For this and other reasons, elected politicians, that is, ministers, are not always interested in exerting control over their departments in all matters. They are apt to have some policies that they wish to carry through, whereas most policies are not only beyond their knowledge but beyond their interest as well.

7 *Decline of parliamentary power* Because of the growing complexity

of issues and their own lack of technical expertise, as well as the short-age in time and numbers of their members and staff, parliaments have been more and more compelled to abandon detailed legislation in favour of general laws. These are little more than frameworks that have to be filled in. Legislative functions have been partly transferred to the administration through delegated powers that allow it to fill these frameworks with detailed regulations. This method of delegated legisla-tion, which entrusts officials with a wide measure of discretionary power, has been fully exploited by them, and most democratic countries have recently produced enormous quantities of ordinances.

Even bills passed by parliaments are generally prepared and proposed by governments, that is, in fact, by top administrators. The parliaments' own role in this legislation is frequently minimal. 'The legislatures sometimes amend, rarely reject, usually ratify [what the administra-tions suggest]' (Grosser, 1964, p. 228).[5] Thus legislative initiative, and the power that goes with it, has passed to a considerable extent from parliament to the administration.

8 *Ministerial turnover* The influence of bureaucrats is often founded on the weakness of the politicians with whom they have to deal. This weakness derives from, among other things, regular turnover of the politicians, while civil servants, of course, enjoy the benefits of per-manence. This implies that ministers are disadvantaged *vis-à-vis* the bureaucracy with regard to both past experience and future perspec-tives. Since ministers come and go, bureaucrats are the only ones who can draw up and follow through on long-term plans.

This is true especially for countries where government instability is proverbial (as was the case for many years in France and still is in Italy). But it holds for other countries as well, simply because of the democratic electoral process. Civil servants, too, may move around in the course of their careers, but usually less so than ministers. Besides, administrative continuity derives not only from the personal stability of officials but also from the accumulated experience of their departments.

Political leaders have various means at their disposal for counter-acting these factors. They might elicit expertise, information, and views on the same topic from various agencies. They might even establish partly parallel agencies for this very purpose (for instance, the Prime Minister's Department in Australia duplicates many of the functions of other departments). They might be able to test internal information and advice against external sources, or they might make use of rivalry between administrative agencies. Often such rivalry derives from administrative 'empire-building', where each agency tries to increase its own size and power at the expense of others. As a result, it is unusual to find bureaucrats unanimously on one side and politicians on the other. Politicians can usually exploit such bureaucratic divisiveness to facilitate the assertion of their own will. They can do so especially since the prevailing codes of ethics force bureaucrats into silence, while politicians are at liberty to speak up and address the public through the media. However, the devices that politicians can use against bureaucrats, can only mitigate, not obviate, the continuing growth of bureaucratic power.

Implications for democracy

This, in turn, poses a grave danger for democracy because it places power in the hands of an appointed rather than an elected elite, one that is not answerable to the electorate. Moreover, in the bureaucracy the process of recruitment is such that bureaucrats appoint other bureaucrats. Thereby the bureaucracy becomes not merely an appointed elite, but largely a self-appointed one. This is not only undemocratic but it also increases dissatisfaction and resentment among the public. Therefore, C. Debbasch (1969) goes as far as to claim that the next revolution will without doubt be not against the government but against the bureaucracy.

It is true, as the pluralists have argued, that bureaucrats (no less than politicians) must be and have in fact been, responsive to interest groups. But while responding to pressure groups, bureaucrats also use them to marshal support for their own programs, thereby increasing their own power. Indeed 'the various activities of pressure groups which the technocrat uses ... [are] one of his best trump cards to further his influence' (Meynaud, 1964, p. 17).

The ascendancy of bureaucracy poses a further danger to democracy in that it intensifies secrecy in policy formation, which is the very antithesis of democracy. Bureaucrats use secrecy not only for the sake of efficiency, but also to augment their own power. Indeed, in many bureaucracies, it has turned into a fetish. Democracy, on the other hand, calls for widespread knowledge of governmental processes to make informed judgment and intelligent electoral choice possible. (See Dogan, 1975a and b; Ellul, 1965; Meier, 1979; Meynaud, 1964; Peters, 1978; Rehfus, 1973; Self, 1972; Strauss, 1961; Thomson, 1965).[6] As Bertrand Russell (1967, p. 37)[7] has summarized the problem: 'The increased power of officials ... has the drawback that it is apt to be irresponsible, behind-the-scenes power, like that of Emperors' eunuchs and Kings' mistresses in former times.'

Despite the problems that bureaucracy creates, it is unlikely that modern society will be able to rid itself of it. As C. Perrow (1979) emphasized, bureaucracy is still the most efficient way to get society's business done. Hence, if we want our prosperity to continue, we will have to put up with and get used to the idea that bureaucracy is here to stay. 'Modern man must live with modern Leviathan, and the question is not how to kill it but how to tame it' (Strauss, 1961, p. 284).

Critique and evaluation

In a way the technocratic view may be seen as a mirror image of the pluralist view: each emphasizes the elements of bureaucracy neglected by the other. Just as the pluralist school has emphasized the fragmentation, vulnerability and responsiveness of bureaucracy, so the technocratic school has emphasized its concerted power and distance from public demands. The main importance of the technocratic conception thus lies in its serving as a counterbalance to the pluralist one. And as will be argued below (chapters 7 and 10) the technocratic view on the growth of bureaucracy's power fits reality in Western societies better than the pluralist view on the dissipation of that power.

However, a certain problem emerges from the school's close identification of bureaucracy with expertise and the idea that a major source of the bureaucrats' power lies in their knowledge. Is this in fact the case? Giddens (1973) writes that the old saying 'knowledge spells power' is oversimplified. Experts do not always hold power on their own; like the scribes of antiquity, the experts may well serve to increase the power of those around them. Following G. Sartori (1971), he adds that there is a fundamental difference between the situation in which the powerful hold knowledge and the situation in which the knowledgeable hold power. When power-holders have knowledge, it certainly adds to their power, but knowledge itself does not confer power. The expert, proceeds Giddens, is undoubtedly more essential to the modern decision-making process than any expert ever was before, but if functional indispensability were to spell power, then in a slave economy, the slaves would be supreme.

Indeed the structure of the modern bureaucratic organization testifies to the incorrectness of this view. It is not the experts but the generalists who hold the highest positions. Expertise may thus be an accessory to, but not the main source of, power. As E. Suleiman (1974, p. 389) put it: 'Civil servants do not rule by their superior technical knowledge . . . If they have power it is based on the establishment of institutions whose chief purpose is to maintain control over a given domain . . .'. Thus the power of bureaucrats rests on their organization more than on their expertise.

Finally, the technocratic school has aptly focused on the threat posed by bureaucracy to democracy. But at the same time it has largely disregarded bureaucracy's positive contribution. Self (1972, ch. 5) has appropriately remarked that there is always some conflict between the politicians' interest in helping their supporters and the bureaucrats' concern with impartial rules and procedures. He also makes the point that in modern democracies the politicians' capacity to secure special favours for their supporters has dwindled, as public services have gradually been purged of political patronage. However, he does not make the additional point that special favours to political supporters disrupt the democratic process. Hence, he does not draw the argument to its logical conclusion, namely that a politically independent bureaucracy that obviates such favours is also an asset to democracy, and that it is in fact indispensable for safeguarding unbiased democratic procedures. This argument will be developed in chapter 7.

Chapter 5

Modern theories:
the corporatist view

A somewhat similar view to that of the technocrats has been expressed by a group of writers on corporatism (commonly known as corporatists) that has become increasingly prolific, well known and popular in recent years.[1] Corporatism is generally defined as an institutional arrangement whereby public policy is worked out through an interaction between top state elites and the leadership of a limited number of powerful corporate organizations (mainly business and industrial corporations on the one hand and labour unions on the other). Under this arrangement, the corporate organizations are granted a deliberate representational monopoly within their respective areas of interest in exchange for submitting themselves to certain constraints imposed by the state.[2] The corporatists are those thinkers who believe that tendencies towards such institutional arrangements have in fact come into being in most modern societies and that the present trends of development are towards greater emphasis on such arrangements.[3]

Like the technocratic view, the corporatist view is in some ways an offshoot of the elitist school of thought. For it, too, maintains that there is a small group (or an interlocking set of small groups) of power-holders, that determines more or less unilaterally what happens in state and society. But for the technocrats this group is composed primarily of top techno-administrative personnel, while for the corporatists, it is composed of top state position-holders in conjunction with the top representatives of the most powerful interest groups. The corporatists thus also have something in common with the pluralists in their emphasis on the crucial importance of interest groups, and in their recognition that the modern state has had to adjust to substantive power centres outside itself. But the pluralist approach implies that multiple, voluntary, competitive, and self-propelled groups have a major impact on state policy, while the corporatist approach posits that only a limited number of non-competitive, hierarchically ordered and state-licensed groups have such an impact. (Another school of thought with which a major subgroup of corporatists overlap is that of Marxism or neo-Marxism, as will be seen below.)

As corporatism puts great emphasis on the top leadership of major interest groups in the formation of policy, it has to face the problem of the relationship between that leadership and the rank and file membership of these groups. According to Schmitter (1979b)[4] corporatist intermediation does not imply that the association's top leadership is necessarily representative of its membership. On the contrary, the association's leadership may well misrepresent the membership's interests, it may represent interests of its own instead, and it may even 'teach' the rank and file membership what its interests are supposed to be.

Corporatist intermediation implies, however, that both employer organizations and labour unions are strongly centralized and that their leadership exerts considerable control over their members. For only under these conditions can bargaining power be concentrated in the hands of that leadership, thus creating 'a sort of interlocking directorate of the competing groups' (Lehmbruch, 1979a, p. 59). Conversely, where a high degree of rank and file autonomy exists, and members use their associations to convey demands upwards, corporatism is not strongly developed and an element of pluralism is introduced.

The development of corporatism

As this group of scholars sees it, corporatism as such is by no means a new development, having been well established in Europe in previous centuries. Despite substantial differences among them, most European countries have been possessed by a set of very influential, traditional associations that were involuntary, exclusive and monopolistic — mainly the guilds. From there, '[w]ith varying degrees of delay, reluctance and reservation' (Schmitter, 1979b, p. 71) most European countries moved (during the first part of the nineteenth century) to the abolition of guild privileges and monopolies and to freedom of contract and liberalism.[5] And thence, these countries moved (around the latter part of the nineteenth century) towards a resurgence of associations and towards the emergence of hierarchies amongst them.

This pattern became visible in Western Europe particularly after the First World War. Evidently 'the most famous — or rather infamous — instance of corporatism in practice [was] that of the fascist states'

(Panitch, 1979, p. 120). But the historical experience with corporatism in this century has not been confined to fascism. In liberal democracies corporatist tendencies developed before, concurrently with, as well as after fascism. They came as a result of, and in conjunction with the centralization of economic corporations, the tendencies towards monopolies, oligolopolies and cartels in the economic market-place, the establishment of employers' peak associations, the development of a well organized trade union movement, the emergence of centralized union confederations, and growing state intervention in the economy.

In the United States corporatism did not develop to the same extent as it did in Europe.[6] This is because peak organizations have been either too weak, incomplete or ineffective to be able to represent their respective sectors in the policy-making process. Also, the state institutions themselves have been too fragmented for a corporatist type of bargaining (Salisbury, 1979).

However, in Western Europe, the tendencies towards corporatism that had been visible during the 1920s and 1930s were accelerated further after the Second World War, reaching their fullest development during the 1960s and 1970s. In recent years corporatist (or neo-corporatist) arrangements have involved the further integration of central trade union and business organizations into economic policy-making. In practice (while varying widely from one country to another), they have found expression in a set of consultative bodies and procedures encompassing both labour and capitalist peak organizations. Such bodies include conciliation and arbitration boards, nationally co-ordinated wage determination boards, labour-management agreements and the like. They have been most prominent in countries such as Britain, Sweden, Norway, West Germany, Austria, the Netherlands and Switzerland.

Types of corporatism

The development of corporatism in the twentieth century was related to its bifurcation into two types, according to the role and relative power of the state *vis-à-vis* that of the other peak organizations. According to Schmitter (1979a) one type is that of state corporatism in which the state dominates the corporate groups by repressive imposition of authoritarian political forces; it exists mainly in fascist or other non-democratic regimes. The other type is that of societal corporatism, in which the dominance relationship is reversed and the corporate groups dominate the state; it exists in Western, capitalist, democratic countries.

According to Lehmbruch (1979b) the second type of corporatism ought to be referred to as liberal corporatism. It is distinguishable from, for example, fascist corporatism by the large measure of constitutional autonomy of the groups involved and the voluntary nature of their integration into the system. Accordingly 'the distinguishing trait of liberal corporatism is a high degree of collaboration among these groups themselves in the shaping of economic policy' (p. 150).

This view, however, does not accord with that of Pahl and Winkler (1974) and Winkler (1976) who hold that under any corporatist arrangement the state controls decision-making by prescribing or limiting the range of choice open to capitalist owners or managers. Indeed, in Winkler's (1976, p. 105) view 'Directive state intervention is the principal defining characteristic of corporatism.' According to Pahl and Winkler (1974, p. 73), even in Western countries corporatism is merely approaching 'fascism with a human face'.

In between these two views is that held by Panitch who argues (1979) that the instability of corporatist arrangements in Western countries in the 1960s and 1970s has led in many cases to a coercive type of state response, in the form of legislation restricting unions' freedom of action. Even so, there is less coercion than under fascism. For, adds Panitch (1981), in Western countries the scope of state intervention is an object of struggle in itself. It is the open and unresolved nature of this conflict that distinguishes corporatism in democratic countries from that under fascist regimes.

Corporatism as reinforcing the ruling class

It is at this point, that corporatism and Marxism or neo-Marxism (discussed in the next chapter) partly overlap. For some (though not all) of the major proponents of the corporatist view see corporatist institutions as having their basis in, and deriving their power from, the capitalist class society in which they exist. They also view corporatist arrangements as an aid to the ruling capitalist class in taming or subjugating the working class when market mechanisms for doing so fail. Under both fascism and Western democracy the state is thus seen as an executor, working on behalf (though not necessarily at the behest) of the ruling class (Crouch, 1979; Panitch, 1979; Jessop, 1979; Offe, 1976). According to Schmitter (1979a), the development of corporatism can be traced primarily to the necessity of a bourgeoisie-dominated capitalist regime to reproduce itself. Under fascism it does so through the out-right repression of the autonomous organizations of the subordinate classes. This arrangement develops when the bourgeoisie is too weak to deal with the situation in a democratic context. In a democracy, cor-poratism still serves the requirements of capitalism, but it does so by incorporating the subordinate classes more closely into the political process.

According to Jessop (1979) and Panitch (1979 and 1980), some corporatists work on the tacit assumption that there is an equivalence of power between trade unions and business organizations. In fact, however, they only appear equal. The true situation is that corporatism requires labour unions to adapt their demands to the existing system, and to confine themselves to demands compatible with its persistence. It thereby reinforces the domination of the bourgeoisie. In practice, business interests have been given prominent weight, and policies have been designed so as to abate the wage pressures of trade unions, and to achieve union co-operation in wage restraint. Unions have thus been incorporated into economic policy-making in exchange for their administering wage restraint to their members (see also Offe, 1976).

Panitch (1981) adds, however, that the wage restraint which unions help administer weakens their legitimacy among rank and file workers. Hence, bourgeois-democratic corporatism is usually fragile, and beset by at least potential instability. This was illustrated by the outbreak of rank and file militancy in Europe in the late 1960s; it resulted either in the decline of centralized union authority (Sweden) or in the tem-porary withdrawal of unions from corporatist structures (Britain, Holland). In response, the state tried coercive measures in the form of legislation designed to restrict the unions' freedom of action. When such measures proved ineffective, the state undertook to integrate the lower levels of the union movement more effectively. This took the form of legislation and state-fostered managerial practices designed to facilitate union recognition in organized sectors of the labour force. Despite the potential instability of corporatist arrangements, efforts to impose or maintain them have thus proved to be pretty persistent in recent years.

As Crouch (1979) sees it, the capitalist state has undertaken to come to terms with autonomous unions which must maintain the support of their (sometimes militant) members by giving working-class interests a more direct role in decision-making. 'A suitable slogan for this develop-ment would be "no moderation without participation" ' (p. 46). Some concessions of power are thus given as a trade-off for greater restraint in economic demands or as Jessop (1978) sees it, in return for curbing industrial action, and thus as a price for stability.

Corporatism and democracy

As many corporatists focus their analysis on corporatism in Western countries, they must face up to the (rather complex) question of the relationships between corporatism and democracy. They usually concur that corporatist arrangements in some ways co-exist with democratic institutions (including parliaments, party systems and elections), and many of them point out that corporatism and democracy both reinforce and contradict each other. They do not, however, seem to have a uniform conception on the nature of the relationship between the two, the manner in which they reinforce or conversely contradict each other and on whether corporatism is about to replace democracy.

In Lehmbruch's view (1979a and b), corporatism in the West has remained embedded in a system of liberal, constitutional democracy and corporations and party systems are interconnected through a symbiosis, though not a stable one. Trade unions frequently have strong ties to labour parties and union leaders exert considerable influence within these parties. On the conservative side, party activists and business leaders also maintain close ties or overlap. At the same time, this overlap on both the labour and the conservative side is only partial; in some cases there is considerable independence of the corporate interest groups from the party system and vice versa.

It is sometimes argued (proceeds Lehmbruch) that corporatist arrangements short-circuit or by-pass parties and parliaments. It would be premature, however, to consider that they displace them. In fact, the relative weight of the party system (as against the corporatist system) varies from country to country: the higher the conflict among the corporate groups, the more important the party system and conversely the lower the conflict amongst the corporate groups, the less important the party system.

According to Jessop (1978 and 1979) both corporatism and parliamentary democracy are necessary for the capitalist state. Corporatism is necessary because it is the most appropriate institution for economic intervention. Parliamentary democracy is necessary because it legitimizes corporatism. Further, while corporatism is appropriate for channelling economic intervention, it is inadequate in other areas such as popular struggles concerning regionalism, immigration, civil rights and the like. Hence pluralist pressure politics and elected parliaments continue to play a central role side-by-side with corporatist structures. Finally, parliamentary democracy and corporatism are combined into a contradictory unity owing to the participation of the parliamentary executive (the government) in both corporate decision-making and parliamentary politics. This participation may form a link between the systems and integrate them with each other. But at times the preferred policies in the parliamentary system may be incompatible with those favoured in the corporate system. Hence the participation of the political executive in both settings may also intensify the conflict between the two.

Like Jessop, Cawson (1978), too, expresses the idea that corporatism is confined mainly to the area of economic policy. In other areas, where the imperative for state intervention has been less insistent, interest representation conforms more to the pluralist model. Advanced capitalist societies thus embrace both a corporate and a pluralist sector of interest representation. He adds, however, that as time goes on there is a growth of the former at the expense of the latter; residual, liberal individualist representation decreases, and thus leads to the eclipse of liberal democracy.

Corporatism and bureaucracy

There is even less uniformity in the corporatists' conception of bureaucracy. As Winkler (1976 and 1977) sees it, under corporatism the role of bureaucracy is minimal. According to his view, the central feature of corporatism in Western countries is the combination of private ownership with state control of the economy. In the exertion of such control, the state works through personnel and organizations that nominally are not part of the state. It also gravitates towards indirect, informal, non-public forms of administration. Thus, contrary to what is commonly thought, state intervention is not necessarily synonymous with bureaucratic intervention, and corporatism is in fact, 'a system of state control without bureaucracy' (1977, p. 50).

Why has the corporate state chosen to exert this non-bureaucratic type of control? One reason for this is its major concern with effectiveness and success, for which flexibility and prompt responses are essential. Formalized rules — which govern the work of bureaucracy — introduce rigidity and delay. Rules constrain not only those subject to them, but those imposing them (i.e. the state) as well. Therefore

'Bureaucratic forms of administration actually weaken the state's capacity to direct the economy' (1977, p. 51). Hence the state avoids formalizing its procedures. It prefers discretionary formulae and optional intervention over clearly spelled out laws and regulations, and voluntary agreements, over formal contracts. 'Indeed, "voluntary" is the euphemism of the corporatist economy, analogous to "free" in a market system' (1977, p. 51). The state uses its financial powers as a bargaining lever to reach all manner of semi-formal 'agreements' with various groups, thus putting 'a patina of legality on what is fundamentally the destruction of the rule of law' (1977, p. 51).

Moreover, since the state is dealing with a limited number of dominant firms, a massive administrative apparatus is unnecessary. Agreements are worked out in informal negotiations between key persons in the state and business sector. Thus, 'The simplest reason why corporatism will not be bureaucratic is because it does not need to be' (1977, p. 53). And once the state reaches agreements with large private bodies, it then obliges them to enforce these themselves, to be responsible for their own members, clients and supporters. Private organizations become agents of the state. The corporatist state thus, in effect, tells its private organizations 'control thyself' (1977, p. 53). And this method appeals to business interests which are hostile to the intrusion of state bureaucracy.

Finally, the corporatist state conducts some of its public administration through quasi-governmental organizations (quagos; for instance, in Britain, the BBC, The Bank of England and the like),[7] and quasi-non-governmental organizations (quangos; for instance the British Press Council and the like) because this enables the central political actors to deny responsibility for what the government is doing. The interests of all major actors thus seem to be best served through a minimalization of bureaucratic power.

According to Panitch (1980), however, this argument cannot be sustained. To the extent that the state imposes policy directives on private associations 'it is inconceivable that this could be done without an autonomous bureaucratic arm with independent access to information and capable of supervising the operations of capital' (p. 165). Cawson (1978), too, thinks that corporatist bargaining institutions are unlikely to replace bureaucracy. Contrary to Winkler, he does not perceive a logical inconsistency between corporatist and bureaucratic principles, and believes that corporatism was itself furthered by increasing rationalization of policy-making.

A similar view has been expressed by Diamant (1981), who believes that there is a bureaucratic side to corporatism. For senior bureaucrats work only under a very thin layer of politicians: 'on the whole the number of political executives sitting atop major state administrative agencies is relatively small' (p. 110). Therefore, in most West European states, relations between societal groups and mandarins (i.e. senior bureaucrats) are bound to be much closer under corporatist conditions than would otherwise be the case and this presumably augments bureaucracy's role in policy-making and therefore its power. An even more extreme view on the increase of bureaucratic power under corporatism has been expressed by Marris (1972) who refers to the corporatist state as a 'megabureaucracy'.

Most corporatist writers, however, see corporatism as related neither to an increase nor to a decrease in bureaucratic power. They have, in fact, little if anything to say on bureaucracy, apparently seeing it as part and parcel of what they usually refer to in general terms as 'the state'. According to Diamant (1981) most corporatists thus tend to reduce the mandarins to automata who act automatically (rather than autonomously) on behalf of the state. Mandarins thus become merely its transmission belts. Rebelling against this common corporatist attitude towards top officials, Diamant (p. 120) writes: 'Will nobody rescue this highly trained and intelligent group of men from a fate they clearly do not deserve?'

Critique and evaluation

The main significance of corporatist writings (like that of technocratic writings) lies in their serving as a counterbalance to pluralism. Pluralist writers have tended to go overboard in their emphatic stress on the multiplicity, fragmentation and power-equivalence of interest groups and on the splintering, overload, bungling and general impotence of the state. Hence the importance of corporatism in swinging the pendulum in the opposite direction by pointing to the unequal and hierarchical nature of interest groups and to some more concerted foci of power at the core of Western states. The fact that corporatist writings have recently become fashionable is also important, for it has enabled them not to obliterate pluralist writings but to help us see them in their proper perspective.

At the same time it must be noted that in relation to elitist theory — as formulated, for instance, by C.W. Mills — corporatism shrinks, if not to insignificance, at least to no more than a modest shift in emphasis.

As will be recalled, Mills posited a power triumvirate consisting of the top state, military and corporate-economic elites (relegating trade unions and their leadership to the middle ranks of power). Corporatists, for their part, do not include top military personnel in their model (or else tacitly assume that it is part of the state elite). Instead, of course, they posit a triumvirate of power composed of the top state, corporate business and trade union personnel. Since many corporatists seem to agree that the power of top trade union leadership is in fact much inferior to that of top capitalist and state personnel, the difference between their and Mills's conceptions is not really overwhelming. Mills applied his conception primarily to the United States while corporatists apply theirs primarily to Western Europe. But both address their analysis to Western, capitalist, democratic countries and the principles underlying the two conceptions are really quite similar. While Mills assumes that those who occupy the 'commanding heights' of society do so because of their control over key institutions, some corporatists locate the source of their power in the capitalist class structure. As noted, however, these latter corporatists have a close affinity with Marxism, so that their view, too, amounts to merely a shift of emphasis.

However, in contrast to Mills, who clearly specified his concepts, corporatists are usually hazy in their dealings with the concepts and phenomena that lie at the centre of their analysis, and rather indeterminate as to the relationships between them. As Nedelman and Meier (1979) have rightly pointed out, it is unclear what corporatists understand by the concept of the state. Is it the government, the administration, parliament or all three? Since the state is one element in the corporatist triangle, an unclear conception of the state also implies a hazy conception of the institutions of corporatism itself. It further implies an unclear conception of the relationship between corporatism and democracy. And, what is especially relevant for the present discussion, it also implies an indeterminate conception on the relationship between corporatism and bureaucracy. Indeed, except for Winkler (whose ideas are rejected by many other corporatists) members of this group have little to say on this topic.

Some queries must also be raised with regard to the faithfulness with which corporatist descriptions of reality accord with actual reality. As Nedelman and Meier have once again indicated, the exclusion of non-economic organizations from the model is not really justified. In many European countries the church has long been one of the central foci of power. While the church's present power cannot be equated to its power in the past (especially before the French Revolution), neither can it be disregarded. Moreover, lately, non-economic organizations representing moral rather than financial interests seem to have become important in influencing core policy decisions (see chapter 9). And so, in a different manner, have multinational corporations,[8] whose omission from so many corporatist analyses is puzzling indeed.

Finally, corporatists posit centralized control of trade union leaders over rank-and-file members. Some corporatists see maintenance of such control as problematic, and some attempt to cope in their analyses with rank and file militancy. But, by and large, corporatists concur, that without a large degree of centralized trade union leadership control over their members, corporatist arrangements cannot be viable. Yet they also maintain that, in many Western countries, tendencies towards corporatism have, in fact, become more pronounced and viable in recent years. They thus work on the tacit assumption that union leadership control of the rank and file has also become more pronounced or at least has remained quite pronounced in recent years. As Diamant (1981) rightly queries, what reason do we have to believe that this is in fact so? Corporatists further assume that labour union leaders are willing to co-operate, and to accept the corporatist deal imposed on them by the state and/or the corporate business elites. Once more: what reason do we have to believe that this is in fact the case? The large number of strikes and other forms of industrial action so prevalent in recent years would seem to indicate, on the contrary, that either the union leaders do not have the degree of control over the rank and file attributed to them by the corporatists, or else are not disposed to display the degree of co-operation with corporatist arrangements similarly attributed to them by the corporatists.[9] If, however, we withdraw the trade unions and their leaders from the power and policy-making triumvirate and see corporate arrangement as merely a coalition between state elites and corporatist capitalist elites, and if we further accept the assertion of those corporatists who claim that in this coalition the capitalist elites hold primacy of power, then we are merely left with a general Marxist theory. This will be our topic in the following chapter.

Chapter 6

Modern theories: the Marxist view

The theory of the state (including that of bureaucracy and democracy) was not the most highly developed part of Marx's work. This has made it both harder and easier for modern Marxists. Harder because they had little (perhaps only one central idea) to go on and easier because it left them more scope for the development of their own ideas.

The state and the ruling class

Marx's central pertinent idea is — as expressed most forcefully in the *Manifesto of the Communist Party* (Marx and Engels, 1969, pp. 110-11) — that 'The executive of the modern state is but a committee for managing the common affairs of the whole bourgeoisie.' As Ralf Miliband (1973, p. 7) has pointed out, although Marx in some of his other writings refined and qualified this view, he never abandoned it.

Using this idea as a point of departure, contemporary Marxists have added to it the distinction between governing and ruling. Governing, they say, concerns the execution of the day-to-day routine work of administration and decision-making, that makes the political process run smoothly. Ruling, on the other hand, implies the holding of decisive power that constrains the political process and determines how it will be run and in whose interests. It makes little difference who *governs* in modern capitalist society, for in any event it is the bourgeoisie, the capitalist class that *rules*; the governing elite (frequently referred to as the state apparatus) merely serves the interests of the ruling capitalist class. Indeed, adds Nicos Poulantzas, the state best serves the interests of the ruling class when the latter is not a governing class and does not participate in the routine, day-to-day running of the political system.

Before the advent of capitalism, Miliband points out, government was in the hands of the then ruling class, the aristocracy. Today, in most Western capitalist countries, the present ruling capitalist class has a significant share in staffing the state apparatus, although it does not monopolize it to the same extent as the aristocracy did in an earlier age. But even though the capitalist class does not govern exclusively, it still rules exclusively, and thus the basic situation is as it was: the political system still works overwhelmingly to promote the interests of the ruling class.

The state apparatus has a relative autonomy *vis-à-vis* the ruling class, but this itself works in the interests of the same ruling class since the state can only serve the common interests of that class in so far as it is not exclusively committed to any of its diverse and frequently warring factions. Only in this manner can the state reach a compromise between these factions' opposing interests. And such a compromise is a basic requirement of their joint rule. Hence, it is precisely this relative objectivity of the state which enables it to organize the hegemony of this class as a whole (Miliband, 1973; Poulantzas, 1975; Mandel, 1975).

This, of course, may raise the query of why the state apparatus should wish to promote the hegemony of the ruling class in the first place. According to Marxist theory, the state does so for three distinct reasons. Firstly, people who are in commanding posts in the state have tended (with some exceptions) either to belong to the dominant classes or to be sufficiently privileged to share their education, social connections and way of life. This results in common attitudes and common perspectives on what is desirable, specifically in the common idea that what is good for capitalism is good for society. Or in the immortal words of a former American Defense Secretary, 'What's good for General Motors is good for America and vice versa.' Secondly, the capitalist class, by virtue of its decisive economic power, has become the dominant pressure group in capitalist society, and the government has no choice but to give in to its pressures. Thirdly, and most importantly, because the state acts in a capitalist system of production, it is structurally constrained to serve the interests of capitalism. 'A capitalist economy has its own "rationality" to which any government and state must sooner or later submit, and usually sooner' (Miliband, 1977, p. 72). And by serving the capitalist economy, the state necessarily serves the class in charge of that economy. Failing this, it would undermine the economy and thereby, the basis of its own power. The state apparatus thus promotes the interests of the capitalist class because by doing so it promotes its own interest, that of keeping itself in power.

The ruling class in a democracy

At this point it may be asked whether this structural bias towards the ruling class has not been counteracted by the development of political democracy, free elections, and especially universal suffrage — as a result of which dominated classes now hold an electoral majority. In view of this, would not the state apparatus, by promoting the interests of the ruling class, increase the chances of being voted out of office? According to Marxist theory, an openly partisan political state would indeed antagonize the working class and undermine its own power. But the capitalist state has managed to promote the interests of the ruling class while *appearing* to be class neutral. It has managed to practise its class character and keep it concealed at one and the same time (Offe, 1974).

Moreover, according to the Marxist view, democracy is designed to lend the electorate a sense of power but only little (if any) actual power to determine policy. As G.W. Domhoff[1] (1978) sees it, election campaigns are largely innocuous: politicians base their appeal on the projection of an image and on meaningless generalities. They frankly admit that you don't raise unnecessary issues in such campaigns. 'Indeed you don't raise any issues if you can help it . . .' (p. 136). According to Miliband (1973, p. 64), the electoral system gives people the illusion that unsurmountable cleavages exist between parties and that momentous issues are at stake:

> The assertion of such profound differences is a matter of great importance for the functioning and legitimation of the political system, since it suggests that electors, by voting for one or other of the main competing parties, are making a choice between fundamental and incompatible alternatives, and that they are therefore, as voters, deciding nothing less than the future of their country.

In actual fact, however, there is a basic consensus among all political parties:

> What is really striking about *these* political leaders and political office-holders . . . is not their many differences but the extent of their agreement on truly fundamental issues . . . the political office-holders of advanced capitalism have, with very few exceptions, been agreed over . . . the existing economic and social system of private ownership.

This being the case, the dominated classes have no choice but to vote for a party that promotes the capitalist system. In fact, it really makes very little difference who people vote for and which party is elected. In any case the victor will perpetuate the system no less than his defeated opponent (see also Offe, 1972).

This general situation is not altered when labour parties come to power. For, once in power, labour leaders have been much more moderate than their followers have meant them to be. They have not shown any marked tendency to transform the system, at least not drastically or immediately. They have assured representatives of prevailing interests that they were 'acutely aware . . . that Rome was not built in a day, and that its building must in any case be approached with the utmost circumspection' (Miliband, 1973, p. 91). They have practically looked for excuses not to embark on the reforms that they had previously promised their electors. And the reforms they did engage in were only those compatible with the reproduction of capitalism. Their first order of business has usually been to revitalize the capitalist economy (Miliband, 1973; Wright, 1978, Conclusion).

It follows that, as G. Therborn (1978) sees it, bourgeois democracy is but the rule of the bourgeoisie through the instrument of free elections and universal suffrage. Although conceived outside the bourgeoisie and accomplished only after long and bitter struggles, universal suffrage actually furthers the bourgeoisie's interests. The popular vote advances one of the bourgeoisie's central aims — integrating all social layers into the political framework of the state without giving up any of its actual power. In fact, bourgeois democracy is a system whereby the acquiescence of the ruled classes is assured *through* their political participation, through taking some account of their interests and through flexibility by which cohesion is maintained. Moreover, 'If these mechanisms ultimately prove to be inadequate, then the more drastic solutions of fascism, military dictatorship or foreign intervention are always available and invariably employed' (Therborn, 1978, p. 77; see also Jessop, 1977).

Despite all this, most Marxists do not hold that democracy counts for nothing. In Miliband's (1977, ch. 4), view, all capitalist states are class states and whenever they intervene in social life, they do so to further ruling class domination. But the *manner* in which they intervene makes a difference. In the bourgeois democratic state the powers of intervention are circumscribed and its police powers constrained in various ways. In the authoritarian state, in comparison, the powers of intervention are much less regulated.

Even in bourgeois democracies, the repressive power of the state is considerable, notwithstanding the hallowed rhetoric of civil freedom. In times of social conflict, this repressive power becomes even more manifest, and it is not absent in peace-time either. It is pronounced especially with regard to the underprivileged — the working class, the non-whites, etc. Even so, there are qualitative differences between such regimes and authoritarian (or fascist) ones; in the latter, dissidence is forcibly suppressed. Some of this occurs in bourgeois democracy but nowhere near to the same extent. Authoritarian regimes make it their first task to destroy the defence organizations of the working class — the trade unions, the labour parties, the co-operatives. Bourgeois democratic regimes, on the other hand, have to accept such organizations and they are defined as democratic in terms of that acceptance. They seek to curtail the rights of such organizations; and to absorb, buy off, or 'co-opt' the leadership of these organizations. But all this is a very different thing from their actual destruction, which is the hallmark of authoritarian fascist (and communist) regimes. Besides, 'Cooptation is a contradictory phenomenon. Entry of the ruled classes into unity with their rulers provides both a means to secure their active and willing submission and a platform for their demands and opposition' (Therborn, 1978, p. 234). So, all in all, bourgeois democracy is still preferable to practically all past and present alternatives. 'The bitter experiences of fascism and Stalinism and the enduring legacy of the latter, have taught the firmest revolutionary opponents of capitalism that bourgeois democracy cannot be dismissed as a mere sham' (Therborn, 1977, p. 3).

Democracy and bureaucracy

It is therefore regrettable that in recent years the institutions of democracy have been receding before those of bureaucracy. This, in turn, is the result of growing state intervention in the economy, which has led to the growth of bureaucracies and an enhancement of their role. Moreover, solutions to the present world economic crisis must involve much more profound state intervention in the production process, and therefore, must lead to even more formidable bureaucracies. Also, the increased dominance of monopolies under advanced capitalism has tended to displace the articulation of bourgeois interests to the upper regions of the state administration, thus further enhancing its role (Mandel, 1975; V. Wright, 1978, Conclusion).

These developments have caused some severe problems for state administration. Once, A. Wolfe (1977) argues, the class struggle and the political process decided who got what. In later capitalism, the administration performs this function. But the formal ideology of bureaucracy is that it is non-political, conflict free and concerned only with administrative rationality. 'Caught between its politicized tasks and its depoliticized rationale, public administration in late capitalism searches for answers to its intractable task wherever it can find them, only to discover that each possible option causes as many problems as it solves' (p. 270). 'The public administration of late capitalism becomes weaker the stronger it appears to be, a contradiction ultimately caused by the gap between its political requirements and its administrative ideology' (pp. 270-1).

Other Marxists believe, however, that bureaucracy has in fact been strengthened, inasmuch as the parliament's previous power over the bureaucracy has been curtailed; its previous power of enacting rules and making political decisions has shifted to the bureaucracy, and the latter has subordinated political parties to itself. Bureaucracy has thus become the dominant state apparatus (Miliband, 1973; Offe, 1972; Poulantzas, 1978).

This ascendancy of bureaucracy has had rather grim consequences for democracy. As C. Offe (1972) sees it, it is questionable nowadays whether parliaments still function to represent the political will of the people. Or, in J. O'Connor's view, the capitalist, bureaucratically organized state is necessarily undemocratic, for in it neither the citizens themselves, nor their representatives, are responsible for devising and carrying out policy. And while 'representatives in elected bodies are once-removed from the people; appointed state officials are twice-removed from the people' (O'Connor, 1978, p. 17).

According to Poulantzas (1978) (who goes into this topic in greater detail), the aforementioned developments mark the growth and imposition of authoritarian statism. This does not mean that the present capitalist state is fascist or approaching fascism. However, 'Every democratic form of capitalist State itself carries totalitarian tendencies' (p. 209). And these tendencies are now apparent to a greater extent than before.

In previous years, proceeds Poulantzas, parliaments had the not-insignificant function of allowing the representatives of the popular masses to give a certain expression to their interests within the state and of serving as barriers to arbitrary state power. These functions have all but disappeared. Now that the bureaucracy has increased its power, the weight of popular demands in policy-making has been greatly reduced. In the past, the deputies were directly involved in decision-making within the administration; today their access to the administration is much more restricted. The administration has thus become distanced from popular representation, shutting itself up in a watertight container.

Also, in the past, when political parties were more powerful, they maintained genuine ties with social classes and afforded some channels for the expression of class interests. Now, however, parties have come to be nothing but conveyor belts for bureaucratic decisions. For their part, the bureaucratic apparatuses, which have taken over from political parties, do not afford channels for the expression of class interests. For they are structured in such a way that the interests of monopoly capital directly impinge upon them, while popular needs and demands are excluded from their fields of perception. In their very structure, these apparatuses thus embody the hermetic insulation of power from democratic control.

Finally, the shift in the centre of gravity towards the state bureaucracy involves a considerable restriction of political liberties. Although in the past such liberties were used by the bourgeoisie in order to submit the state to its own interests, they also afforded some public control over state activities. Now this control has all but vanished.

Power is thus being concentrated in tighter structures: governmental and bureaucratic summits. This process is now replacing the limited distribution of power among various centres that used to characterize the bourgeois state. This development embodies 'the specifically bureaucratic logic according to which statism begets statism and authoritarianism begets authoritarianism' (p. 227).

One reason why the strengthening of bureaucracy has such grim consequences for democracy is that the increasingly powerful bureaucracy is becoming more politicized. In France, the plurality of parties is being subjugated by the administration, and one party, the dominant one, has an increasing share in controlling it. Hence, the administration is less and less successful in maintaining the fictitious distinction between administrative and political decisions. 'Of course it [the administration] was never neutral in any real sense; but it is now being openly and massively politicized . . .' (Poulantzas, 1978, p. 234).

This, in turn, has subverted democratic processes, in that the dominant party has managed to monopolize the command posts of the administration for its members and sympathizers. At the same time senior civil servants gravitate towards the dominant party, just as much as the party propels its trusted men towards the senior posts in the administration. A veritable symbiosis is thus created between the state apparatus and the dominant party. The result: the bending of state institutions so as to create the best conditions for partisan action and the diversion of public funds for party aims. Loss of government power would strip away a whole series of material rewards for party faithfuls (Poulantzas, 1978, part 4, chs 1, 2, 3).

Bureaucracy is basically an arm of the state, and as such it is no different from the rest of the state in the degree to which it promotes ruling-class interests: it can gain some, but not unlimited, autonomy from these interests. Nevertheless, the growing power of bureaucracy is significant in this respect too because bureaucrats tend to have distinctly conservative inclinations. Insulated as they are from popular pressures, which politicians must at least partially heed, bureaucrats mostly play the role of advocates of the *status quo*. Further, recruitment procedures, screenings and security checks prevalent in all capitalist countries favour people with a conservative stance. This, in turn, is reinforced by more favourable career prospects for conservative civil servants while 'Outside that spectrum, there lurks the grave danger, and in some countries the absolute certainty, of a blighted administrative career or of no administrative career at all' (Miliband, 1973, p. 111).

Thus, if civil servants seem to be party neutral, it is because parties in power (including social democratic ones) have never tried to implement policies at variance with conservative interests. 'For the loyalty they [the social democratic leaders] praise is much less an expression of the infinite ideological and political adaptability of civil servants as of the infinite adaptability of social democratic leaders to conservative purposes' (Miliband, 1973, p. 109).

Substantial numbers of those on the lower rungs of the bureaucratic ladder are potential allies of the working class. But the top of the hierarchy resists these forces and tends towards conservatism. And since it is this level that holds the power, the bureaucracy as a whole tends to reinforce the conservative bent of the government. Thereby it becomes a crucially important element in the defence of the structure of power and privilege inherent in advanced capitalism. Contemporary capitalism has no more useful servants than the administrative elite (Miliband, 1973, ch. 5; Poulantzas, 1975; V. Wright, 1978, Conclusion).

Critique and evaluation

Contemporary Marxism[2] has several engaging qualities. It consists of a general framework whose various parts interrelate and interlock with each other; it thus presents a unified and coherent explanation of all aspects of social reality. It presents a dynamic and forceful view of society, with major emphasis on socio-historical change and revolution, as against the exceedingly static view put forward in many contemporary writings of 'mainstream'[3] social scientists. It calls (or recalls) our attention to economic factors, conflict (and in particular class conflict) as major factors in understanding social life and social change, a set of factors that for many years has been sadly neglected by 'mainstream' social scientists. It points to the importance of class interests in explaining social action even in areas that are seemingly unrelated to it. It demystifies many established ideologies and shows them up for what they are — attempts to legitimize class interests. Through all these features it has made a truly substantial contribution to our understanding of modern, especially capitalist society. Last but not least, it shows more serious concern with socio-economic inequality than many other schools of thought in the various disciplines of the social sciences. For all these reasons it holds (and justifiably so) a strong appeal especially for the young and even more so for young intellectuals.

In relation to bureaucracy the contribution of modern Marxism (like that of Marx himself) lies in its seeing this establishment as engaged in promoting distinct interests and as entangled in power struggles — something that Weber despite his genius never came to terms with. It also lies in the conception that bureaucracy, through the power it amasses, its non-democratic nature and general distance from the public — poses an increasing threat to democracy.

The problem seems to begin, however, with the Marxist idea that the state (and with it the bureaucracy) serves the interests of the ruling class. The problem with this idea is not merely its content but the fact that it has turned into a dogma. Whether it ever was a hypothesis that could be tested (and therefore possibly invalidated by empirical evidence) is not clear, but it certainly is no such thing today. Empirical developments in Western countries are invariably interpreted as supporting this tenet. If the state elite is conservative in its policies then, obviously, it works in the interests of the ruling class. If, on the other hand, it introduces reforms that benefit the lower classes (e.g. universal suffrage or extensive welfare and social security systems), this too is interpreted according to the Marxist view as serving merely to co-opt these classes and make them more willing to accept the capitalist system. Hence, this too, is done in the interests of the ruling class.

It cannot be denied that in many countries (whether capitalist or of another persuasion) a certain overlap of interests between the politically ruling elites and the economically dominant classes is evident: both are interested in maintaining the socio-political system from which they derive their dominant positions. Hence, each must, to some extent, serve the interests of the other, in order to promote its own interests. The Marxist view brings out only one side of this dual relationship: the manner in which the state elites, by serving their own interests, serve the interests of the ruling classes. The opposite, however, is equally correct: the dominant classes, by serving their own interests, frequently serve the interests of the state elites. Rather than viewing the state elites as the servants of the ruling class, it would be more realistic to view them as two groups, each of which is intent on using the other to serve its own interests.

Moreover, while the interests of the two groups may frequently coincide, they are by no means identical. Whenever those interests diverge, can there be any doubt that each group will give clear preference to its own interests as against those of the other? If the political elite in a capitalist country should find that it can survive better by promoting working- and lower-class interests or by exploiting the capitalist class, can there be any doubt that it will in fact do one or the other or both? In the second part of this book, an instance will be cited in which the latter has, in fact, occurred (see chapter 13).

Thus, the Marxist view of the class nature of the state apparatus suffers from excessive dogmatism, from insufficient flexibility to see the other side of the coin and take into account incongruous developments. At the same time, the Marxist view of democracy suffers from excessive vacillation and uncertainty. On the one hand, democracy is conclusively shown to afford little (if any) choice, discretion or power to the public; on the other, it is praised as being preferable to practically all other existing regimes, and its alleged recent weakening through the strengthening of bureaucracy is sincerely lamented. One may well ask: if democracy is so worthless then why is it so desirable? If democracy is so innocuous, then why lament its alleged decline? If democracy affords no real power to the public in curbing the power of ruling elites, then how has it avoided the atrocities of nazism, fascism, Stalinism and other like-minded regimes? For although Marxists seem to believe that democracy is preferable to these regimes, they never explain *why*.

Miliband states that democracies have a lesser tendency to suppress dissidence, and in contrast to authoritarian regimes tend to accept working-class organizations. He adds that they are defined as democratic in terms of that acceptance. This, however, merely begs the question. It describes the phenomena that call for an explanation but does not furnish such an explanation. Which is another way of saying that this analysis (like other Marxist analyses) does not really add up to a theory of democracy.

The indeterminacy and vagueness that characterize the Marxist analysis of democracy are characteristic of its analysis of bureaucracy as well. It has been argued (Krygier, 1979a) that Marxists believe bureaucracy (and the state of which it is part) has no real power, such power being exclusively in the hands of the ruling classes. So, although Marxists may revile bureaucracies as much as anarchists did, they do not really regard them as centrally important. From the foregoing analysis it seems, however, that Marxists are not as consistent on this point as Krygier assumes them to be, that the clearcut view on the powerlessness of bureaucracy which Krygier imputes to Marxists is simply not there.

For at the same time that Marxists assert that bureaucracy (as part of the state) is merely a servant of the ruling class, they also assert that bureaucracy is amassing more and more of the state's decision-making power, and they are deeply concerned about this development. They see it as insulating the state from popular pressure and bringing to the fore the state's most conservative elements. If bureaucracy holds no real power, why be concerned about the increase of that power? If bureaucracy holds no central importance, why worry about the growth of that importance? This means, in other words, that Marxists (like Marx himself) do not really present a well-developed theory of bureaucracy either.

Finally, while Marxists point to the dangers of bureaucracy for democracy they (like many other theorists) fail to bring out its positive contributions; they fail to show the indispensability of bureaucracy for democracy. To this, among other things, we turn in the next chapter.

Chapter 7

Bureaucratic power –
a democratic dilemma

On the background provided thus far by the theories reviewed, some additional theses can now be proposed. To make these intelligible, it is necessary first to present some working definitions of the main concepts to be employed and some assumptions on their context. As has been remarked, concepts mean what we tell them to mean. To avoid confusion, we must therefore establish what we do, in fact, tell our concepts to mean in this analysis.

Definitions and assumptions

Bureaucracy is defined as a hierarchical organization of officials appointed to carry out certain public objectives (the discussion will be restricted to state bureaucracy). The extent to which such an organization does or does not fit Weber's model (for instance with regard to the appointment and promotion of officials by objective criteria and the general, objective, impersonal rules guiding their actions) can thus be left open for empirical investigation.

Power is defined as control over (or ability to determine) the allocation of resources on which others are dependent; and therefore, ability to influence other people's life chances.[1]

Elites are defined as those people or groups of people who wield such power. State elites are those people who wield power by virtue of their position in the institutional structures of the state (they include political elites – or senior politicians – and bureaucratic elites – or senior bureaucrats).

My assumption is that the people holding power positions commonly work to entrench themselves in these positions, and that many of their actions can be explained in that light. This is so because power opens access to various material and social rewards (such as high salaries, fringe benefits, prestige and celebrity) besides being a reward in its own right. This implies that elites (like other persons) act in their own interest; it does *not* imply, however, that they are motivated *only* by self-interest, taking no account of other considerations. As Downs (1967, p. 84) put it:

> Under normal conditions, men accept certain constraints on their pursuit of self-interest imposed by the widely shared ethical values of their own cultures. . . . Thus the prevalence of self-interest . . . does not imply that people will pursue their own interests without any ethical or other constraints.

Politics is defined in the broadest sense as the process whereby power is contested for, obtained, maintained and exercised. In the modern state the contest for, and the exercise of, power frequently takes place within and through certain organized groups known as political parties. The contest for, and the exercise of, power also takes shape through the design, promotion and implementation of policies — policies being the general guidelines for the allocation of resources. Thus, both party-related activities and policy-related activities are in the broadest sense political.

Democracy (or a democratic political structure) is defined as the institutional arrangement whereby two or more organized groups of people (or parties) participate in the contest for power (or for elite positions) on the strength of their advocated policies and/or their projected images and whereby they acquire such posts on the basis of free elections by the whole of the adult population.

This definition presupposes certain civil liberties as implied in the concept of free elections. It also presupposes that free elections, by making it possible for the public to replace elites, afford a significant channel of public influence on those elites' decision-making. However, it is, on the whole, a realistic (or descriptive) rather than an ideal (or prescriptive) definition.[2] Even so, it is not necessary to assume that any regime actually embodies this institutional arrangement. It is sufficient to assume (as I do) that most Western states come closer to doing so than non-Western states and that some Western states come closer to doing so than others.

It is a widely held assumption (which I share) that in a democratic political structure, the contest for and exercise of power take place according to certain 'rules of the game' that have been worked out through previous power struggles, have developed over several centuries and have been incorporated into constitutions, statutes, laws and unwritten conventions. These rules serve as normative constraints on the pursuit of the elites' self-interest, they serve to circumscribe the elites' struggle for power and to restrain their exercise of that power.

At the same time there are limits to the efficacy of these rules and ethical constraints themselves. When political survival or other important interests are at stake, they may well be countervened or circumvented. Also these rules are not always clearly defined; they are sometimes ambiguous, inconsistent, controversial or all three. Whenever this is the case, the power of elites is augmented, the power struggle becomes fiercer, carries more dire consequences for the losers and poses a threat to the democratic institutions in whose framework it takes place. It is in part for this reason that democracy is, in fact, a rather fragile institutional arrangement.

Bureaucratic power and democracy: the theoretical context

In light of these definitions and assumptions, I now argue that the role of bureaucracy in a democracy is problematic because this is precisely one of the areas in which the democratic rules of the game are ill-defined, ambiguous, self-contradictory and controversial. Thus, it is my first thesis that *bureaucracy generates a dilemma for democracy*: bureaucracy is becoming more and more independent and powerful and the rules governing the exercise of that power are not clearly defined; hence bureaucracy poses a threat to the democratic political structure and to the politicians who run it. And yet, a powerful, independent bureaucracy is also necessary for the prevention of political corruption and for the safeguarding of proper democratic procedures. Bureaucracy is thus a threat to, but also indispensable for, democracy.

It is my second thesis that, by the same token, *democracy generates a dilemma for bureaucracy* and the bureaucrats who run it, because democratic rules are self-contradictory and put bureaucracy in a double bind. By such rules, bureaucracy is expected to be both independent and subservient, both responsible for its own actions and subject to ministerial responsibility, both politicized and non-politicized at one and the same time.

It is my third thesis that *these dilemmas exacerbate strains and power struggles on the political scene*. And because these power struggles (unlike many other democratic power struggles) take place at the point at which the democratic rules of the game break down, they are especially problematic for democracy.

These theses will be explicated below, but first their connection with the theories reviewed so far must be spelled out. They are most closely akin to Weber's conception, for it was he who pointed to the importance of rules for the regulation of bureaucratic action, even though he did not emphasize the importance of rules for democracy and the problems that may come from the ambiguity or breakdown of such rules. Furthermore, it was he who alerted us to the dilemmas generated by bureaucracy in a democracy by pointing out that bureaucracy was the most effective tool for the implementation of any (including democratic) policy, while it also posed a potential threat to such implementation.

The arguments here presented also draw on Mosca. For he was the one who pointed to the danger inherent in the unmitigated power of bureaucracy, because of its tendency to result in an absolutist regime, but he was also the one who pointed to the danger inherent in the uncurbed power of elected politicians, because of its tendency to bring about party-related political corruption.

Marx's idea (emphasized in his early writings) that bureaucracy and the bureaucrats who staff it represent interests is accepted as one of the premises of the present analysis. But Marx's idea (developed especially in his later writings and subsequently accepted by his followers) that such interests ultimately represent ruling-class interests and that political struggles necessarily represent class struggles is found to be less than useful in the present context. Instead, the view adopted here is that bureaucratic in-fighting and out-fighting are to be seen as power struggles within and between state elites, in which each group represents its own interests. The interests of one or more of these embattled groups may well coincide with the interests of the capitalist class, but this is not necessarily the case and certainly cannot furnish the explanation for the struggles among them. Indeed, since it is the Marxist view that the state as a whole, including its various apparatuses, ultimately represents ruling class interests, it is hard to see how struggles within and between those apparatuses can logically reflect class struggles.

One of the more controversial issues among contemporary theorists has been the degree of actual power bureaucracies have recently accumulated and can therefore deploy in their struggles for even greater power. Some pluralists have maintained that Western bureaucracies (and the governments of which they form part) have been overloaded with conflicting interests and conflicting demands with which they have been unable to cope effectively. Bureaucracies themselves have become internally fragmented and thus unable to come up with coherent policies. Bureaucracies have thus become vulnerable, splintered and bungling.

On the other hand, both the technocrats and some Marxists have held (from different vantage points) that the power of Western bureaucracies has increased and become formidable in recent years. I would argue that although these conceptions appear to be contradictory, they actually are so only in part.

Bureaucracy has in fact increased its power because the modern state, in its expanding capacity of monitoring the economy and of providing a greater variety of services to the public and especially in its expanding capacity as a welfare state, is in charge of allocating ever-growing resources. A growing number of individuals are more and more dependent on these resources for their livelihood and sometimes for their very lives. Bureaucracy, which allocates these resources, thus has ever-growing numbers of people ever more dependent on itself. By definition, then, it wields more power. A monolithic and concerted internal structure would certainly be a bonus for such power but – beyond certain limits – not its prerequisite. Thus, bureaucracy may be both bungling and powerful, both fragmented and formidable at one and the same time.

Another controversial issue has been the extent to which bureaucratic power poses a threat to democracy. As Kamenka and Erh-Soon Tay (1979, p. 112) have pointed out, 'The fear of bureaucracy ... creates strange bedfellows.' Thus some pluralists maintain (by implication) that bureaucratic power has not jeopardized democracy, while the pluralists concerned with governmental overload, as well as the technocrats and the Marxists (who are opposed to each other in their general outlooks), concur that it has. But none of these contemporary theorists has suggested that the development of bureaucracy has actually favoured democracy. What none of them has brought into relief is that historically, in most Western countries, bureaucracy and democracy developed almost simultaneously. More precisely, state administrations began to swell with the development of the absolute monarchies in Europe. But with the retreat of absolutism before democracy, administrations did not instigate a similar retreat. On the contrary: as parliaments gained in power, as multiple party systems emerged and as the franchise was extended, state administrations continued to grow in size, budget and power. And as bureaucracies became more powerful, democratic institutions developed even further.

The question immediately poses itself of whether this near-simultaneous development was merely a historical coincidence. In other words, did bureaucratic and democratic developments occur at roughly the same time only because they were both the outgrowth of modernization, or was it because there is a more direct connection between the two?

The first thesis: bureaucracy as a dilemma for democracy

As noted before, I argue that there is in fact an intrinsic connection between bureaucracy and democracy, although it is of a paradoxical or self-contradictory nature. On the one hand, the growing power of bureaucracy does indeed pose a threat to democracy, as some schools of thought have pointed out. On the other hand, a modern democracy cannot exist without a relatively powerful and independent bureaucracy,[3] a point which the various contemporary schools of thought have neglected to emphasize.

Bureaucracy poses a threat to democracy because it may serve as a tool for the enhancement and greater efficacy of state domination, and in some cases of state repression. As will be seen in the next chapter, it has, in fact, done so in several historical cases. More recently, observers have pointed to the growing pervasiveness of all bureaucracies as well as the evolving technology of ever more sophisticated devices of collecting, storing and retrieving ever-larger amounts of information. Because of these combined developments, bureaucracy has increasingly gained the potential of encroaching on the autonomy, liberty and privacy of the individual — immunities which are of the very essence of democracy. Moreover, while bureaucracy has the power to invade the domain of the individual, it is (as various theorists have emphasized) intent on guarding information and preserving the utmost secrecy in its own domain. Yet, as Ralph Nader has said, information is the currency of democracy. And this holds especially for information on the institutions of government themselves.

Bureaucracy also poses a threat to democracy in that it has increasingly gained the potential to exempt itself from the control of elected politicians and to infringe on their domain. The technocrats have argued that this is due, among other things, to bureaucracy's monopolization of expertise and information and to the decline in the power of parliament. My argument is that it is also due, among other things, to the ambiguity of rules which demarcate bureaucracy's sphere of competence. In any case, as Freedman (1978) has pointed out, government by elected politicians ensures political accountability through the electoral process and the resultant threat of replacement. Such accountability is the public's insurance against the abuse of power. Thus, bureaucracy's ability to exempt itself from the control of elected politicians means that it can exempt itself from the democratic process. Its ability to infringe on their domain is also the ability to infringe on the democratic process.

Given those threatening effects of bureaucracy for democracy, what is it, then, that makes the very existence, power and independence of bureaucracy a necessary requirement for democracy? It is the above-mentioned fact that the modern state is in charge of allocating enormous resources. For democratic procedures to work properly, the modern state must have at its disposal an organization that will not only allocate the resources but will do so by non-partisan criteria. Such criteria must be based on general categories of need or entitlement, or indeed on anything other than the potential or actual political support of the recipient for the donor and his party. Failing this, the political-democratic process would necessarily be based on an exchange of material benefits (ranging all the way from jobs to contracts, subsidies or tax exemptions) for political support. Thereby contending politicians and political parties would compete for office not on the basis of their advocated policies or projected images (as per the above definition of democracy) but rather on the basis of the resources they can marshal and deploy for the personal benefit of their supporters. This would be nothing but open or disguised bribery – a type of political corruption that would turn the electoral process into a mere farce.[4]

Politicians, and the political parties with which they are aligned, gain office and stay in office by winning elections. It is natural that they should seek to do so by whatever means are at their disposal. Anybody under the direct and unchecked control of politicians and political parties would thus be under continuous pressure to allocate resources in return for political support so as to maximize their chances of re-election. It is only in a body of people who are permanently appointed rather than elected (who therefore have no need to mobilize electoral support for themselves and their parties) and who are free from pressure by those who are themselves elected that the potential of passing out resources by non-partisan criteria exists.

To put it differently, in any body composed of, or directly controlled by, elected politicians and their parties, the structure of self-interest, indeed the interest of political survival, must necessarily be such as to favour allocation of resources to citizens by criteria of party political support. Only in a strong and politically independent bureaucracy is the structure of self-interest such that one may reasonably expect partisan criteria to be kept out of the process of allocation. Thus, only a full-fledged, politically independent bureaucracy can safeguard full-fledged democratic procedures.

Bureaucracy thus presents a dilemma for democracy. There is on the one hand the *threat* of a powerful bureaucracy that will exempt itself from political control and thereby from democratic accountability. There is on the other hand the *necessity* for a powerful bureaucracy that will exempt itself from political control in order to prevent the disruption of the democratic process itself.

The second thesis: democracy as a dilemma for bureaucracy

I further argue that by the same token, and partly for the same reasons, democracy poses a dilemma for bureaucracy. By democratic rules, bureaucracy is in a double bind: it is expected to be under the control of elected politicians and yet exempt from such control; it is expected to be subject to ministerial responsibility and yet accept responsibility for its own actions; it is expected to implement the policy devised by its elected political head and yet participate in the formulation of policy in its own right; it is expected to participate in the formulation of policy and yet be politically neutral; which is another way of saying that bureaucracy is expected to be politicized and non-politicized at one and the same time.

To the extent that bureaucracy takes part in the formulation of policy, its senior participants take part in decisions on the allocation of resources. It therefore participates in the exercise of power and is (by definition) engaged in politics. Moreover, in this capacity it is necessarily subject to the pressure of interest groups and must respond to, or manoeuvre between such pressures. Thus, it is a participant in the struggle for control over resources – or the power struggle – and, therefore, once more (by definition) engaged in politics. In this sense, then, it is clearly politicized. Indeed, this type of politicization is regarded by many participants and observers as legitimate and even beneficial for the democratic process. It is clearly part of the role expectations of bureaucracy in a democratic society.

On the other hand, if a bureaucracy favours one political party over another in its policies or in its appointments and promotions, it gives that party an enormous advantage in the electoral process. And this type of politicization is considered illegitimate in most democratic countries and is certainly detrimental to the democratic process.

The problem, however, is that policies frequently have some, if only covert or indirect, implications for partisan interests. The boundaries between the politics of policy on the one hand and party politics on the other are therefore hazy and vulnerable and may easily be approached or crossed advertently or inadvertently, and this, in fact, has frequently happened.

The dilemma of bureaucracy in a democracy, as expressed in the ambiguities and contradictions built into bureaucracy's role definition, has not been greatly emphasized by contemporary theorists of bureaucracy. Yet it surfaces quite clearly in the comments of other observers of bureaucracy: it figures prominently in reports of official enquiries into bureaucracy and in the insights of actual participants in the bureaucratic-political process.

For instance, in the Report of the Fulton Committee of Inquiry into the British Civil Service (1968) the following statements can be found:

> Because the solutions to complex problems need long preparation, the service must be far-sighted; from its accumulated knowledge and experience it must show initiative in working out what are the needs of the future and how they might be met. A special responsibility now rests upon the Civil Service because one Parliament or even one Government often cannot see the process through.
>
> At the same time, the Civil Service works under political direction. . . . [It] has also to be flexible enough to serve governments of any political complexion. (p. 11)

In other words, the public service must itself work out what the needs of the future are, and yet must serve different governments which may have totally opposing conceptions of what such needs might be.

In their book *The Civil Servants* (1980) Peter Kellner and Lord Crowther-Hunt (a journalist and a member of the Fulton Committee, respectively) illustrate similar contradictions in the prevalent conception of bureaucracy's role by quoting the following excerpts from *The Times*. In a leading article on 15 February 1977, the following assertion appears: 'The constitutional position is both crystal clear and entirely sufficient. Officials propose, Ministers dispose. Officials execute.'[5] Yet in another statement in the same newspaper, dating from December 1977, the position of the civil service does not emerge as quite so 'crystal clear':

The Civil Service needs somebody to speak in its defence. It is no good officials expecting their ministers to protect them. Many ministers share the popular prejudices against their servants, often superimposing a self-serving one of their own which imagines civil servants as engaged in a kind of continuous *coup d'etat* against the manifesto pledges of elected governments. . . . It [the civil service] is a sheet anchor of the constitution and a great bulwark against change of the worst kind.[6]

As Kellner and Crowther-Hunt (1980, p. 14) point out, this state-ment is 'pregnant with contradiction',

for while it contemptuously dismisses the idea of Whitehall[7] mounting a 'continuous *coup d'etat* against manifesto pledges', it also describes the Civil Service as 'a great bulwark against change of the worst kind'. . . . [But] one man's solemn manifesto pledge is another man's worst kind of change. If it is wrong to resist the first, you cannot logically be a bulwark against the second.

A similar dilemma regarding the role definition of bureaucracy emerges from the Coombs Royal Commission of Enquiry on the Australian Government Administration in whose Report (1977) the following pronouncements appear:

The Westminster model envisages a government chosen from elected representatives and responsible and accountable to them. It presents the bureaucracy as simply an extension of the minister's capacity: it exists to inform and advise him; to manage on his behalf programs for which he is responsible.

A consultant, Professor H.V. Emy, draws attention in his paper to the increasing unreality of this picture as a description of either how Australian government works or how it should work. It is true that the Australian Constitution (section 64) enshrines the principle of ministerial responsibility in its provision for 'departments of State' under the control of ministers. Nevertheless, Professor Emy points out, ministers do not accept, nor does Parliament or the public expect them to accept, a blanket responsibility for the acts of their officials. (pp. 11-12)

Clearly there is a dilemma here which must be faced. On the one hand, if ministers involve themselves in decisions to a degree necessary for them to accept responsibility for them, officials are likely to feel less personally responsible and the outcome may therefore be less efficient. On the other hand, attempts to acknowledge and give precision to the responsibility of officials and to hold them accountable for its exercise may be seen as weakening direct ministerial responsibility and therefore political control . . . the realities of contemporary government require that the bureaucracy be seen as exercising some powers in its own right; the independence of those powers requires that those exercising them should be held accountable. (p. 13)

The Commission observes that, for purely practical reasons, the administration inevitably plays a role in determining the character of the processes of government and that there is a lack of definition and clarity about the nature and extent of that role. Such lack of precision can be a significant source of misunderstanding and cross purposes. (p. 19)

The Commission believes that the administration should serve a government dedicated to . . . change or reform as competently and devotedly as one which aims to preserve the *status quo* or to achieve a more gradual rate of adaptation. (p. 22)

There remains the vexed question of whether there is or should be an 'ethos' . . . among officials. . . . This issue arose in the Commission's work most frequently in relation to the claim that officials should be 'neutral' on political issues. On the one hand, such neutrality was seen as basic to the capacity of the administration to serve equally well governments of different political persuasion. On the other hand, it was argued that a claim to be neutral frequently was either false or reflected merely a singular lack of self-awareness. (p. 24)

Ostensibly countries such as the United States and France have solved the problem by differentiating between political executives (in US, political appointees, in France, members of ministerial cabinets[8]) and career bureaucrats. Thus, in the United States, the Report of the Hoover Commission on the Organization of the Civil Service (1955) states:

> Political executives who are leaders in public life and career administrators who are civil servants are both essential in modern government. Each group has a function that complements the function of the other. . . . This joining of different functions . . . is of fundamental importance in representative government.
>
> In the National Government, it is the function of political executives to represent within the administration the policy purposes of the President . . . to provide leadership in developing national policy . . . in short to take responsibility for governing. . . .
>
> It is the function of the complementary group of career administrators in the National Government, who must serve whatever responsible officials are in office . . . to keep the government operating as effectively as possible at all times. (Task Force on Personnel and Civil Service, pp. 1-2)

Apparently, things do not work out quite as smoothly as that in practice, however, for the Commission then goes on to state:

> Despite the need for clarity, the functions of political executives and career administrators have become excessively confused in practice. The confusion is not deliberate, but is rather the inadvertent consequence of a combination of circumstances. . . . [Among other things] the difficulty of finding satisfactory criteria for distinguishing the role of political executives and career administrators. (p. 4)

Although the Commission made some specific recommendations on how to disentangle the confusion, the problem has not been solved. This is evident from the remarks of some recent observers that even now 'the distinction in roles between political and higher bureaucratic executives is muddled in Washington both formally and informally' (Heclo, 1978, p. 173).

In France, a similar differentiation between members of ministerial cabinets and career civil servants has not brought clarity in the definition of roles either. Haziness and controversy seem to be concentrated especially in the role definition of the senior career civil servants — the directors. This becomes evident from the views of directors and ministerial cabinet members, as reported by Suleiman (1974).

The conflict between [ministerial] cabinet members and Directors manifests two diametrically opposed role perceptions: for the Directors, politics and administration are distinct domains that only infrequently come into contact with one another, and which, in any case, ought always to remain strictly separated. For the cabinet members, the two domains cannot be separated at the highest levels of the administrative system. (p. 222)

Directors prefer to think of their work as being more or less purely administrative. (p. 223)

But cabinet members disagreed. As one cabinet member noted,

The Directors want to have the image of a 'pure administration' that doesn't get involved in politics. But . . . every aspect of the Directors' work has a political element. Theirs is not, nor can it be, a purely administrative task. (p. 226)

Here, too, then, the role definition of bureaucrats and bureaucracy is unclear.

The third thesis: the bureaucratic dilemma and political friction

Finally, I argue that the dilemma of bureaucracy forms a significant source of strain, friction and outright conflict in the political arena of modern democracies. The contradictions and ambiguities built into the role definition of bureaucracy in a democracy seem to be a source of friction and conflict especially between senior bureaucrats and senior politicians (both ministers and members of parliament). Because the role of bureaucracy is not clearly defined, senior bureaucrats have been able – and indeed have sometimes felt obligated – to branch out into the bureaucratic-political no-man's land which does not fall clearly within the domain of bureaucracy nor clearly outside it. This, however, is disputed territory. Its penetration by bureaucracy has therefore led, at times, to an adverse reaction by politicians who lay claim to this territory as well. Thus, the problem bureaucracy causes for democracy lies not only in the power it has amassed, but also in the power struggles it has generated.

This holds in particular for bureaucracy's participation in politics. As noted before, in this respect bureaucracy is in a double bind: it is expected to be involved in policy formation and yet to be neutral as far as party politics is concerned. Clearly, there is a disputed territory here. For the boundaries between policy and party politics are hazy; they are easily approached or crossed. I argue that whenever this occurs it is apt to lead to especially severe tensions and power struggles, which sometimes contribute to the downfall of senior politicians or even entire governments, to the dismissal of senior bureaucrats or even to the abolition of entire bureaucratic agencies.

To be sure, politics, by definition, involves power struggles. But, as noted, democratic power struggles are usually circumscribed by rules and this holds especially for struggles among politicians or political elites themselves. Indeed, the adherence of political elites to such rules in the course of their power struggles is widely considered to be the very essence of democracy. Because the power struggles generated by bureaucracy occur at a point at which the rules are inadequate or at which they break down, they are potentially more ruthless and disruptive.

Moreover, by the rules of a democracy, the outcomes of power struggles are ultimately decided by the electoral process, whereas the power struggles created by bureaucracy clearly are not. For this reason, too, such struggles are especially problematic for the already fragile arrangements that constitute democracy.

Part II
Empirical perspectives

This part of the book is designed to furnish empirical support for the theses developed in the foregoing chapter, while also presenting an overview of the development and current position of bureaucracy in Western societies. Chapters 8-10 trace the development of bureaucracy and its power in Western societies and illustrate how a powerful and politically independent bureaucracy poses a threat to democracy. Chapters 11 and 12 present a comparative review of the relation between bureaucracy and party politics in various countries; they bring evidence to show that a powerful and politically independent bureaucracy is not only a threat but also a necessity to democracy. Chapter 13 presents case studies on the relationship between bureaucracy and politics, bureaucrats and politicians. It also illustrates the hazy demarcation lines between bureaucratic policies and party politics and shows that whenever they are approached or crossed this causes strain and friction on the political arenas of Western societies.

Chapter 8

The development of Western bureaucracy: overview and explanation[1]

In medieval times, despite substantial differences between various countries, Western Europe was generally characterized by a decentralized system of political rule and administration. 'Apart from the dream-picture of the Holy Roman Empire and the actual extension of the temporal sway of the Church ... centralized government was everywhere at a discount. Administration had become drastically localized' (Gladden, 1972, p. 1). This was necessitated by the poor system of communication, furthered by the relative self-sufficiency of the local agricultural economy, and buttressed by the feudal system of stratification. Because of the poor communications, the stability of society depended largely on the ability of the feudal lords to maintain order. But this ability also made it possible for them to resist the encroachments of the crown into their domains of power.

The feudal lords thus maintained quasi-autonomous socio-political units of which they were not only the economic masters, but the political masters and judicial authorities as well. The basic power and administrative units were thus centred in the lord's manors. Eventually, these came to be supplemented by local administrative units and the beginnings of central (royal) administrations, although these too, were small and relatively weak.

All over Europe, the church provided other important centres of local administration.[2] And so, too, did the towns that were revived or sprang up with the revival of commerce and gradually gained independence from the seignory.

Centralization

Thus, feudalism was based on various independent or semi-independent administrative units. It was also based on an uneasy balance of power and intermittent struggles among three power centres: the crown, the feudal lords and the church. In this power struggle the crown did not necessarily emerge as the victor on all or even most occasions. It was only with the beginning of modernization that the balance gradually shifted in its favour; and as the king's power successively increased, that of the church gradually decreased while that of the feudal nobility was increasingly bent to the king's purpose. This is not to say that the power of the aristocracy was eliminated, but rather that it was increasingly incorporated into the structure of the state and became one of its major bases.

In this way, a two-sided process of centralization occurred: a process of territorial centralization whereby quasi-independent feudal domains, localities and towns became incorporated into the state and a process of functional centralization, whereby military, judiciary, and other functions previously carried out independently by these domains, successively came to be monopolized by the states' governments.

Not surprisingly, the process by which autonomous entities lost their power to central governments and by which independent administrative units were incorporated into central state administrations, was not continuous or smooth. For centuries the feudal lords tenaciously resisted the state's usurpation of their independent power. But eventually many of those nobles were placated; they were compensated for the loss of political independence by prestigious and sometimes powerful offices in the king's or prince's administration.

Towards the end of the medieval period and at the beginning of modernity the most developed administrations were those of cities — especially in fourteenth-, fifteenth- and sixteenth-century Germany. There, every detail of everyday life was regulated by the local administration and this was done more effectively than in the king's or prince's court. But gradually, the towns, too, lost their independence. Their military authority, judicial and police systems and eventually their finances, too, passed into the hands of the central administration. With the development of commerce, the cities were themselves increasingly interested in the development of a central authority in charge of security of traffic and markets.

The changes summarized so far in a few words only were actually exceedingly complex and protracted processes that lasted for several centuries and culminated in the emergence of the European territorial nation-state with its absolute ruler. By the end of the sixteenth century, Western Europe included a number of such states and absolutism had budded, developing further in the seventeenth and eighteenth centuries.

Absolutism involved the further siphoning of power from the church, the local aristocrats and the municipal or provincial units in favour of the central, usually royal administration. But the strength of absolutism varied widely. In England, by the sixteenth century, the royal administration had grown relatively strong but the Puritan Revolution inflicted a blow which weakened it considerably.

Thus, in eighteenth-century England, local government proceeded on its own, with little reference to central administration. Also, office was a property for which consideration was paid and officers were concerned less with administration than with drawing good dividends from their investments. Moreover, much of the administration was conducted by boards that seldom had real powers of direct administrative action.

In France, by contrast, the centrally controlled administration developed significantly in the seventeenth and eighteenth centuries. The crucial institution in this development was the provincial *intendant*. Previously, royal emissaries had been appointed only for specific purposes on a temporary basis. During the seventeenth century, however, *intendants* were sent to almost all French districts and they were established as permanent provincial officials, turning from inspectors into administrators. By the end of the century they headed a hierarchy of provincial officials, that was linked to the central administration. Under Louis XIV (1643-1715) the *Secretaires d'État* in Paris and the *intendants* in the provinces became the chief elements in a royally controlled system of administration which extended virtually over the whole of France.

Even so, central control was not wholly effective. According to Krygier (1979b) the *intendants* constantly vied with independent officials and local notables and their powers did not always match their responsibilities. Also, they themselves were not always easy to control. And in the eighteenth century, under Louis XV (1715-74) and especially under Louis XVI (1774-92) the central direction of the *intendants* became even less effective.

In Prussia, from the mid-seventeenth century, traditional local associations, provincial governments and independent estates were gradually brought under the authority of a central government, and the foundations of a new, centralized administration were laid. A General Directory was established as the central administrative apparatus, a body of centrally controlled officials was created and commissioners were appointed to control towns or groups of towns (thus doing away with municipal autonomy). However, Frederick the Great (1740-86) reintroduced decentralizing elements into the administration by curtailing the power and unity of the Central Directory, by breaking the central administration into many units and by sanctioning the re-emergence of non-bureaucratic agencies of corporate self-government.

In both France and Prussia centralization thus advanced, but was still only partially effective and even suffered a temporary setback. But it soon made further strides forwards following the French Revolution, its repercussions and aftermath throughout the Western World and the consequent decline of absolutism. Overall, the ascent of absolutism had furthered a certain degree of bureaucratic centralization, but the descent of absolutism did not effect a reversal of this trend. On the contrary, the abolition of feudal privileges through the revolution in France (and the gradual decline of such privileges elsewhere) only helped to strengthen the trend towards centralized administration; 'indeed one year of the Revolution had accomplished more for royal authority than had all the many years of absolutism' (Jacobi, 1973, p. 53). For, according to Jacobi, absolutism had been more successful in destroying the local, decentralized administrative units than it had been in enforcing its own decrees. The administrations evolving in the nineteenth century proved much more adept in this respect than their autocratic predecessors.

This was particularly evident in France. After a few years of revolutionary upheavals Napoleon (1799-1815) erected a centralized, hierarchical administration, designed to consolidate his rule. Accordingly, officials were strictly controlled from above; the prefects (who were the heirs of the *intendants*) were put in charge of the departments and through them, effective control of those departments was gained. 'While Louis [XIV] could only delude himself into thinking that he controlled this basis, Napoleon ... was actually in control' (Barker, 1944, p. 14).

The French bureaucracy remained centralized under the restoration and the Third Empire and even in the twentieth century continued to be based on the foundations laid by Napoleon. (This, despite some inconsistent elements to be discussed in the next chapter.)

Rationalization

The centralization of bureaucracy was also related to a trend of growing rationalization. That is to say, bureaucracy became more clearly differentiated, more methodical, coherent and effective in the execution of its tasks; in other words, it came to adhere more closely than before to the model of bureaucracy spelled out by Weber.

In feudal society each of the smallest entities was responsible for its own legislation (if any), for judicial tasks and for its own administration, and the various activities were fused with each other and took place on an haphazard basis. The king's (or prince's) administration was part of the royal household. It subsequently became more elaborate, in an attempt to cope with administrative tasks with which the simple household organization was not capable of coping, but it remained partly fused with the household until the beginning of modernity.

According to Gladden (1972), the sixteenth century marked a watershed between feudal and modern administration. During this century administration was still based on personal relations; but with increasingly complex administrative problems a differentiation between personal ties and administrative tasks became more noticeable. Also, functional differentiation between the judiciary and the administration, and among administrative units themselves, became more emphasized.

Further specialization occurred during the seventeenth and eighteenth centuries. In France, at the time of Louis XIII (1610-43) and Richelieu (1624-42), it became the custom to give some of the secretaries subject areas such as those of Foreign Affairs or War, in addition to their territorial spheres. During the rule of Louis XIV, the administrative apparatus was more clearly divided into functional ministries with links to the *intendants* and other provincial officials. But by the time of Louis XV government agencies once more proliferated in a haphazard manner.

At that time, the Prussian administration, too, made some advances towards internal specialization. At the beginning of the eighteenth century the administration was organized on a territorial rather than a functional basis. Under Frederick the Great territorial units were not abolished, but they were surrounded and subverted from within by new, functionally specialized ministries. However, the king feared the power of the central administration and therefore complicated matters by introducing a cabinet of private advisers, and by generally splitting administrative power and functions between rival organizations.

Side by side with these developments some advances were made in the institutionalization of bureaucratic processes and more definite procedures of selecting, training, grading and promoting officials came into being. But here, too, the realization of the new principles was slow, intermittent, beset by setbacks and, in several areas, only partly successful.

The most far-reaching developments occurred in Prussia. At the beginning of the eighteenth century, exact rules were introduced covering officials' conduct and duties; a group of professional administrators was trained; qualifications for office were specified and a system of entrance examinations was introduced. Even so, the protégés and kin of influential people still had a headstart in selection and advancement. Strangely, a synthesis developed between the new principles of merit and the old favouritism and 'With the connivance of Frederick William I, this synthesis between the new and the old order was consolidated into a long enduring "system" ' (Rosenberg, 1958, p. 75). At that time, the purchase of office was also common and this too, hindered the advancement of the merit system.

Under Frederick the Great specialist training for administration was administered on a larger scale, its standard was raised, and regularized recruitment of public servants made further headway. By 1770 a centralized recruiting system for the whole bureaucracy and a superior examinations commission for that purpose began to operate and standardized civil service examinations were introduced. By the end of the eighteenth century a merit system applied to all posts in the Prussian bureaucracy.

The legal code of 1794 gave officials the right to permanent tenure and to due process of law in relation to questionable conduct. It also furthered the process of depersonalization of administrative procedures and rules which had began to take effect with the ascent of absolutism. As Barker (1944, p. 18) saw it, 'Prussian absolutism almost redeemed its nature by its impartial impersonality.'

Yet as Rosenberg (1958) emphasized, even these processes and innovations proved compatible with advantages to the upper classes, favouritism and nepotism. Not even the civil service examinations introduced in 1770 brought an immediate change. Moreover, by that time, the Prussian bureaucracy had acquired some additional less-than-endearing qualities. As Chapman (1959, p. 24) characterized it, 'by 1794 the Prussian organisation had degenerated into a caste system . . . [characterized by] exclusiveness, contempt for outsiders . . . social discrimination, aloof paternalism'.

In the seventeenth- and eighteenth-century French administration, the personal and the impersonal, the private and the public were still interlinked to an even greater extent than in Prussia. During the reign of Louis XIII, for instance, it was Richelieu's firm policy to procure appointments for as many members of his family as he could, and afterwards, too, favouritism and nepotism continued to prevail. So, too, did the purchase of offices, and government posts (except those of the *intendants*) were still the private property of officials. This gave officials the licence to exploit those under their authority, so as to realize maximal profits from their purchase. Also, while this 'selection method' was financially expedient, it did nothing to ensure that officers possessed the personal abilities and technical expertise for office.

At that time, too, in France as well as in England, the aristocratic society inevitably undermined all general laws and regulations, because privileges consisted of personal exemptions and exceptions and the personal always prevailed over the general. To this must be added the regional variations, and the crown's efforts to maintain control of officials, all of which produced a bewildering array of governmental agencies, many becoming almost useless.

In general, under absolutism, the bureaucracy had made great strides forward, but it was still rudimentary and unsystematic. According to some observers, it could hardly be referred to as a bureaucracy at all[3] and according to Eisenstadt and Von Beyme (1972) it scarcely had the rationality later attributed to it by some sociologists. Only in the nineteenth century, with the decline of absolutism, did a systematic bureaucracy in the modern sense emerge.

The French Revolution brought with it administrative upheavals, and changes which quickly superseded each other. But these were themselves superseded by Napoleon's building up a more effective administration than had previously existed, as an instrument for his centralized and authoritarian state. Officials now became public servants and were paid regular salaries. The local departmental systems was re-established, but on a more coherent basis. Authority was concentrated in the hands of the prefects (who now replaced the *intendants*). Their selection was made by the emperor himself, and administrative capabilities were now an important element in this selection. The prefects, in turn, nominated the lesser administrators on a similar basis.

The coherence of Napoleon's administration was aided by the codification of the law which Napoleon initiated and which resulted in (among other things) the *Code Napoléon* in 1807. It was basically conservative but its clarity and logical consistency helped further the coherence of the administration that was guided by it. Napoleon placed great emphasis on security and police administration became highly effective, especially in the elimination of the regime's opponents. In other areas administration was also regularized. This included the introduction of an annual budget, the submission of exact accounts by each administrative unit, and the rationalization of the tax collection system. A coherent judicial system was established as well.

Napoleon's efforts at shaping a more systematic administration were not confined to France. 'By a judicious selection of ancient institutions modified to the purposes of the world he was moulding right across Europe, he brought order out of chaos and achieved a level of administrative efficiency far above that of the preceding era . . .' (Gladden, 1972, p. 297). This system still depended on the emperor's personality, and therefore it foundered as soon as his authority was withdrawn; but subsequent regimes drew on it.

In Prussia, for instance, the reform initiated by Napoleon after the country's defeat in 1806 was short-lived 'but its legacy was a remarkably modernized and rationalized administrative structure' (Krygier, 1979b, p. 8). A new simplicity was introduced into the previous confusion, when definite departments under the responsibility of ministers were instituted, the array of overlapping agencies was straightened out, and the connections between the ministries and the administrative agencies in the provinces were clarified and organized in an hierarchical manner. Also, by that time, a hierarchy of career bureaucrats headed by the king and selected through rigorous examinations had come into being.

The nineteenth-century British administration followed its own path to greater rationality. The previously existent multiplicity of boards disappeared, a more logical articulation of functions took place, and administrative departments for each of these functions was created. Also, towards the end of the century, officials came to be recruited by open, competitive examinations.

In general, the present division of the executive and its bureaucracy into a series of ministerial departments on a functional basis, supplemented by a variety of territorial divisions, has its basis in the administrative system that evolved and was being reformed in the nineteenth century, and was unquestionably more rational and effective than its predecessors. Even so, the subsequent growth and increasing complexity of tasks, especially in the twentieth century, did not necessarily lead to even greater rationality and effectiveness. The optimum of bureaucratic effectiveness (though not necessarily the maximum of bureaucratic power) may thus have been passed by now. These topics are taken up in chapters 9 and 10.

Throughout most of the period described, the administration had still been wholly or partly intermingled with politics. In the ninteenth century, with the appearance of political parties, this took the form of the interpenetration of administration and party politics. In Prussia, for instance, at the beginning of the nineteenth century, personal and family considerations in administrative appointments often gave way to political patronage, and talent often came to mean political talent or the holding of the right opinions. Towards the end of the century, marked discrimination against liberals and social democrats took place, so that the higher ranks of the administration were dominated by conservatives. In several countries a gradual differentiation between administration and party politics eventually took place, but in others, the two remained partly interlinked, and in all Western countries the relationship between bureaucracy and party politics has continued to pose some intractable problems. This will be our concern, in chapters 11, 12 and 13.

Growing pervasiveness

With centralization and rationalization, government bureaucracy also branched out into a whole new range of activities. As de Tocqueville had observed, while the forms of government changed from feudalism to absolutism and from that, gradually to democracy, bureauracy continued almost uninterruptedly to accumulate more functions and wider responsibilities and as it did so, it intervened in, and regulated wider spheres of social life.

In the seventeenth and eighteenth centuries government bureau-cracies first made the attempt to control all economic activities in detail. Government control increased in the area of coinage, weights and measures, and royal trade and production ordinances replaced guild and municipal regulation. Governments instituted monopolies and privileges, fixed wages and prices, and regulated imports and exports.

Bureaucratic pervasiveness made further inroads in the nineteenth century. In addition to the expansion of bureaucracy's traditional activities in the areas of administering the police, the judiciary, the military and foreign affairs, novel functions were added. These included responsibility for roads, canals, bridges, harbours, railways, building standards, water supplies, sanitation, education and culture.

In addition, government bureaucracy began dealing with the social problems created by modern industry: the regulation of working hours and conditions, workers' compensation and the like. Bureaucracy also branched out into large-scale provision of social welfare, including poor relief, social services, social insurance and public health.

In the previous centuries, whatever social welfare services existed, had been provided by the church. Their transfer to the state was a long and gradual process. In France, under the old Régime, the state had been participating in the provision of such services to a small degree, but up to the revolution the king could still count on the co-operation of the wealthy church which maintained hospitals and other charitable organizations. Under Napoleon, however, special attention was given to public assistance. With the reduced wealth and status of the church (brought about by the revolution) relief could no longer be left in its hands and had to be taken over by the public administration. And

> Although the relief system never had access to sufficient resources to render it really effective . . . there can be little doubt that the Napoleonic régime built up a social security system that was well in advance of the age. (Gladden, 1972, p. 296)

And towards the end of the nineteenth century, the provincial and local administrations administered asylums, institutions for destitute children and hospitals.

In Britain, the Poor Law Amendment Act of 1834 introduced central administrative control in the sphere of public assistance, and during the second half of the nineteenth century welfare legislation and bureaucratic involvement in the provision of social services were greatly expanded, as was the case in other European countries as well.

At that time, governments also moved into the area of social insurance. In Germany, the foundations of the modern social security system were laid towards the end of the nineteenth century: old age pensions and social security were provided by an act of 1889. In Britain, the foundations of such a system were laid at the beginning of this century. In the United States welfare legislation and government involvement in welfare and social security came later. Legislation introduced in the 1930s represented a federal generalization of the measures previously introduced in some States to provide old-age pensions and unemployment insurance. Especially from the 1960s, however, welfare legislation made massive headway in United States as well and government (bureaucratic) involvement in such welfare significantly increased.

Looking back once more into the nineteenth century, we see that at that time, the state stepped up its intervention in the economy as well.

The liberal, *laissez-faire* ideology prevalent at the time, called for a contraction in state-bureaucratic intervention in the economy, and yet, in actual fact, such intervention was expanding rather than shrinking. According to Jacobi (1973, p. 55), the growing pervasiveness of bureaucracy in a period of economic individualism 'was one of the greater ironies of history'.

The economic system commonly referred to as *laissez-faire*, and which culminated towards the middle of the nineteenth century, was characterized by a relative freedom for the play of economic forces. In several European countries and especially in England, many of the traditional restrictions of movement, choice of occupation and production were abolished. Also, there was a trend towards free trade as duties were reduced, shipping restrictions were eliminated and other free-trade measures were introduced.[4]

But, as Karl Polanyi (1957) pointed out:

laissez faire itself was enforced by the state. The [eighteen] thirties and forties saw not only an outburst of legislation repealing restrictive regulations, but also an enormous increase in the administrative functions of the state. (p. 139)

The road to the free market was opened and kept open by an enormous increase in continuous, centrally organized and controlled interventionism. (p. 140)

Economic intervention was stepped up even further towards the end of the nineteenth century, and even more so during the twentieth. State credits, investments and expenditures increased to such an extent that through their administration government bureaucracy came to exert considerable influence on the course of the economy, reflecting a determination to guide the economy rather than being guided by it.

Such guidance came to be especially pronounced in France, with its five-year plans somewhat reminiscent of those in socialist countries. But state intervention penetrated all Western economies and was constantly growing. It was least pronounced in the United States, where it has been countered by a traditionally strong ideological opposition. But even here, the government was eventually drawn to increase its economic role. For instance, Galbraith (1967) reports that federal, state, and local government activity accounted for 8 per cent of economic activity in 1929, and for about 25 per cent of such activity in 1967.

By the beginning of the present century, the European public administrations had become concerned with anything from building highways to the administration of old-age pensions. The American bureaucracy lagged somewhat behind, but throughout this century has made considerable strides in the same direction; it took over the regulation of more and more areas of social life and administered ever tighter and more complex regulatory laws and ordinances.

For instance, as Schultze (1977) indicates, under the 1972 Federal Water Pollution Control Act Amendments, the Environmental Protection Agency is charged with establishing effluent limitations and issuing effluent permits for some 62,000 point-sources of water pollution. Recently the federal government has also entered in a big way the field of health, regulating health and safety in work places, and social services. It provides heavy financial support for health care through Medicare and Medicaid and actively influences the structure of the private health care system through various grant-in-aid programs. Twenty-five years ago there were virtually no federal manpower programs; by the mid-1970s the government was spending $9 million a year on such programs in an attempt to influence the structure of the labour market. In the field of energy and the environment the objectives of national policy now imply a 'staggeringly complex and interlocking set of actions, directly affecting the production and consumption decisions of every citizen and every business firm' (Schultze, 1977, p. 9).

Proliferation and growth

For the growing intervention in all these social spheres bigger and additional bureaucratic agencies had to be provided and those multiplied and proliferated all over the modern world.

In the United States, for instance, the original bureaucracy consisted of the War, Navy, State and Treasury Departments along with the Office of Attorney General and these departments were extraordinarily small. After the Civil War further developments occurred, the existing agencies grew and new agencies were created to deal with specific problems. The Justice Department was created in 1870 and its powers were expanded (under the Sherman Act of 1890) to deal with the rising restraints on trade and the growth of monopolies. The Interstate Commerce Commission was created in 1887 to supervise the railroad industry. The Post Office Department was established in 1882, and the

Department of Agriculture in 1889. But even then the administration was relatively small.

The real proliferation and growth of bureaucratic agencies came in the twentieth century, when the existent agencies were entrusted with additional tasks and many new ones were brought into being. For instance, the Federal Reserve Board was established in 1913 to stand at the head of a Federal Reserve system; the Federal Trade Commission was created in 1913 to supervise trade and restrain deceptive business practices; the Federal Power Commission was formed in 1920 and the Federal Radio Commission was instituted in 1927.[5] Further proliferation took place during the New Deal, with the establishment of the Securities and Exchange Commission in 1933, the National Labor Relations Board in 1935, the Civil Aeronautics Board and Civil Aeronautics Administration[6] in 1937 and the formation of new bureaus in existing departments (Woll, 1966). Subsequently, the proliferation continued, so that in 1954 the federal government embraced no less than 2,133 different agencies, including departments, bureaus, and divisions (MacNeil and Metz, 1956, p. 7). After that, the number of social programs carried out by the government administration proliferated as well. According to Bell (1975) in the early years of the Kennedy administration there were about 200 such programs. By the mid-1970s they had proliferated to about 1,100. The proliferation of federal regulatory agencies has been almost as striking. In the mid-1950s the federal government had a major regulatory responsibility in only four areas: antitrust, financial institutions, transportation and communication.[7] In 1976, no less than 83 federal agencies were engaged in regulatory activities (Schultze, 1977, p. 7).

The expansion in the volume of government-bureaucratic activity is also evident from the persistent rise in government expenditures. Thus, in the United States, for instance, public (all levels of government) expenditures rose from 7 per cent of gross national product (GNP)[8] in 1890 to 24.6 per cent in 1950 and to 37.9 per cent in 1974. In the United Kingdom, such expenditures rose from 8.9 per cent of GNP in 1890 to 34.1 per cent in 1950 and to 59 per cent in 1974. In Sweden, they rose from 31.2 per cent of GNP in 1950 to 63.8 per cent in 1974 (see Chirot, 1977, p. 194; Musgrave, 1969, p. 92; and Peters, 1978, p. 18).

Much of the growth in government expenditures is, of course, due to rising military outlays. However, the same trend is visible when non-defence spendings only are taken into account. In 1929, some 9 per cent of the American Gross National Product was spent by state,

Table 8.1 *United States, United Kingdom, Canada and Australia:[a] central government employment[b] per thousand of population[c]*

Year[d]	United States (Federal)	United Kingdom[e] (Non-industrial)	Canada (Civil Service)	Australia (Common-wealth)
1821	0.7			
1831	0.9			
1841	1.1			
1851	1.1			
1861	1.2			
1871	1.3			
1881	2.0			
1891	2.6			
1901/2	3.1	1.4		
1910/11	4.3	1.5		
1920/21	5.3	2.6	5.2	
1924/25				4.6
1930/31	5.0	2.4	4.2	4.7
1939/40		3.4	4.3	10.0
1941	11.0			
1950/51	16.0	8.6	9.3	24.0
1960/61	14.0	7.2	9.9[f]	21.0
1968		8.6		
1970/71	14.0		11.3	26.0[g]

Sources: Compiled and computed from: (for the US) Nachmias and Rosenblum (1980, p. 39); *Statistical Abstract of the United States*, (1978, Table 27, p. 28); (for Britain) *British Labour Statistics, Historical Abstract 1886-1968*, Table 154, p. 299; *Annual Abstract of Statistics*, Vol. 117, 1981, p. 7; (for Canada) *Canada Year Book*, 1946, Table 10; p. 1141; 1951, Table 7, p. 1140; 1961, Table 1, p. 119; 1970-1, Table 1, p. 212; 1972, Table 11, p. 167; *Vital statistics*, 1952, Table 2, p. 10. (for Australia) *Official Year Book of the Commonwealth of Australia*, nos. 19-64, 1926-1980.

Notes
[a] The purpose of the table is to establish change in the size of government employment over time in each of the countries. It cannot be used for a comparison of the size of government employment among the countries since the types of employees included are not identical for the four countries.
[b] For Canada, part-time staff are included; for the UK they are counted as half units from 1939; for Australia they are not included; for the US their status is not specified.
[c] Population figures on whose basis computations were made relate to the same years as employment figures or to the closest years for which figures are available. The population figure for Britain in 1939 is an estimate. For Australia, population figures exclude full blooded Aborigines until 1961.

Notes to Table 8.1 (contd)
d When two years are listed the data pertain to either one or the other.
e For the UK, post office employees have been excluded. Northern Ireland
  figures have been included from 1948 onwards.
f For Canada the surveys for 1960/1 and 1970/1 have been more inclusive than
  the previous statistical series. Also, the figures for 1960/1 pertain to
  departments only, the figures for 1970/1 pertain to departments and
  departmental agencies. An accurate comparison between 1950/1 and the
  following years is therefore not possible. However, the data do show that from
  1950/1 onwards there has been only minor growth in the Canadian Public
  Service, relative to population.
g It should be noted, that not all government employees are strictly speaking
  bureaucrats. It is assumed, however, that changes in numbers of government
  employees in general would also furnish a rough indication of changes in the
  number of government bureaucrats.

federal and local governments for purposes other than defence and foreign affairs. By 1960, the proportion of GNP spent on domestic programs had risen to 17.5 and by 1976 to 28 per cent (Schultze, 1977, p. 7). The same trend is once again visible when government expenditures without transfer payments are looked at. Transfer payments represent sums given to private individuals or organizations for consumption (e.g. social security payments). Government expenditures without transfer payments thus represent those sums for which the government bureaucracy itself makes the final consumption decisions. In the United States these expenditures rose from 13.6 per cent of GNP in 1950 to 22.7 per cent in 1974; in the United Kingdom they rose from 20.1 per cent of GNP in 1960 to 38 per cent in 1974, and in Sweden from 25 per cent of GNP in 1960 to 28.9 per cent in 1974 (Peters, 1978, p. 18).

The increase in the volume of bureaucratic activity is most directly evident in the numerical growth of government employees. This growth in its turn gives rise to a need for more internal management and supervision. Thus, the administration of administration becomes more extensive, which leads to a further growth in the number of bureaucrats. Technological changes such as the growing utilization of computers in bureaucratic activities would seem to have counteracted this trend by making some manual tasks obsolete. This trend, however, is itself counteracted by the enhanced possibilities for ever new types of bureaucratic activities which these computer systems have provided, the additional tasks thus created, and the further controls they require.

The net result seems to be a trend of ever-growing numbers of bureaucrats, at least until fairly recently. For instance, in the United States, the number of civilian employees of the federal government has gone steadily up from around 7,000 in 1821 to over half a million in 1921, soaring to almost 2,750,000 in 1977. Moreover, this growth far outdistanced the growth of the population which the federal bureaucracy was supposed to serve (or govern). And this holds for a number of other countries as well, as can be seen from Table 8.1.

The development of Western bureaucracy: an explanation

Following the brilliant (albeit humorous) analysis by C. Northcote Parkinson (1979) and like-minded critics, it is now widely believed that the development of modern bureaucracy has been a self-feeding process in which the vested interest of bureaucrats has played a far-from-insignificant role. But even Parkinson (when not at his most flippant) would probably have to admit that a variety of factors other than bureaucrats' drive for self aggrandizement and 'empire-building' have been at work as well. He would also have to admit that several of these were historical factors over which bureaucrats themselves had little control even though they fed into their own interests. And just as the development of Western bureaucracy was exceedingly complex so, too, were the factors leading up to it. Some of these have been included in Weber's classical analysis (see chapter 2), and these need not be reiterated here. Additional factors, to be held accountable, include those following.

Economic development and taxation

The advent and maturation of modern capitalism was marked by unprecedented economic development and growth. This process not only required[9] but also facilitated the growth of bureaucracy. For only the growing economic surplus made it possible for larger and larger numbers of people to be set aside for the 'non-productive' tasks of administration. Economic growth 'took off' especially from the time of the industrial revolution and onwards. It is of particular interest, however, that during this period growth in volume of bureaucratic activity by far outpaced economic growth.

As noted before, one indication of the volume of bureaucratic activity can be found in its deployment of financial resources, or in other words in (especially non-defence) government expenditures. Economic development can be best measured by growth of GNP[10] and although GNP was rising briskly from the second part of the nineteenth century onwards[11] the volume of bureaucratic activity grew to a far greater extent: the data cited above show that it comprised a progressively larger percentage of GNP. At least, this was the case up until the mid-1970s.[12]

The explanation for this lies in part in the evolution of taxation, which was itself closely related to the general trend of economic development but outpaced it by far, as will be seen below. As Jouvenel (1952) points out, neither the centralization of administrative functions nor the expansion of bureaucratic intervention, nor the unprecedented growth in the size of the administration could have come about without an enormous increase in the government's financial means through the development of taxation.

In medieval times, the ruler usually could not marshall the funds for extensive government operations. He was limited mainly to the revenue that accrued from his own land. When under major pressure, for instance because of war, he could turn to the church, and if the latter concurred with the objectives of his campaign, it would hand over to him a certain percentage of its own revenues, for a limited period of time. Another source of revenue were the towns, where the rudiments of taxation were pioneered. But the towns emphasized their independence; taxes could be obtained only with their consent, and they were not very forthcoming with that.

Hence, in the Middle Ages, the ruler's revenues sufficed only to replenish his privy purse; he was usually under much financial pressure and therefore very limited in what he could accomplish. These straitened financial circumstances prevented him from employing salaried agents, and thus from developing his own military forces, administration and judicial system.

In the thirteenth and fourteenth centuries the rulers increased the pressure on various segments of the population for the extraction of payments at progressively shorter intervals. However, such payments had to be consented to by the people. Hence the kings or princes were obliged to visit the major population centres periodically in order to convince the people to make their monetary contributions. As parliaments developed, the rulers succeeded in mobilizing those for the extraction of taxes from the public. But in return they had to make various concessions to their demands in the matter of policy and justice.

Eventually, taxes turned into a permanent feature of political life, but even at the peak of absolutism, the public's resistance to the payment of taxes was strong, and a continuous struggle on this issue was taking place between that public and the monarchy. Indeed, dues and taxes of all kinds imposed on the peasantry were one of the prime causes of the French Revolution. It is only with the advent of democracy that the public reluctantly acquiesced in the paying of taxes. Hence, it is in particular in the nineteenth and twentieth centuries, that taxation soared and far outpaced economic development – as measured by growth of gross national product (GNP) or gross domestic product (GDP).[13] Thus, US internal (federal) revenue collections totalled 1.3 per cent of GNP in 1880-1, 3.3 per cent in 1930-1 and 18.1 per cent in 1960-1. Australian (Commonwealth) taxation collected totalled 4.2 per cent of GNP in 1902-3; 8.6 per cent in 1932-3 and 17.1 per cent in 1960-1. And the trend of taxation growing in excess of economic development continued in practically all Western countries, as can be seen from Table 8.2. It is this trend which enabled the volume of bureaucratic activity to grow in excess of economic development as well.

Table 8.2 *Total tax receipts as percentage of GDP (at market prices) of sixteen Western countries – 1955-80[a]*

	1955	1965	1975	1980	1980 minus 1955 (% points)
Federal Republic of Germany[b]	30.8	31.6	35.7	37.2	6.4
Italy	30.5	27.3	29.0	30.1[c]	−0.4
Austria	30.0	34.6	38.5	41.5	11.5
United Kingdom	29.8	30.8	36.9	35.9	6.1
Norway	28.3	33.2	44.8	47.4	19.1
New Zealand	26.8	24.3	30.0	31.7	4.9
Finland	26.8	30.1	36.2	34.5	7.7
Netherlands	26.3	35.5	45.8	46.2	19.9
Sweden	25.5	35.6	44.2	49.9	24.4
Belgium	24.0	31.2	41.1	42.5	18.5
United States	23.6	26.5	30.2	30.7	7.1
Denmark	23.4	30.1	41.1	45.1	21.7
Australia	22.6	23.8	29.1	29.8[c]	7.2
Ireland	22.5	26.0	32.5	37.5	15.0
Canada	21.7	25.9	32.9	32.8	11.1
Switzerland	19.2	20.7	29.6	30.7	11.5

Source: OECD (1981b, p. 11).
Notes
[a] France and Luxembourg have been excluded since data for 1955 are unavailable.
[b] Countries have been ranked by the 1955 figures.
[c] 1979 figures.

The development of the nation-state

Although this may not seem evident at first glance, another explanation for the augmentation of bureaucracy may be found in the development of the modern nation-state. In medieval Europe there existed the rather weak supernational empire on the one hand and the sub-national or non-national minute political unit on the other hand. Towards the end of the medieval period, as the empire disintegrated and the smaller units were increasingly integrated into the larger political entity, their many languages were incorporated into, or replaced by a single, national language. This language then became the carrier of the new national culture and both together became the identifying marks of the nation. The nation, in turn became the focus of intense identification (Berger, 1971, p. 27). In this manner the first European nation-states emerged in France, Spain and England. By the sixteenth century, several European political entities had emerged as nation-states; others were added throughout the following centuries through the unification of smaller units (for instance in Italy towards the end of the nineteenth century) and through the dismantling of the Austro-Hungarian Empire following the First World War. Today practically all Western states are variations on the nation-state.

The importance of this development for the expansion of bureaucracy lies in the ability of the nation-state to mobilize a much higher level of commitment of its citizens than any prior political unit was capable of doing. It is this type of national-political identification (or patriotism, if you will) that apparently makes citizens willing (or at least less unwilling) to serve the state, for example through increased taxation (or military conscription), while it also makes people more willing to accept the government's leadership and authority and its (and hence bureaucracy's) decrees in matters of resource allocation.

It has sometimes been claimed that in recent years, nationalism has lost its importance in the Western world. In fact, however, the evidence does not support this conclusion. Wherever different national minorities have been incorporated into one state this has been a source of conflict or at least pressure to change, as the case of the United Kingdom eloquently illustrates. While in the United States (and possibly in other Western democracies as well), young people have become wary of compulsory conscription, in general the allegiance of citizens to their states is apparently still stronger than it was before those states could draw on nationalism for their legitimation.

The advent of democracy

The centuries in which bureaucracy was gradually developing were also the ones in which Western democratic institutions − parliaments and elections − were gradually evolving. As could be seen, the development of bureaucracy was accelerated especially from the nineteenth century onwards. This was also the time in which democratic institutions made considerable progress in several Western countries. In Germany, for instance, this was not yet the case. But in the United States, Britain and several other Western states, political parties took shape, the electoral franchise was extended, gradually approaching universal suffrage, the secret ballot was introduced, and voting participation was massively increased. (See Etzioni-Halevy, 1981, ch. 7.)

Paradoxically, and contrary to what common-sense would lead one to expect, another explanation for the development of bureaucracy − with the advent of democracy − has been given in terms of that democracy itself. Musgrave (1969, p. 96), for instance, claims that the transition to democratic government changed the public's perspective as to what it was entitled to and hence strengthened the public's effective demand for government services. It was, in other words, the preamble or even the beginning to what Bell has subsequently termed the revolution of entitlements (see chapter 3). These growing demands for government (i.e. bureaucratic) services stimulated the supply of an increasing number of such services and, as inevitable correlate, bureaucratic pervasiveness.

It has also been claimed (Jouvenel, 1952) that Western individualism involved grave popular suspicion towards, and widespread reluctance to accept state power. As long as the people felt that they were ruled by the alien forces of absolutism they opposed, to the best of their ability, any moves on the part of the ruler which might conceivably result in the augmentation of such power. The gradual development of constitutions served no other purpose than this. But with the advent of democracy, people came to feel that they themselves were now the masters of their rulers. Consequently, they no longer feared the encroachment of government on their lives, and even welcomed it. So it is because of democracy and under the cloak of democracy that bureaucracy has become more pervasive than any Western government establishment could have hoped to become before.[14]

The development of bureaucracy, for its part, had a two-sided effect on the development of democracy. In some countries over-developed bureaucracies played a crucial role in arresting the development of democracy. In Germany, before and in Bismarck's time, the bureaucracy (in alliance with the army and court circles) fulfilled a dominant role in making the emergence of a democratic leadership impossible. The repressive and anti-democratic qualities of the French bureaucracy under Napoleon I and Napoleon III have also been well documented.

But where bureaucracy did not assume such repressive qualities, its development, growing specialization and increasing power and independence favoured the development of democracy. Ostensibly, historical evidence does not support this claim. The United States and, to a lesser extent, Britain, are sometimes cited as examples of countries where the development of democracy proceeded without the benefits of a powerful, independent, bureaucracy. In point of fact, however, in both Britain and America, throughout the nineteenth century, democratic electoral procedures were highly deficient and electoral corruption flourished. And in both, proper democratic procedures did not evolve until the respective bureaucracies were well developed and had gained power and considerable independence from party politics. And the same holds for several other Western countries — (as will be seen in chapters 11 and 12).

Historically, the development of bureaucracy and democracy in the West thus had a mutual though complex relationship with each other: the development of democracy generally favoured the growth of bureaucracy. And bureaucracy — except where it overshot its mark and became repressive — had a similar effect on democracy. The complex relationship between bureaucracy and democracy in more recent years, will be dealt with in the following chapters.

Economic and social crises

No less complex than the relationship between bureaucracy and democracy was the relationship between bureaucracy and economic development. While, in general, bureaucratic growth and pervasiveness have been facilitated by economic development, they have, paradoxically, also been stimulated by economic setbacks and crises and the social problems connected with them. And the deeper the crises, the quicker the upheavals, the greater the government-bureaucratic intervention to cope with them or smooth them over.

One of the prime features of capitalism as it reached the peak of its development in the nineteenth century was the recurrence of economic crises. These crises had figured prominently in Marx's theory. He saw them as the result of some basic contradictions of capitalism, and as part of the constellation of factors which threatened its very existence and must eventually hasten it to its inevitable doom. There were, in fact, spells of general depression and slump between 1873 and 1879, 1882 and 1886, 1900 and 1901, 1907 and 1908, 1912 and 1913. These crises reached their peak with the crash of 1929 and the subsequent depression in which, in the United States, for instance, GNP declined from $104 billion in 1929 to $56 billion in 1933[15] and nine million savings accounts were lost as the banks closed their doors. But contrary to Marx's conception the crises did not (so far at any rate) lead to the demise of capitalism. Instead they led to growing state (and bureaucratic) intervention into the economy in an attempt to counter the threat they posed to the capitalist economies. It is, no doubt, in part as a result of these crises that state intervention in the economy grew massively from the latter part of the nineteenth century, and in several countries reached new peaks with the great depression.

It has been argued that initially, the situation was aggravated by a misplaced restrictive economic policy by the United States government − entailing raised interest rates and diminished investment − and that this helped transform a normal recession into a major depression. According to this view, even the New Deal Policy (introduced specifically to counter the depression) was anything but helpful initially. Only towards the later 1930s, when Keynesian-type economic policies came to be applied, were these errors corrected. Indeed, it is widely agreed that the depression only receded through the preparations for war which led to full employment.

Nevertheless, as Jacobi (ch. 6) indicates, governments were eventually forced to intervene extensively, in America as well as Europe. They did so by means of price supports, bulk buying, the creation of jobs, the regulation of credit and interest rates, monetary controls, and import and export quotas. These measures marked a watershed; many of them became permanent, thus giving the government bureaucracy an unprecedented foothold in the guidance of the economy.

The Second World War, though it helped end the depression, created a crisis of its own, leading government bureaucracies to even further intervention. As Jacobi summarized this process:

World War II and the problems it produced only furthered this process. The state had to maintain full employment and institute a monetary and credit policy to prevent an economic crisis; it participated in public investments and nationalized banks and industries. Departments were established to plan and direct the economy, and agriculture received aid in the form of subsidies and price support.

But state action soon moved beyond internal economic affairs. Collapsing world markets — a result of the financial crisis — and post World War II anti-colonial revolutions became matters for governmental measures. In previous centuries, private export of capital to noncapitalist, nonindustrial nations had helped stabilize the world economy. Now the export of capital was a state responsibility, undertaken partially by aid programs to 'underdeveloped' countries.

Since the war, the economic crises have, in fact, been brought under a certain degree of control. Or at least this seemed to be the case until the early 1970s (see next chapter). But whether or not government intervention precipitated by the crises has in fact been successful in curbing them, it has in any case been a major source for the growth of bureaucracy. This emerges quite clearly from Table 8.1 above which shows that in the United States only a very slow growth of the federal bureaucracy (relative to population) took place from 1821 to 1871. But between 1871 and 1921 (the time of the recurrent spells of economic crisis) bureaucratic growth was much accelerated. Also, no growth (and even a relative decrease) in the federal bureaucracy took place in the 1920s. But during the depression, the war and immediate post-war years, the federal bureaucracy grew immensely relative to population, and after that, until the beginning of the 1970s, its growth was once again very small.[16] A similar trend is evident for the Australian bureaucracy as well, while the British and Canadian bureaucracies grew mainly during the war and post-war years, after which, their growth, too, was greatly slowed down.

The redistribution of resources and class interests

Bureaucratic proliferation and growth, especially from the nineteenth century onwards, occurred not only through increased state intervention into the economy but also through the growth of state-provided welfare and welfare-related services, thereby bringing about a certain redistribution of economic resources. I would argue that such a redistribution (and the bureaucratic growth related to it) occurred because it was not only in the interests of the underprivileged but also in the interests of the privileged groups, the capitalist classes and the ruling elites – to bring it about.

It must be recalled that during the first part of the nineteenth century the standard of living of the working classes was on a sub-human level. The nineteenth-century European economy was faced with massive population growth and with the requirement of feeding an unprecedented number of people. Whether this led to a decrease in real incomes, or whether the incomes of the bulging working popula-tion nevertheless rose slightly at the beginning of the nineteenth cen-tury, is still a matter of debate. But the quality of life was certainly dismal. With the industrial revolution, the rapid flow of labourers and their families into the industrial cities had created urban slums in which overcrowding, smoke, inadequate water supplies, lack of sanitation and the consequent epidemics had made life unsupportable.[17] Working hours for both adults and children were generally from dawn to dusk, working conditions were unbearable and job security or unemployment benefits were as yet unknown. Those who were incapacitated by illness, work accidents or old age were not compensated but dismissed, and they, as well as the great masses of workers who were periodically hurled into unemployment, or could not find work to begin with, had little to subsist on. As a result, working-class grievances were rife, and resentment mounted. Violent clashes were not as frequent and perva-sive as might have been expected under the circumstances, but they did occur periodically.[18]

These conditions, too, had figured prominently in Marx's theory and he saw them, too, as part of the constellation of factors which would hasten capitalism to its doom by bringing about a socialist revolution. As E.J. Hobsbawm (1962) concurred: 'Nothing was more inevitable in the first half of the nineteenth century than the appearance of labour and socialist movements, and indeed of mass social revolutionary unrest. The revolution of 1848 was its direct consequence' (p. 243). And as Dahrendorf (1959) convincingly argued, a much more sweeping and fateful revolution, the kind that Marx predicted, would indeed have been imminent, were it not for the fact that capitalism was able to make certain adaptations which made life more tolerable for the disadvantaged.

This happened through the fact that towards the latter part of the nineteenth century the organization of labour (which had previously been prohibited) made great strides forward and as labour organizations became more powerful they pressed for a change of the previous condi-tions and for a redistribution of resources. It also happened, however, because it was in the interests of the ruling elites, the capitalist classes and the more privileged groups in general, to bring about some redistribution of resources so as to maintain the system and their own privileged positions in it.

This is not to say that all members of the privileged groups were necessarily aware of this. Indeed, the increasing regulation of working conditions and the expanding welfare measures met with strong opposition from some business and industrial circles and from some of the state elites as well. But not from all.

In Britain, in the latter part of the nineteenth century, the more doctrinaire liberals, who still adhered to doctrines of free trade and *laissez faire* were slow in meeting the mounting social problems — but found themselves pushed from the left by more radical minded liberals and by growing socialist movements and labour organizations. 'For this reason many of the social welfare measures passed in these years were the work of conservative parties, or of liberal parties obliged to yield to the pressure of their more radical supporters' (Thomson, 1966, p. 356). Thus, Tory politicians co-operated in the fight for child protection and the reduction of working hours despite resistance from factory owners. And around the turn of the twentieth century, both conservative and liberal governments undertook successively more progressive social welfare legislation.

In France, Napoleon III (emperor from 1852 to 1870) was active in implementing various paternalistic measures of improving working conditions and wages. 'Napoleon . . . has been called "Saint-Simon on horseback", and there is no reason to doubt either the sincerity of his desire to improve material conditions or the reality of the benefits his rule conferred. . . . "Today" he had written before coming to power, ". . . you can govern only with the masses" ' (Thomson, 1966, p. 271).

And in Germany, Bismarck (chancellor from 1871 to 1890) 'had contrived to steal the thunder of socialists' (Thomson, p. 356) by similar and even more far-reaching paternalist action on behalf of the workers, expressed in welfare and social security legislation.

More recently, a British Conservative leader, Stanley Baldwin, is reported to have said: 'If you want people to be conservative, then give them something to conserve.' And (as the previous examples show) he apparently was not the only European or Western politician to become aware of this, or to have such awareness foisted on him. Moreover, as several of the more astute politicians rightly appreciated, and as Disraeli for one urged on the Tory party — private charity no longer sufficed, and it took the state (and its bureaucracy) to cure the dire poverty and diminish the immense inequalities of the nineteenth century.

To a certain (though limited) extent, then, the interests of the working classes and the underprivileged to improve their lot and bring about a redistribution of resources coincided with the interests of the more privileged classes and the state elites, to prevent the radicalization of the underprivileged and avert possible rebellions and revolutions by means of a certain redistribution of resources through the instrumentality of the state. The partial coincidence of interests was therefore one of the major sources for the growing pervasiveness and proliferation of bureaucracy. And this still continues to be the case today — as will be shown in the next chapter.

The result of all this was the redirection of greater resources to social welfare and social services and this trend continued until the mid-1970s as can be seen from Table 8.3.

Table 8.3 *Percentage of spending going to defence and social services in three Western countries — 1950-74*

Country	1950	1960	1970	1974
United States				
Defence	26.3	29.9	23.8	17.3
Social services	31.6	36.2	43.5	50.4
Sweden				
Defence	17.6	17.9	13.5	11.4
Social services	38.9	45.0	58.8	61.0
United Kingdom				
Defence	18.8	19.5	11.3	10.2
Social services	29.4	33.1	37.6	45.2

Source: Peters (1978, p. 22).

This, in turn, has resulted in a certain decrease in inequalities. For as Wilensky (1975, ch. 5) concluded from data on a large number of countries, the payout of the welfare state has been overwhelmingly progressive while its financing through taxation has been mildly progressive or only mildly regressive.[19] Hence its net effect has been definitely egalitarian.

The development of bureaucracy has thus been related to a certain decrease in economic inequalities. At the same time it has also been interrelated with an *increase* in power inequalities. For the development of bureaucracy has been related to the disproportionate growth of some power — namely its own. An attempt to substantiate this claim will be made in chapter 10. But first it must be seen whether the trends of development traced so far have not been counteracted by some apparent counter-trends in recent years.

Chapter 9

Recent developments: some apparent counter-trends

Fragmentation and incoherence

The preceding analysis of the centralization and rationalization of bureaucracy was not meant to imply that these developments have necessarily attained new heights in recent years. Many observers maintain, in fact, that certain counter-trends have now become apparent. For one thing, it has been maintained that many functional subdivisions of government bureaucracies have been brought about for prestige and power reasons, rather than for real administrative necessity, and thus have brought overlap and duplication rather than effectiveness. Also, consistent principles have not always been followed in allocating functions to different units; examples of illogical groupings are not rare and (as the pluralists have been adept in showing) instances of disunified control, insufficient co-ordination and internal fragmentation are not hard to come by either. To this must be added the outside pressures and demands and the consequent necessity for bureaucracy to maintain liaison with various sections of the community. This, in combination with the general mounting complexity of administrative tasks (chapter 2) has led bureaucracies to become exceedingly cumbersome in their structures and operations. The recent technical advances from photocopying to computer-processing have helped bureaucracy cope with the complexities. But even with their aid some bureaucracies cannot hope to do more than 'muddle through'.

In America, for instance, it has been observed that bureaucracy's lines of command have been fragmented (among other things) by a combination of congressional and interest-group intervention. Congress and congressional committees have certain powers of review and supervision over bureaucratic agencies. Such agencies must consequently gain the support of pertinent interest groups (and interested sections of the public) which, in turn, influence Congress. Bureaucratic agencies thus maintain formal and informal contacts with, and even forge independent alliances with, congressional committees and interest groups, to the detriment of internal bureaucratic coherence. Partly as a result of this, bureaucratic agencies may themselves form elements in the internal fragmentation of bureaucracy by pulling that establishment in different (sometimes irreconcilable) directions (see Meier, 1979, ch. 3; Rehfus, 1973; chapters 2 and 3 in this book).

Equivalent observations have been made by F. Ferraresi (1980, pp. 183, 235) with regard to Italy. According to these, the recent developments of Italian bureaucracy have not followed logical principles. After the Second World War welfare-state activities and economic intervention by the bureaucracy have expanded and multiplied, as have the bodies designed to deal with these activities. But the new bodies were introduced as partial modifications, undermining the old structures without creating consistent new ones. The consequence is that administrative regulation of social interests has grown in most areas, but has done so in a haphazard way. The resultant bureaucratic structure appears as a loose, disjointed collection of ministries, lacking coherence and co-ordination. Fragmentation, overlapping and conflicts are the normal state of affairs. Financial matters, for example, are dealt with by three ministries as are industrial policies, while matters concerning public transport are dealt with by no less than four ministries, with each ministry going its own separate way.

Observations of the same order have been made even with regard to the French bureaucracy which is widely considered as highly centralized and concerted in its power. Countering this as a myth, Wright (1978, ch. 4) claims that the French bureaucracy actually has elements of fragmentation and decentralization built into it. Under the fifth Republic (he writes) there have been a number of administrative reforms, but they have been characterized by lack of internal logic and coherence. 'Indeed, it would be no exaggeration to say that there has been a total lack of system, since the reforms have sought to reconcile or to juxtapose or even to superimpose basically conflicting ideals' (p. 95) namely: more efficiency, more subordination and more democracy. Some reforms were intended to reduce duplication and have undoubtedly achieved that end — especially with regard to regional administrative services. There are many areas, however, where the problems of co-ordination have not been solved or have even been made to deteriorate.

Most of the evidence (continues Wright) also points to internal diversity of the French bureaucracy and suggests that it is prone to domestic tensions and dissensions. There are deep seated personal, ideological and interest cleavages; so much so that the clashes between them are often carried out in the open. Four main groups are involved in decision-making: the *Grands corps de l'État*, the technical *corps*,[1] the top-ranking administrators and the middle-ranking bureaucrats, and they all have different ideas on how the administration should be run and what its policies should be.

Conflicts also occur between ministries: 'There is continuous struggle between the Finance Ministry, the watchdog of the nation's wallet, and most of the spending ministries' (p. 99). Conflicts between other ministries and within ministries are no less frequent (as some of these are federations of practically autonomous divisions) and rivalries amongst the various *corps* are also a normal feature of French administrative life. Attempts at co-ordination are made, for instance, by ministerial cabinets[2] and by interministerial committees, but these efforts are clearly inadequate.

The centralizing tendencies of the French administration have been accentuated during the twentieth century, decision-making has become increasingly concentrated in Paris whence a strong, centralized authority has radiated to the provinces. But while decisions are taken at the centre, the provinces carry considerable weight in influencing and shaping them. In general, the rigours of centralization are tempered by various factors: centre-periphery relations are usually subtle and complex and based on mutual dependence, provincial elites are able to exploit differences of opinion in Paris and the power of prefects (the representatives of central government in the provinces) is not as great as it is often thought to be (see also Hanly *et al.*, 1979, ch. 3; Machin, 1977 and Thoenig, 1978).

A potentially far-reaching reform towards greater independence and powers to the regions and local authorities, as over those of the central bureaucracy, has been introduced in 1981, under President François Mitterrand. A law transferring economic powers from Paris to the regions has been enacted by parliament. The power of prefects has further diminished. They retain authority over the police and will continue to act as the government's chief political agents in France's 95 mainland departments. But they will no longer be able to make the key economic decisions there, or in the 22 larger administrative regions. From now on these decisions are to be made by elected local assemblies, whose presidents will take over many of the powers that used to belong to the prefects. However, it is still too early to tell what the long-term effects of this reform will be in practice.

In any event, the observations on decentralizing trends in Western government and bureaucratic structures have been met by various counter-claims. They include the point that not all Western bureaucracies are splintered to quite the same extent. And even those that are, have their fragmentation and decentralization confined to secondary issues, while a much more concerted and centralized power hierarchy prevails underneath, shaping decisions on the most fundamental issues (see chapters 3, 4 and 5). It is clear at any rate that a historical perspective (such as the one presented in the foregoing chapter) sheds a different light on the problem than does an analysis focused on recent years only. For in historical retrospect it can be seen that despite all counter-trends bureaucracy is still more institutionalized and coherent today than it was even in the preceding century; it is certainly more centralized and rationalized than was the haphazard administration that existed in earlier periods. Recent trends have not necessarily been towards even greater coherence and rationality. But the overall historical trends in the last few centuries have undoubtedly been in this direction.

The New Right and anti-statism: a curb on the growth of bureaucracy?

In contrast to centralization and rationalization, the trends of increasing bureaucratic pervasiveness, proliferation and growth have continued, unperturbed, almost up to the present. But even here there has lately been a seeming reversal of this trend with the advent of anti-statist movements and regimes, especially in the United States, Britain and Australia (where such a regime prevailed until the last election).

In the United States this ostensibly new counter-trend was ushered in by Neo-Conservatism and the New Right, adding their power to that of the more established right. These movements rose at the end of the 1960s and the beginning of the 1970s, as a reaction to the 'New Left', the counter culture, and the disappointment with President Lyndon Johnson's 'great society' programs in the 1960s.[3] They also came as a response to the downturn of the economy and rising inflation and unemployment following the oil-price shock of 1973-4. Specifically, they were a response to the perceived inability of the government to solve these and other persistent socio-economic problems, despite its ever-growing interference in the economy and society.

One of the groups which made itself noticeable, was that of the

Neo-Conservatives, composed of former liberal Democrat intellectuals and centred around such magazines as *Commentary* and *The Public Interest*. A prominent member of this group, Irving Kristol, is reported to have said that Neo-Conservatives were liberals whose dreams of an egalitarian Utopia, painlessly brought about by increasing government action, had turned into nightmares of bureaucratic interference. Accordingly, the Neo-Conservatives focused their critiques on what has recently been referred to as the 'New Class', that is, the 'intelligentsia' (located at universities, and at the government bureaucracy) which has been exerting pressure for greater government intervention. For their part, the Neo-Conservatives have concentrated their efforts on, among other things, opposing the expansion of government bureaucracy, taxation and the public sector of the economy.

While Neo-Conservatism is predominantly an intellectual movement, the New Right is basically a populist one, concerned mainly with mobilization of lower-middle-class, and middle-class people. In the 1970s it took shape in the sustained expansion of interlocking single-issue rightist movements focused, for instance, on the defence of the family, opposition to school-busing, anti-gay rights campaigns and the 'Right to Life' crusade. Among other things, the New Right (like Neo-Conservatism) centred on criticism of the New Class and government bureaucracy. It 'couches its political appeals in rhetoric that mixes patriotic and conservative slogans with opposition to elites and "big" this or that – big business, big labor, big government' (Philips, 1979, p. 142).

This movement has gained substantial influence; after the 1978 mid-term election, it came to control 10 per cent of Congress – forty members of Congress and ten senators. In the Senate, this represented a five-fold increase since 1972. The movement had an especially strong representation in the mountain States, California, the Midwest and the South. The movement's influence is also evident from opinion polls; most of these show the prominence of opposition to bureaucracy, government intervention and taxation. In Kaufman's (1981, p. 1) words, 'Anti-bureaucratic sentiment has taken hold like an epidemic. More and more people are apparently convinced that bureaucracy is whirling out of control and are both infuriated and terrified by the prospect.' Its most conspicuous triumph was the victory (in June 1978) of Proposition 13 in California, which lowered that State's property taxes;[4] this was followed by a move of tax-cutting crusades in other States as well, notably in Massachusetts in 1980.

The New Right has been dominated by small businessmen –

entrepreneurial rather than corporate capitalists. But in recent years there has also been an expansion of corporate lobbies, employer associations and a powerful new alliance of the largest corporations. The 'Business Roundtable' was organized to co-ordinate congressional lobbying, and 'The Wall Street Right' sprang up as a closely allied group. While Neo-Conservatives and the New Right have not actively identified with the Republican Party, the latter groups are close to, or part of, the G.O.P. establishment.

There is an additional right-wing group, the Libertarian Party, formed in 1972. 'Like other conservatives, the Libertarians want − as Reagan put it during the presidential campaign − "to get the government off our backs". Unlike other conservatives, the Libertarians mean what they say' (Miller, 1981, p. 12). The number of libertarians is insignificant, but they have some influence in California and Alaska 'where many people appear to hate government with extraordinary intensity' (Miller, p. 12).

All in all the New Right has become a formidable force in American politics. In the absence of effective counter-pressure from the left, right-wing activism seems to have pushed the centre significantly to the right and to have influenced the agenda of issues for public debate. Even Democratic congressmen have had to show sensitivity to their pressures (Davis, 1981; Miller, 1981; Philips, 1979).

Similar developments have been evident in Britain and in Australia in response to the 1973-4 economic downturn. With the spread of economic instability the reputation of government for successful economic management with the aid of Keynesian economics has waned amongst British intellectuals. Hence there has been a revival of certain key themes of (nineteenth-century) liberalism, which had dropped into the background with the ascendance of Keynesianism.

The gist of these themes is the distrust of government bureaucracy and the call for a return to a free market economy. Government planning (it is held) promotes the intrusion of politicians and bureaucrats into the sphere of the individual. The market, on the other hand, sets definite limits on that intrusion and promotes individual autonomy. State agencies ought to be strong in protecting the market and the individual, but they ought to be constructed so as to supply the least possible scope for interference into their domains. Consequently, the advantages of drastic restrictions on government economic activities and cuts in taxes and public expenditure are exhorted.

These ideas − prominent among intellectuals − and variously known as Monetarism, Social Market doctrines and economic, *laissez-faire*, liberalism[5] – were popularized by leading writers in the press and influential economic commentators. They struck a popular chord and in turn became linked with other movements, most importantly the Populist Right within the Conservative Party. This movement's advocates have concentrated their assaults on taxation, the abuse of welfare, government proliferation and inefficiencies and the threat to public order posed by immigrants and minority groups. They, too, have called for the rolling back of the interventionist state and the retreat of government power (although, as critics have pointed out, all New Rightists favour the strengthening of law enforcing agencies and increased defence spending). The Populist Right, in combination with its more intellectual counterpart, has exerted an influence on centrally located politicians in the Conservative Party (such as Sir Keith Joseph) who were resolved that the Conservative government should adhere to its prescriptions (Gamble, 1979; Sawer, 1982).

In Australia the New Right has attributed the economic crisis of the early 1970s and other current social problems to several factors including high wages, industrial unrest and the growing public sector that has allegedly been destroying incentives in the private one. The Australian New Right has been particularly resentful of the growth in welfare expenditure, the number of bureaucrats employed by the welfare empire and the rising tax burden on citizens all this entails (Head, 1982). As one of its spokesmen, Viv Forbes, summarily expressed this idea, the average Australian working man 'supports a wife, two children and three bureaucrats' (*The Courier Mail*, 7 October 1980).[6] Their policy prescriptions have accordingly included reduction in real wages, facilitation of free market mechanisms and cuts in taxation and government spending. 'Pruning the welfare sector in favour of income tax cuts, has become their catch cry' (Head, 1982, p. 108).

The idea that the state is the source of all evil and that salvation lies in its reduction in favour of the free market has been emphasized especially by *laissez-faire* liberals, commonly known as Libertarians. A Libertarian party – the Workers' Party (later the Progress Party[7]) was formed in Australia in 1975. Its political success was minute[8] but it has invested large efforts in an attempt to gain influence and win the 'battle of ideas' amongst the public at large. On this front its success has been considerably greater: its ideas have gained support among mining, small business and farming circles, amongst members of the liberal professions and in some University Economic Departments (Kasper *et al.*, 1980, p. 208). It has also gained influence within the major political parties. The Progress Party had stressed the idea of a uniform 20 per cent flat-rate income tax and this policy was adopted by the Queensland branch of the National party in May 1980. In the Liberal Party there is now a group of some thirty *laissez-faire* liberals on the back bench of the federal parliament and both it and the Australian Labor Party organized its 1980 election campaigns around low taxation rather than around increased welfare spending (Sawer, 1982). In May 1982 the Liberal Party adopted a platform that is more clearly libertarian in spirit than the platform it replaces, which suggests that for the time being at least *laissez-faire* liberals have gained ascendance in it.

In the United States the ascendancy of the New Right was signalled by Ronald Reagan's election. The new President pledged himself to what came to be known as the four lesses: less money supply, less spending, less tax, less regulation. He pledged to 'get the government off our backs' by reducing the size of the bureaucracy and some of the services the bureaucracy was providing. He repeatedly stressed that 'the best view of big government is a rear-view mirror as we leave it behind' (*The Australian*, 16 January 1982). Accordingly, his advisers and members of his administration have been drawn in large proportions from the New and Far Right.

In Britain several key ministers and especially the Prime Minister Margaret Thatcher have represented a similar stance. In the words of *The Economist* (17 May 1980, p. 9), 'she carries in her ideological knapsack a passionate belief that the bureaucracy ought to be reduced not only in size but in interventionist potential. To her, the civil servant is not merely an intransigent item of public expenditure; his self-aggrandizement is a symbol of what is wrong with Britain.'

In Australia, the then Prime Minister Malcolm Fraser was another kindred spirit. He repeatedly characterized the public sector as unproductive and 'big government' as a source of inflation. He repeatedly expressed the commitment to cut government spending and government bureaucracy. And in Canada the Liberal government has also become known for its (albeit milder) Neo-Conservative economic policies. Despite criticism from some provincial premiers, Prime Minister Pierre Trudeau has recently insisted that a policy of restrictions on government spending was what Canada needed (*Canberra Times*, 4 February 1982, p. 4).

To translate this New Right stance into actual policy President Reagan has been waging a campaign in Congress to cut government spending in all areas but defence. He has recently been criticized by New Right Supporters for his push to increase indirect taxes, but decreased government spending remains one of his major, declared policy objectives. Prime Minister Thatcher has announced in the House of Commons her intention of cutting the number of government officials to what is apparently the lowest level since the war and Prime Minister Fraser set up a Committee of Review of Administrative Functions popularly (or unpopularly) known as 'the Razor Gang' — whose charter was to look into areas of waste and redundancy. When it recommended closing some agencies, selling some government enterprises to private individuals and cutting staff ceilings in the public service by 2 per cent, Fraser wholeheartedly adopted the recommendations.

Has the growth of bureaucracy been curbed?

In this case, however, announcing intentions and adopting recommendations is easier than carrying them out. How, then, did the announced cut-backs fare in practice? How much 'big government' have these regimes actually trimmed? Has the trend of bureaucratic growth been reversed? An indicator for the volume of bureaucracy's activity may be found in its deployment of financial assets or, in other words, in government expenditures. In the previous chapter it could be seen that these expenditures have been rising up until the mid-1970s. Has the tide turned since then? One way of measuring government expenditures would be in relation to level of economic development as indicated by Gross National Product (GNP) or Gross Domestic Product (GDP).[9] Table 9.1 presents the developments in recent years in countries with pronounced anti-statist regimes, the United States, the United Kingdom and Australia (until the last election).

It can be seen that in all three countries there was a slight decrease in non-defence expenditure and/or social services expenditure, as percentage of GNP (or GDP) in recent years. Possibly, the cuts were mainly in social services, while government outlays for economic activities were not affected. But in any case, in all three countries, bureaucracies had less funds at their disposal in relation to the level of economic development in their respective countries, and thus, in a sense, had to curb the volume of their activities.

Since Table 9.1 reports on the situation in the United Kingdom up to 1979-80 only, it is here supplemented by an additional table, leading up to 1981-2.

In Table 9.2 government expenditure is measured in constant prices by size of population, another valid measure of volume of bureaucratic activity. From the table it can be seen that by that measure, government expenditure in Britain, per head, has been expanding slightly in

Table 9.1 *United States, United Kingdom and Australia: central government expenditures as percentage of GNP (GDP for Australia)[a]*

	United States (Federal)			United Kingdom		Australia (Commonwealth)	
	Total expenditure	Total non-defence expenditure	Social services[b] expenditure	Total expenditure	Social services[b] expenditure	Total expenditure	Total non-defence expenditure
1960[c]	18.2	9.3	6.6				
1970	20.0	12.0	8.0	27.3	16.8	24.0	20.9
1975	21.3	15.7	11.0	34.3	26.6	30.1	27.5
1979	20.8	15.9	11.0	32.1	25.1	27.7	25.1
1980	22.1	16.9	11.5				
1981						27.6	24.8
1982[d]	21.7	15.8	11.3				

Sources Compiled and computed from: (for the US) *Statistical Abstract of the United States*, 1980, pp. 259, 261; *The United States Budget in Brief, Fiscal Year 1982*, p. 79; *Facts on File*, 1981, p. 304; *The World Almanac*, 1981, p. 167; *OECD Economic Outlook*, 1981, p. 64; *Conference Board Statistical Bulletin, Sept. 1981*, p. 8; (for Britain) *Annual Abstract of Statistics 1981*, pp. 7, 56 and 378; (for Australia) *Budget Statement 1981-82, Budget Paper*, no. 1, pp. 265, 287.

Notes
a The purpose of the table is to establish size of expenditure in each country over time. It cannot be used to compare size of expenditure in the different countries, for instance, because in the US and Australia, State expenditures, too, would have to be taken into account and because for Australia expenditures are expressed as percentage of GDP (rather than GNP).
b For the US social services include: (1) education, training, employment and 'social services'; (2) health; (3) income security; (4) veteran benefits and services. For Britain, social services include: (1) education; (2) national health services; (3) personal social services; (4) school meals, milk and welfare foods; (5) social security benefits; (6) housing.
c The time-spans covered each year are not identical for the three countries: for the United States they relate to financial years ending on 30 June up to 1977. From 1977 onward they relate to financial years ending on 30 September. For the UK they relate to financial years carrying over to 31 March of the following year. For Australia they relate to financial years carrying over to 30 June of the following years.
d The US material for 1982 is based on President Reagan's budget and the modifications introduced to it by Congress, as ratified by Congress on 20 and 21 May 1981. Possible subsequent modifications have not been taken into account. The GNP for 1982 is based on a projection by the UCLA Business Forecasting Project as published in the Conference Board, Statistical Bulletin, September 1981, p. 8.

recent years, although the picture might be different if non-defence and especially social services expenditure only had been included.

Table 9.2 *United Kingdom general government expenditures*[a]

	£ billion	Population[b]	£ per capita
1979-80	77.9	55,883	1,394
1980-81	79.0	55,900	1,413
1981-82	79.5	56,020	1,419

Sources: Compiled and computed from: *Financial Statement and Budget Report 1981-82*, p. 17; *Annual Abstract of Statistics*, 1981, p. 7.

Notes
a   At 1980 survey prices.
b   For 1980-1 and 1981-2, projected population figures have been used.

The most direct measure of the volume of bureaucratic activity is evidently the size of the bureaucracy itself. In the previous chapter it could be seen that Western government bureaucracies have been growing steadily up to fairly recently. Has this trend been countered in the last few years? As in the previous chapter, size of government bureaucracy has been measured by number of government employees per 1,000 population. This has been done on the assumption that the size of the bureaucracy is most meaningful in relation to the size of the population it is intended to service (or govern). The relevant data are presented in Table 9.3; they show that by this measure, all three countries examined, have in fact had a small decrease in the size of their government bureaucracies in the last two or three years.

Countering the counter-trends

Thus, there have recently been small cut-backs both in non-defence government expenditures (relative to level of economic development) and in the bureaucracies (relative to population) in the countries in which the New Right has been influential. I would argue, however, that this trend is temporary, that it is likely to be halted and that, quite possibly, the tide may once more turn in the opposite direction, at least for the near future.

For, in the first place, it is not clear that the pressure exerted by the New Right will uniformly be in the direction of government cut-backs.

The call for such cut-backs is very much part of the movement's[10] rhetoric. And the movement does, in fact, press for deregulation, for instance in some areas of the economy, in environmental and consumer protection and the like. But the movement's pressure for contraction in government intervention in these areas may be partly counterbalanced by its call for more regulation in other areas, especially in the maintenance of law and order. It may also be counteracted by the New Right's special concern with abuses of the welfare system, with 'bludging' and fraudulent obtainment of benefits. Hence its tendency to press for more inspection and investigation. And these, of course, besides requiring additional staff, are especially intrusive types of bureaucratic activity, now aided by computerized methods of storing, processing and retrieving information.

Table 9.3 *United States, United Kingdom, Australia: central government, state and local employment per 1,000 population[a]*

	United States		United Kingdom			Australia		
	Federal	State and local	Non-indus-trial	General	Local authority man-power	Under Public Service Act	General	State and local
1975	13.3	47.4	9.4	12.5				
1976						11.5	28.1	74.8
1979	12.9	49.8	10.1	13.1	43.3	10.7	27.5	77.6
1980[b]	12.6	58.7	9.8	12.6	43.1	10.5	27.1	77.7
1981	12.2	57.8	9.6	12.3	42.3	10.4	27.1	77.1

Sources: Compiled and computed from: (for the US) *Statistical Abstract of the United States*, 1980, pp. 279, 321; *Monthly Labor Review*, August 1981, p. 78; information supplied by American Information Center, Canberra; (for Britain) *Annual Abstract of Statistics*, 1981, pp. 7, 159, 1982, pp. 7, 159; *Monthly Digest of Statistics*, no. 429, September 1981, p. 26; (for Australia) *Annual Labour Statistics 1979*, p. 71; information supplied by the Australian Bureau of Statistics; *Australian Demographic Statistics Quarterly*, June 1981, p. 4.

Notes
a   The purpose of the table is to establish change in the size of government employment over time in each of the three countries. It cannot be used for a comparison of the size of government employment among the countries since the types of employees included are not identical for the three countries. For the US and UK the figures are for full-time employee equivalents. For Australia, part-time employees have not been included.
    It should also be noted that not all employees are, strictly speaking, bureaucrats (actual bureaucrats can be teased out only for the British and Australian central governments). It is assumed, however, that changes in numbers of employees in general would also furnish an approximate indication of changes in the number of state and local bureaucrats.
b   For the UK 1980 and 1981, projected population figures have been used.

Some New Rightists (e.g. Milton Friedman, Arthur Seldon and others) have suggested that people should be enabled to choose between government-supplied and privately supplied (or among privately supplied) social services in the areas of education, health, care for the aged, and so forth. They have also suggested that beneficiaries should exert their choice and at the same time pay for the services (or part thereof) through a system of government-supplied vouchers.[11] This system, if adopted, would eventually have the effect of increasing the private sector at the expense of the public one, especially in areas where most services have previously been rendered by the government. Thus, it would have the effect of reducing the government bureaucracy's size and power.[12]

Several education and welfare services are even today carried out by the private sector with financial support from the government (for instance private schools and homes for the aged in Australia). Quite possibly, a push will be made to transfer more services to the private sector in the near future. But there seems to be only a remote chance that the voucher system proper will be adopted on more than an experimental scale, even by New-Right-influenced governments, in the near future. In Australia, for instance, the voucher system in education has been publicly debated for several years. Liberal and National Country Party (the former coalition partners) policy statements from 1975 call for an investigation into the feasibility of introducing the system in Australia. In fact, however, no such investigation has taken place. In the United States, only a small-scale experiment of vouchers in education (at Alum Rock in California) was carried out, and even this was subsequently terminated. In Britain, a New-Right-winger, Sir Keith Joseph, is now minister for education, but so far there are no signs that he is about to implement the voucher system on a large scale. And the chances of its introduction in other areas of government activity seem even more remote at the present time.

In part, the reason for this is that some powerful vested interests oppose it, not least amongst them the government bureaucracies themselves. Also, spearheading the introduction of such a system may not be an electoral asset for even a right-wing government. For large blocks of voters may see the proposed system as jeopardizing whatever processes of redistribution of resources have so far been taking place through the present version of the welfare state and through the services the government has so far been rendering to its citizens.

A similar argument has been presented in a recent paper by A.H. Meltzer and S.F. Richard (1978) entitled, 'Why Government Grows (and Grows) in a Democracy'. The authors argue that not only has government grown in the past but it will continue to do so. Periodic dissatisfaction with high taxes and 'big government' may slow down, but cannot end, the growth of government. This is so because of the nature of the political process in a democracy: with nearly universal suffrage, the market produces a distribution of income that is less equal than the distribution of votes. 'Consequently, those with the lowest income use the political process to increase their income. Politicians have an incentive to attract voters with incomes near the median by offering benefits that impose a net cost on those with incomes above the median' (p. 117). The process of such redistribution, in its turn, spells big (and growing) government.

This analysis does not take into account the fact that in most democratic countries, even with universal suffrage, voting is not compulsory, and electoral turnout is usually far from universal. People of higher than average socio-economic position tend to be over-represented amongst the voting population. This, however, is counterbalanced by the fact (noted in chapter 8) that some redistribution of resources is not necessarily against, but in fact favours the interests of the more privileged classes, for it is instrumental in preventing the radicalization of the underprivileged. It is also counteracted by the fact that the process of redistribution benefits not only the most underprivileged. As has often been observed, some of the prime beneficiaries of present government welfare and other services are lower-middle and middle-class people. Hence, any attempts by governments to introduce far-reaching changes into the supply of such services – changes whose consequences cannot be fully predicted at the moment – may antagonize very large sections of voters indeed. Since lower-middle- and middle-class people form the New Right's most formidable bases of support, the movement itself has to be careful with regard to its pressures for contraction of government services. Hence, when the crunch comes, it is doubtful that the movement will be able to push these pressures to their logical conclusion.

To this may be added what Daniel Bell has termed the 'revolution of entitlements' (see chapter 3), that is, the tendency of more and more people to have higher and higher expectations as to the government's responsibility to supply them with services and, generally, to solve their problems. These people oppose increases in bureaucratic size and power, but simultaneously favour increased bureaucratic services. As Kaufman (1981, p. 3) put it: 'so the rapid and unpopular growth of administration does not prove that our bureaucracies are uncontrolled;

on the contrary, one could more persuasively contend that *responsiveness* of the system to the myriad demands on it ... accounts for phenomena we all deplore'.

This, in turn, is supplemented by a trend of increase in the proportion of the population that is in need of and/or entitled to special government or government supported services by present criteria. Thus, for instance, there is in recent years all over the Western world a growing proportion of aged people[13] and a diminishing readiness of families to care for them on their own; further, there is in recent years all over the Western world an increase in the proportion of unemployed[14] — another category of people in need of, and entitled to, special government services. (The Australian government, for instance, is currently running no less than nine training, education and community work schemes for the unemployed at the cost of several hundred million dollars.)

In addition, there is in recent years, a steady increase in recorded crime rates[15] in many Western countries, an increase that precipitates the growth of government law-enforcing and custodial agencies. Because of recently growing divorce and separation rates, there is also an increase in the proportion of 'single-parent families', another category of people at least potentially in need of government support.[16] Assuming these trends continue in the near future, they spell an increase in bureaucratic services (and personnel) and thereby, bureaucratic intervention in the lives of a growing number of people.

Finally, as has been argued (chapter 8), increased government intervention in the economy (as well as an increase in government services) is frequently precipitated by economic crises. Such crises not only increase the number of people dependent on, and entitled to, government services, as well as the demands on government law-enforcing agencies, but they also exacerbate the public's demands on the government to 'do something' to solve the crises. Governments tend to react by giving birth to new 'programs' (the 'New Deal' of the 1930s in the United States being a prominent example). Whether or not such programs are effective in solving the problems they were meant to solve, or whether they merely consist of 'throwing money at problems', they do in any case involve an increase in the volume of government-bureaucratic activity.

To be sure, the continued growth of bureaucratic activity forms an increasing burden and a growing drain on the Western countries' economies. Eventually, therefore, this growth must reach a saturation point. And ostensibly this point must be reached sooner when the economies are in difficulties and economic growth is halted or reversed. But the point at which the burden that bureaucracy imposes on the economy becomes unbearable is by no means clearly fixed or easily recognizable. By contrast, the louder clamour for more government action at times of socio-economic crisis has, in the past at any rate, been more clearly recognizable and strongly audible at the political level.

Hence the recent difficulties in Western economies, where relatively high unemployment and inflation have been coupled with relatively low economic growth, and the social problems thereby created, would seem to indicate (the New Right notwithstanding) greater public demand for further government intervention and greater government response to such demands. Paradoxically, then, the economic crises which have caused the New Right to call for a *decrease* in government intervention, are the same ones which, in actual fact, are likely to bring about an *increase* in government intervention, which in turn spells the further growth and increasing pervasiveness of bureaucracy.

Chapter 10

Bureaucratic development and the power of bureaucracy

This leads us back to the question: has the growth and increasing pervasiveness of bureaucracy (at least up to the most recent years), and will the probable further growth of bureaucracy in the near future spell an increase in its power as technocrats, and some Marxists have argued? Or has the growth of bureaucracy merely caused it to become fragmented and splintered, overloaded with pressures and demands, thus making it more and more vulnerable and barely allowing it a capacity to 'muddle through', as the pluralists have maintained? Could it be that bureaucracy is merely a self-inflating balloon with a large and growing volume, but little weight? And has its growth merely been 'Parkinson's Law' in operation?

Parkinson, it may be recalled, in a humorous characterization of bureaucracy, formulated the 'law' that the work of bureaucracy expands in proportion to the time (and manpower) available for its performance. Could it be that the growth in the volume of bureaucratic activity has, in fact, been merely a work-creation scheme for a growing number of educated people?

Hard and fast empirical evidence on the power of bureaucracy (or any other group of people) is difficult and perhaps impossible to come by. Empirical measures of power (e.g. role in decision-making) proposed by some observers have been promptly rejected by others (see chapter 7, note 1). The fact that different schools of thought have adamantly held on to diametrically opposed views on the power of bureaucracy is itself an indication that decisive empirical evidence is not readily available. Therefore, some general comments and anecdotal evidence will have to suffice as a preliminary approach to the topic.

In line with Parkinson's ideas, it has been argued for instance, that modern bureaucracy merely creates verbosity 'It is not for nothing that the Lord's Prayer contains only 56 words, the Ten Commandments

297, the American Declaration of Independence a crisp 300 words, while the EEC regulations on the export of duck eggs contains nearly 27,000' (Neal, 1978, p. 115). It must be noted, however, that verbosity is not inconsistent with power. On the contrary, the fact that regulations issued by a bureaucracy are exceedingly long-winded and (presumably) complex means that this bureaucracy is prescribing and proscribing citizen's actions in great detail, thus affecting not only the details of what they can or cannot do but also the details of what they can or cannot get.

The same line of reasoning applies to bureaucratic services. Many people would like to see an increase in bureaucratic services but balk at an increase in bureaucratic power. However, more bureaucratic services lead to what is merely the other side of the coin: bureaucratic control over what those services provide. And as more and more people obtain more and more services from the bureaucracy, their life-chances are also increasingly affected by it or, in other words, they become more dependent on it. Therefore, the increase in bureaucratic services, by putting the bureaucracy in charge of more resources, and by making more people more dependent on these resources *is in itself* an increase in bureaucratic power.

Pressure groups and the power of bureaucracy

What, however, about the various interest, pressure or 'veto' groups which supposedly countervail the power of government bureaucracy and on which the pluralists have largely built their case? Empirical observations of bureaucracies in Western societies frequently support pluralists in their claim that such groups apply pressures not only to government politicians but to bureaucrats as well. But this does not imply that such pressures have necessarily detracted from the power of bureaucracy, or that they have done so to a greater extent than in the past.

It is clear, on the one hand, that pressures on governments by various representatives of organized interests have taken place all through history. Estates, guilds, professional organizations and local communities were some of the more recent forerunners of modern interest groups. It is also clear, on the other hand, that the increasing heterogeneity and complexity in modern society implies the multiplication of specialized interests and is therefore reflected in the unprecedented proliferation of groups representing such interests.

But the increase in the number of interest groups does not necessarily spell an increase in their power. Indeed, to the extent that interest
groups multiply, some of them may well countervail each other's
pressures thereby granting the bureaucracy greater leeway in exercising
its power than would otherwise have been the case.

Moreover, as has been pointed out (chapter 3), interest groups
clearly have a bias built into them. Although in some manner they
channel influence from 'below', they do not necessarily do so in a
representative fashion. For not all interests are organized and represented; at the extreme, some elements of the population may be
entirely excluded from representing their interests in matters that
deeply concern them, or else may be at a relative disadvantage in doing
so, while others – especially the more prosperous, the more articulate,
the better organized, the ones that have a leverage over crucial resources,
are at a distinct advantage. Interest groups are thus skewed in favour of
the most powerful sections of the community (McConnell, 1966, p. 7).

Consequently, one may safely assume power differentials or even a
power hierarchy of interest groups. As the corporatists have rightly
pointed out – the most formidable groups, those at the top of the
interest-group hierarchy, those whose power is truly compelling and
relates to a country's most central policy issues – are very few indeed.
And while they are very powerful, I would argue that there is no
evidence to support a claim that they are more powerful than equivalent groups (such as those of large landowners) in earlier times, and that
they have eroded bureaucracy's power to a greater extent than their
predecessors have done in the last few centuries.[1]

Assuming, then, that some of the lesser pressure groups may well
cancel each other out, that the power of some select pressure groups is
great but not necessarily greater than that of their equivalents in the
past, and that, on the other hand, bureaucracy has clearly become more
pervasive and interventionist, it would seem that the technocrats and
Marxists have a stronger case than the pluralists and that the power of
bureaucracy over the public has indeed been increasing.

Furthermore, the very fact that interest groups tend to aim their
pressures at the bureaucracy is itself an indication of that establishment's power. For if bureaucracy were not powerful in controlling the
allocation of resources why waste time and effort in pressuring it as to
the allocation of such resources? In the same vein it has been observed
that bureaucrats and bureaucracies have a great deal of discretion in the
selection of the interest groups they will allow themselves to be pressured by. And that, indeed, bureaucratic agencies sometimes initiate

and organize interest groups to pressure them, in order to gain public support for the policies they were set on engaging in anyway. Or else, that they organize interest groups to exert pressures on other sections of the government — on their behalf. Thus, bureaucratic agencies may develop symbiotic relationships with interest groups in which they not only serve those groups' interest but also use them to further their own.

Fragmentation and the power of bureaucracy

What, however, about the fragmentation of bureaucracy on which the pluralists have also built their case? Here, it seems that things can be argued both ways and the arguments which the pluralists have used to support their case can also be turned against them and used to support the opposite point of view. Certainly, many observers agree that the American bureaucracy (and some other Western bureaucracies) have certain elements of fragmentation built into them. But not all agree that this fragmentation is as far-reaching and fundamental as the pluralists have made it out to be, and not all agree that such fragmentation — to the extent that it exists — has necessarily detracted from bureaucracy's power. In relation to the United States, for instance, Kaufman (1981) writes:

> the federal bureaucracy is such a collection of diverse, often competing and contradictory, antagonistic interests that many of its components check and neutralize each other. (p. 5)
> As a result of such divisions, rivalries, and opposing missions and interests, one of the principal barriers to an assumption of dominant power by bureaucrats is other bureaucrats. (p. 6)

But he adds that fragmentation also spells bureaucratic autonomy:

> Bureaucratic autonomy is also evidenced by the agencies within the executive departments . . . that have carved out their own missions and their own ways of performing them so successfully that they seem immune to interference by outsiders. (p. 3)

And this includes their formal superiors. It holds especially when fragmentation and interest-group alliances go hand in hand:

bureaus within the executive chain of command often became so skillful at forging alliances with congressional committees and with powerful interests outside the government that they are likely . . . to heed their allies rather than their nominal superiors. (p. 2)

Or as Meier (1979, p. 51) put it:

Fragmentation permits sub-system politics — a triumvirate of a bureau, committee and interest group — in specialized areas that, in normal political times, can act without interference from other political actors. . . . Bureaucracy, therefore, has opportunities to exercise political power because American government is fragmented.

In some cases the alliances between bureaucracy and interest groups may degenerate into a transfer of bureaucratic power to private groups. But more often, the transfer of power is in the opposite direction, so that interest groups have enabled bureaucratic agencies to increase fragmentation and thereby to increase their autonomy or their independent control over the allocation of resources.

Similar observations have been made about the Italian bureaucracy. Here, too, fragmentation and lack of coherence have been observed. But the result is not (as might have been thought) a decline of bureaucratic power. On the contrary: according to Ferraresi (1980, p. 258), lack of effective organization spells the wielding of strong arbitrary powers as each ministry is run as a fiefdom by politicians and a small number of top-level administrators. The irrationality of the system further strengthens the position of the bureaucrats because they are the ones who have the authority to interpret the norms and decide which must be enforced and which may be evaded. In this manner the general inefficiency of the bureaucracy allows the senior ranks of bureaucrats to transform into negotiable items what should have been institutional duties. This enhances their bargaining position and thus their ability to influence the allocation of resources to their own benefit.

Elected politicians and the power of bureaucracy

The remarks made so far pertain to the power of bureaucracy in relation to all its role-partners: politicians, interest groups and the public. Of special importance to the argument developed in this book, however, is the question of the power of bureaucracy as against that of elected politicians. Hence this topic deserves some further and more detailed comments. Has the development of bureaucracy made this establishment so formidable that its power, and especially the power of senior bureaucrats, is now surpassing that of elected politicians? And is bureaucracy thereby posing a threat to democracy as the technocrats and some Marxists have claimed?

Some accounts by participants and observers

It might be useful to start out with statements made in recent years by some actual participants in the government process of Western democracies. For instance Suleiman (1974), on the basis of interviews with senior French civil servants, concluded that those civil servants' main power lay in obstruction. As one director observed: 'When a minister wanted something unfeasible done, we only had to say "fine" and chances were that we would hear no more of it.' The minister simply could not follow up every idea that he proposed to them (p. 167).

Similar statements with slight variations have been made about the administration in Britain. Thus Joe Haines (1977) who was prime minister Harold Wilson's Press Secretary and close adviser in 1969-70 and 1974-6, commented that the civil service's power of timing committee meetings, frequently allows it to manipulate their results:

> The Civil Service does not like delay which is not of its own making. There must always be the temptation, sternly though it would be resisted, to arrange committee meetings to take place when a minister who might be awkward was due to be abroad. In other words, meetings could be arranged to fit the inconvenience of ministers. (p. 18)

Other statements by the same participant-observer include:

> This determination [of Treasury] that the opinion of the machine should prevail — and it exists in other departments, too, notably the Foreign Office, but also in Defence and Environment — . . . is reflected in the contempt with which the manifestos on which a Government has been elected are held. (p. 29)

> Politicians . . . regard the Treasury knights with something of the reverence with which Red Indians approached their totem poles.

(p. 40) With a certainty which successive Chancellors have invariably mistaken for wisdom, these financial Fu Manchus have presided over, nurtured, cossetted and brought to flower almost every kind of economic crisis . . . they managed to achieve the worst unemployment since the war, deflation and inflation, recession, rising prices and falling living standards, and all at once, and yet their supremacy is rarely challenged. (pp. 40-1)

And the Chancellor traditionally defends his advisers right up to the moment that he is sacked for their getting it wrong. (p. 41)

Further statements in the same vein come from Lord Balogh, a state minister of the Department of Energy in 1974-5, as quoted by Kellner and Hunt (1980, p. 226). For instance, on the power of inter-departmental official committees, Lord Balogh has this to say:

Most decisions of any importance involve more than one ministry. First they go to one interdepartmental committee at Assistant Secretary/Under Secretary level. Then they go to an official committee of Permanent Secretaries chaired by the head of the Treasury or the Cabinet Office. Usually some compromise is reached there before it comes to ministers. For a cabinet minister to reverse a document that has been through these stages requires the intellect of a Newton and the thrust of an Alexander the Great combined with a Napoleon. Such people are seldom met.

Balogh also makes the point about civil servants keeping information from ministers and trying to rush them into decisions:

The question is whether and when you get papers, especially interdepartmental papers. Sometimes you get complicated papers which require a decision within twenty-four hours or even on the same day at a committee meeting. Sometimes you query something being done in the department and the office says the 'Cabinet has decided it.' You then ask for the Cabinet minutes, and they say you can't have them, 'they are confidential'. Occasionally there's a row and it goes to the Secretary of State. Sometimes you get your way. But after a while you say 'Oh . . . it' before you start.

Similar statements have been made in Britain by an outstanding personality from the other side of the fence. In two statements (quoted from *The Times* 15 November 1976, by Sedgmore, 1980 (p. 32)), Lord Armstrong, who as Sir William Armstrong was head of the civil service, gave the following description of his and his colleagues' roles:

> Obviously I had a great deal of influence. The biggest and most pervasive influence is in setting the framework within which the questions of policy are raised. We, while I was in the Treasury, had a framework of the economy which was basically neo-Keynesian. We set the questions which we asked ministers to decide arising out of that framework and it would have been enormously difficult for my minister to change the framework so to that extent we had great power. I don't think we used it maliciously or malignly. I think we chose the framework because we thought it the best one going.

And further:

> Choosing people, X and not Y to be the new Permanent Secretary of this department, or Y and not Z to be the Deputy Secretary of that department, then I reckoned it was my business to know these people and I would make a definite recommendation. I wouldn't say to the Prime Minister 'there is A, B, C, D and it's up to you to choose' because I think I knew them better than he did and so in that area I reckon I had greater power in that sense.

While an abundance of such statements emanate from Britain, the American political scene seems to be a fertile ground for such statements as well. Many observations in this vein by presidents have now become widely known (see for instance Kaufman, 1981). No less instructive are some statements made by Henry Kissinger (1979) in his memoirs, describing the period in which he was President Richard Nixon's Assistant for National Security and close adviser on foreign policy (1969-73):

> This is a particular problem of a Secretary of State. He is at the head of an organization staffed by probably the ablest and most professional group of men and women in public service. . . . When there is strong leadership their professionalism makes the foreign service an invaluable and indispensable tool of policy making. . . . But when there is not a strong hand at the helm, clannishness tends to overcome discipline . . . officers . . . will carry out clear-cut instructions with great loyalty, but the typical Foreign Service

officer is not easily persuaded that an instruction with which he disagrees is really clear cut. . . . When I later became Secretary I discovered that it was a herculean effort even for someone who had made foreign policy his life's work to dominate the State Department's able machine. Woe to the uninitiated at the mercy of that extraordinary and dedicated band of experts. (pp. 27-8)

While bureaucracy has been known to drag its feet in implementing directives with which it disagrees, its alacrity in carrying out instructions that it favours . . . is wonderful to behold. (p. 376)

How much confidence can we place in statements like these? They stem from people with first-hand knowledge but quite obviously have some problems attached to them. These relate mainly to subjectivity and are well summarized by Randall (1979, p. 808): 'Many students . . . stress the obstacles to presidential control of the bureaucracy, basing their findings on the recollections by presidents, their aides and bureaucrats. This research approach runs the risk of letting the respondents write the conclusions.'

Another approach would be based on accounts of various cases (reported either by participants or by outside observers) in which bureaucrats pitted their will against that of elected politicians, formally their superiors. According to these accounts, bureaucrats, in several instances, did in fact succeed in thwarting the purpose of those politicians.

Thus, Peter Kellner and Lord Crowther-Hunt (1980) analyse the manner in which the Fulton Committee's[2] recommendations on the reform of the British Civil service, accepted for implementation by the Prime Minister and the government, were 'successfully blocked' (p. 23) by the civil servants themselves. According to the authors, the battle between the would-be reformers and the civil servants started in 1968 with the appointment of the Fulton Committee. It ended in 1978 when a government White Paper stated that the recommendations had been implemented. In fact, this was the reverse of the truth, for 'by then, the main Fulton attacks had actually been defeated' (p. 24).

The committee had found the civil service inadequate in several aspects, most importantly in that generalist administrators had a monopoly over the top positions. The committee's intention was to break this monopoly. 'But from their command positions in the service the mandarins were able to deflect Fulton's fire' (p. 45). The top civil servants did not condemn the Fulton recommendations. But while

paying lip-service to their acceptance and claiming that they were being implemented, they set out to subtly erode them. They did so through several manipulative devices:
— procrastination, stalling, or deferral of action;
— redefinition of the recommendations to suit their own wishes;
— selectivity in implementation, ignoring some recommendations altogether and selecting for implementation only those that met with their approval.

The authors describe how several of the committee's recommendations were thwarted in this manner. They then go on to say that the committee's most important recommendation was that the large number of separate civil service class divisions be abolished, including the horizontal lines, but emphasizing especially the vertical lines, separating the administrative and executive classes from the scientific and technical officer classes. These vertical barriers had confined specialists to the narrow range of posts within specialist fields and kept them out of departmental command structures — the preserve of generalists. Instead, the committee proposed an open, single grading structure. Each job was to be filled by the best qualified — whether specialist or generalist.

Once the recommendations had been accepted by the government, a joint committee was established to implement them under the chairmanship of Sir William Armstrong. The problem was that many of the committee members were themselves generalists — thus they were themselves part of the problem to which they were now supposed to find a solution. Not surprisingly, the committee was apprehensive about the proposed abolition of vertical barriers, because generalists would now have to face competition from specialists as well. Hence the committee proposed to approach the task in stages. In practice this consisted of implementing what seemed to them practicable — immediately — and postponing the rest 'regretfully but indefinitely' (p. 67). Thus the committee proposed to remove the *horizontal* class divisions and presented this as the first stage of a two-stage reform; but the second stage was never reached.

By 1978 a Civil Service Department (CSD) White Paper said that the acceptance of the Fulton recommendations had resulted in radical changes in the public service. On the face of it this was true. The vast majority of Fulton's 158 recommendations had been or were being implemented. But these recommendations had been constructed around a central criticism of the dominance of generalists. The CSD checklist dealt solely with the means and ignored the end. The complex old structure had been simplified but the essential vertical barriers remained; below under-secretary level the administrative (generalist) group retained its hold on all policy-making jobs. Thus the battle for giving specialists a better chance of advancing in the public service was lost.

The second case, related by Haines[3] (1977, ch. 5) concerns an attempt to solve some of Britain's housing problems for low-income earners. A large number of such people were living as tenants in council houses but were not permitted to buy those houses. This arrangement was problematic in that with inflation, rent payments rose, while at the same time home owners' mortgages remained constant, and thus in real terms, declined drastically. Partly for that reason, as well as for other psychological reasons, many people were anxious to own their homes. In 1975 the Conservative Party representative advocated that council tenants of more than twenty years' standing should obtain ownership of their houses free of charge.

The author was concerned that the advocated Conservative Party policy would give that party a significant advantage in the next election. The Labour prime minister then authorized him to put forward a proposal for a new policy of that issue. The gist of that proposal[4] was that 'a tenant would be offered the opportunity to buy his house at its *original cost*, minus the amount already paid off on the loan. In other words he would take over the debt' (p. 110). The prime minister was enthusiastic and called the proposal 'historic'.

A series of meetings with officials at the Department of the Environment was then arranged to see if the scheme could be implemented. Initially, the expected opposition from the Department's officials did not materialize, and they were even eager to help. However, objections came in from special political advisers who managed to take evasive action so as to stall progress on the scheme.

The author then spoke to the prime minister who said he was still adamant to carry it through. By 24 March 1976, the prime minister's intention to resign had already been announced. Those advisers who favoured stalling knew they had only to hang on a little longer and prime ministerial pressure on the proposal would be removed.

> But the death blow to our scheme came from an unexpected source: the civil service who until then had been so helpful . . . These schemes were 'novel' Ministers were warned. 'Novel' is the sort of word civil servants will use about proposals coming from Mr Tony Benn.[5] It is what 'sin' means to a bishop. (p. 109)

Thereupon these civil servants put forth various objections to the scheme. And when papers for a ministerial meeting on the subject were circulated to ministers (most of whom had known nothing about the item until then), the proposal had been changed by the civil servants. Instead of the initial version the civil service version of the scheme was laid before the ministers, and this was done without consultation with anyone at No. 10 Downing Street. The modified proposal now read:

To pay to the local authority a premium based on the net rent (excluding maintenance and management) making assumptions about future rent increases and taking account of the life expectancy of the tenant and his named dependants and subject to a minimum charge. (p. 110)

Ministers were not told that a fundamental change had been made in the scheme.

There was a brief discussion of the proposal. The prime minister was apparently not willing to put up a fight for it. After a few minutes he suggested moving on to the next item, 'abandoning a scheme which six months earlier he had said could be historic' (p. 110).

Another case reported on by Higley *et al.* (1975) concerns the Norwegian Treasury's influence on economic policy overriding that of politicians – through its control of the budget. In Norway Treasury civil servants are the ones to collect and analyse the mass of data on whose basis the budget is constructed. This gives them a virtual monopoly over the relevant information. Civil servants also have the prerogative of defining the questions that need to be answered politically through the budget. Ministers have little time and motivation to consider issues on which no questions have been asked. Frequently Treasury officials themselves even come up with the answers. Thus they virtually instruct the government on how the budget should be composed.

Ministers have the responsibility of examining the budget submitted critically, but investigation shows that they rarely do so. Exceptions occur when powerful interest groups direct their attention to it, but this happens very rarely. Examination of the relevant archives from 1947 to 1969 revealed that government discussions of preliminary budgets delivered by Treasury have been meagre. Parliament does not appear as a serious check either because of the sparse expertise it commands. The staff of parliament's Finance Committee consisted entirely of one economist. A total of ten aides served parliament but these were employed by parties rather than by committees. When questioned, members of the Finance Committee tended to admit that they lacked the knowledge that would enable them to evaluate the budget seriously. For their parts, civil servants described parliamentary criticism of the budget as too general and vague to be of use.

In an unusual reversal of this pattern in 1969, the government simply rejected a contractive budget prepared by Treasury — as politically inopportune. Officials were instructed to discard it and draft a new one. Although many of them disagreed with this order — they followed it. Thus the government proved that it does have the power to control the process, but the exertion of this power has been the exception rather than the rule.

More clear-cut cases in which politicians managed to get their way over bureaucrats have been reported in the literature as well. Two such cases are reported by Suleiman (1974) with respect to France. The first concerns E. Pisani, the Minister for Agriculture (1961-6), who sought to undertake a far-reaching administrative reform in his ministry. He saw the ministry as too compartmentalized and blamed the numerous *corps*[6] existing in the ministry for this. He sought to combine some of them so that the ministry might produce more integrated policies. This met opposition from the *corps*, which were adamant in preserving a monopoly over their own domains.

At first Pisani proposed to regroup the ministry's numerous *Directions* into three large ones. This project did not materialize, as all the *corps* were firmly opposed to it. But the reform that was eventually carried through was only slightly less extensive. It entailed a reorganization of the ministry and the fusion of two *corps*. The minister was able to carry through the reform, partly because of his own persistence and skills and partly because of the backing he received from the government and the Elysée. Also, despite vigorous opposition, the *corps* were not united in their stand and, instead of joining forces, were busy fighting each other.

A more traumatic case was the drawn-out battle between A. Chalandon, Minister of Equipment and Housing (1967-72), and the higher civil servants in his ministry. This ministry was the province of one of the most powerful and prestigious *corps* in France — the *Corps of Civil Engineers* — and it is against the opposition of this *corps* that he attempted to introduce his reforms.

Chalandon took the view that France was stifled by excessive power of the state and by 'administrative totalitarianism'. He believed that a shift of power from the bureaucracy to the minister and from the state to the private sector was called for. Accordingly, he strove to change the method by which departmental directors and regional service chiefs were appointed. He objected to the existing practice of appointment to those posts on the basis of rank and seniority in the *Corps* of Civil Engineers, and proposed that non-members be appointed as well. He also wished a minister to have the power to appoint his own senior officials, so as to be in better control of the department. Finally, he proposed to change the existing highway-building policies: he sought to remove highway and construction from the state and place it in private hands.

The *Corps* of Civil Engineers felt threatened by these reforms, since they involved losses of important domains that had traditionally been under its jurisdiction. Not surprisingly, it fiercely opposed them. A serious conflict, fought more or less publicly, ensued. Since the minister was strongly backed by the Prime Minister and the Minister of Finance, he was in a strong position and eventually succeeded in carrying through his proposals.

Conclusion

Some of the observers reporting on the cases here cited were actual participants in the proceedings described, others were not. Many other cases reported by both types of observers could be cited.[7] Clearly they point in various directions: in some instances, bureaucrats asserted their will over that of elected politicians, in others, politicians won out over bureaucrats, in others again, the outcomes were mixed. Evidently there is a great variety in the manner in which bureaucrats and politicians cope with each other and in the balance of power between them. Ostensibly, then, we are back where we started, and no clear-cut conclusions can be drawn.

However, it must be recalled that the first thesis presented in this book (see chapter 7) is not that bureaucracies (and the bureaucrats who staff them) have become more powerful than elected politicians. Rather, it was part of this thesis that bureaucracies (and bureaucrats) have become sufficiently powerful to pose a threat to democracy.

Hence, what is significant in the cases reported is the very occurrence of power contests between bureaucrats and politicians – no matter in whose favour they were resolved. Admittedly, some observers of these cases were less than wholly objective. But other cases have been relayed by outside and presumably more objective observers. Indeed, the number of cases and the variety of observers attesting to such contests is simply too large to leave any reasonable doubt on this score. Clearly, in many instances ministers wanted one thing, civil servants wanted another and (as *The Economist*, 31 May 1980, p. 118) put it, 'Officials moved heaven and earth to try to ensure that their view prevailed.'

The very fact that elected politicians were forced to put up a struggle to promote their aims against those of (non-elected) public servants — no matter who emerged victorious — is itself an indication of bureaucracy's power and its ability to pose a threat to electoral-democratic procedures.

In this vein, this chapter may best be concluded with the words of another less-than-objective, but knowledgeable participant, Richard Crossman,[8] and this is what he (1972) had to say:

> If Whitehall gangs up on you it is very difficult to get your policy through or even to get a fair hearing for a new idea (p. 65) . . .
> the next thing is to select a very few causes and fight for them. The greatest danger of a radical minister is to get too much going in his department. Because, you see, departments are resistant . . . it does not pay you to order them to change their minds on everything. . . .
> Select a few, a very few issues, and on those issues be bloody and blunt because, of course, you get no change except by fighting. . . .
> But you can't afford to have fights on many things. You must have them on one or two or three issues. (pp. 66-7)

In other words, because a minister must fight top civil servants to push his programs through, he can hope to succeed on only a small number of issues. This evidently could not have been the case, were it not for the massive power of bureaucracy; it clearly indicates the potential threat that bureaucracy poses to democracy and it is indeed precisely what technocrats (and some Marxists) have claimed to be the case.

Chapter 11

Bureaucracy and party politics

The technocrats and some Marxists have argued that bureaucracies in the Western world have become powerful enough to gain independence from elected politicians and that they have thereby posed a threat to democracy. The cases cited have corroborated, or at least widely illustrated this point. Chapters 11 and 12 are designed to show that a bureaucracy that gains independence from elected politicians is also, paradoxically, a necessity to democracy. These chapters show that politicians' control over the bureaucracy has frequently subjected that institution to party politics, that whenever this has occurred it has found its counterpart in manipulation of the electoral process, and that only where bureaucracy has gained immunity from party political intrusion have proper democratic procedures developed. Accordingly, this chapter traces the penetration of elected politicians and party politics into the bureaucracies of seven Western-style countries and the subsequent decline of this penetration in some of them. The next chapter depicts certain malpractices in the electoral-democratic procedures of the same seven countries and the subsequent decline of these forms of manipulation in some of them. It concludes by showing that trends of development and decline in these two areas have been practically identical.[1]

Britain[2]

The first bureaucracy to be dealt with is the British one, which today is renowned for its relative immunity from party politics and is frequently set up as a model for other countries in this respect. It was not always so, however.

In the eighteenth century administrative departments were regarded as the private establishments of ministers. Consequently, there was no clear-cut distinction between bureaucratic and political activities, and for many public servants they blended into each other. Even low rank-ing public servants frequently had political tasks to perform, such as canvassing for parliamentary elections. And even administrative activities were subordinated to political considerations. Ministers tended to give preference in appointments to their political supporters; but although political patronage in the civil service[3] thus grew, no spoils system[4] developed. For a time the government created openings for its sup-porters by dismissing the appointees of its predecessors — but the practice subsided before it became firmly entrenched.

From 1780 onwards administrative reforms proceeded on a consider-able scale, and by 1830, the trend of divorcing the administration from partisan considerations was well under way. The leaders of the party in office still allocated jobs to their supporters, but the more flagrant subordination of administrative efficiency to political utility had diminished. Moreover, by that time, the supply of patronage in the civil service fell far short of demand. As Parris (1969, ch. 2) noted, for every friend a politician gained through the award of an administrative post, one or more enemies were made by the refusal of their requests. Many politicians thus came to consider patronage as more of a burden than a boon. These developments set the stage for the further reforms that were based on the Northcote-Trevelyan Report (submitted in 1854). Their essence was the separation between temporarily elected politi-cians and permanent, appointed, non-political public servants. Recruit-ment to the public service was to be solely by merit. It was to be based on open, competitive examinations conducted by a central board, without intrusion of political considerations.

The implementation of these prescriptions was a protracted process. For a time, the civil service commission (appointed in 1855), had to be content with a system of limited competition — a compromise between the older system and the Northcote-Trevelyan recommendations. It was not until the 1870s that open, competitive examinations were estab-lished as the regular method of entry for most of the large administra-tive departments.

Even then, civil service patronage was still tenacious. In the next decade, 20,000 posts were still used for this purpose. But both parlia-ment and public opinion were increasingly critical of patronage. These were two of the major reasons why the practice declined steadily throughout the second half of the nineteenth century and with the close of the century was practically eliminated.

The new system, based as far as possible on merit, non-political appointments and promotions, and partisan neutrality of the public service has been perpetuated into the present. According to Birch (1973, ch. 3) the Labour government of 1955 gave temporary appointments in the civil service to a limited number of economists with left-wing views, but it was assumed that these appointments would not be permanent. Permanent appointments are sometimes offered to persons of known political views, but care is taken not to confine these offers to members of the government party. According to Richards (1963) there are no such clear-cut barriers to patronage with regard to ministerial or administrative boards, public companies, Royal commissions, the bestowal of honours and the like. But as far as the civil service proper is concerned the possibilities for political patronage are very limited indeed.

Many observers concur that there are in present-day Britain some consensual conceptions – common to both politicians and public servants – that set the framework for the activity of the public service. These include the view that party-political control of the service is detrimental to good administration and that civil servants are servants of the crown, who are bound to serve with impartiality whichever government happens to be in power. Civil servants usually have their own views on matters of policy but are not free to indulge their partisan sympathies freely. Their allegiance to one party or another is subordinated to the requirements of their profession.[5]

In the 1960s further reforms were introduced into the British civil service. The foremost of these resulted from the Fulton Report of 1968.[6] Among other things the Fulton Committee recommended that ministers be entitled to give temporary posts to a small number of experts serving as their personal advisers. None of the changes recommended, however, re-ordered the political roles of civil servants in any but marginal ways, and the partisan neutrality of the service was not tampered with.

Australia[7]

Australia (like Britain) presents an example of an administration that has attained a large degree of immunity from party politics. Initially, Australia inherited the pre-reform British administrative structures: five of the six Australian colonies became independent States in the middle of the nineteenth century, in the same decade in which the Northcote-

Trevelyan Report was submitted, but before it was fully implemented. Thus, although administrative structures differed from State to State, all were permeated by the intervention of politicians and of party political considerations in administrative matters. The new States did not immediately introduce far-reaching changes and only towards the end of the nineteenth century did significant reforms come about.

The politicization of the States' administrations was most clearly evident in political appointments. Researchers agree that such appointments occurred, although there is no consensus on their dimensions. Some researchers mention that they were only a relatively small percentage of all appointments. Others claim they were practically the order of the day (see, for instance, Bland, 1944, p. xi). Politicization was apparently an important factor in promotions as well. For New South Wales, towards the end of the nineteenth century, for instance, Knight (1961) reports that seniority was the ruling factor in promotions. None the less, politicians had enough politically motivated promotions at their disposal to cause considerable dissatisfaction among public servants.

Towards the latter part of the nineteenth century, public service acts introduced in several States provided for public service boards to ensure appointments by merit. Initially, the acts did not have much success in ridding the bureaucracies of political influence. Eventually, however, the British administrative reforms had some impact in Australia. Gradually, politicians lost control over appointments, and the States moved towards public service boards that became gradually more effective in safeguarding the political neutrality of appointments. In some cases the public service boards had no control on public statutory corporations such as the railways, and there, political appointments continued. Nevertheless, Parker (1960) maintains that in New South Wales, at any rate, standards of recruitment and promotion became more neutral around the turn of the century. Politicians themselves were now glad to surrender patronage within the public service because, with the growth of that service, it had become too bothersome. In Queensland, however, it was not until 1932 that an effort was made to close the door against patronage appointments.

The Commonwealth public service, created after federation in 1901, was based on principles of p-litical neutrality from the beginning. To avoid political influence, recruitment was by competitive examinations under the control of the Public Service Board, which served in the Commonwealth as in the States as the major bulwark against patronage. As Encel (1970, ch. 13) points out, promotions, too, have come to be influenced to a much greater extent than before by objective criteria. In the

Commonwealth Public Service, permanent heads of departments are in charge of promotions, but since 1945 such promotions may be appealed against by other candidates within the public service who believe they are better qualified. Appeals are heard by a committee that includes a staff representative.

Does all this mean that the present-day Australian bureaucracy is neutral as far as party politics is concerned? Some observers argue that heads of department and other senior bureaucrats are still motivated to promote those who share their views and are loyal to themselves in order to solidify their power bases. But observers usually agree that the Public Service Board and the appeals system lead to greater objectivity than would otherwise be the case; that great pains are taken to remove politicians' interference in appointments and promotions and that these are generally made on criteria of merit more than in many other bureaucracies. Spann (1973, p. 590) concurs that as a rule, politicians cannot use posts in the administration as political rewards and that political patronage in the bureaucracy 'is not a serious problem in Australia, though there are a few cases, especially on statutory boards, of "political" appointments to administrative jobs'.

Recently, Weller and Grattan (1981, p. 77), on the basis of a series of thirty interviews with senior public servants, reached a similar conclusion on how things actually work out in practice:

> What permanent heads strongly opposed was any suggestion that ministers should be able to select candidates for promotion. They insisted that the public service makes the choice and that any ministerial protégé had to run the gauntlet of the merit principle. One minister wanted to get involved, but was warned off by his permanent head. But anyway such problems seldom arise.

Nevertheless, it is recognized that a few of the very top appointments have occasionally been made through political influence. It has been reported, for instance, that Liberal governments have sometimes made political appointments to top diplomatic posts. When Labor came to power in 1972, it made what *The Sydney Morning Herald* (22 November 1976) termed 'blatant' political appointments by introducing three former private secretaries to the Prime Minister, Gough Whitlam, as permanent heads of government departments.

However, in fact, the dimensions of political appointments are very modest indeed, especially when compared to what takes place in some other countries such as Israel or Belgium (see below). In 1977, legislation was passed according to which an incoming government is allowed to choose department heads from outside the professional public service, but such appointments may not be permanent, being limited to a maximum of five years. This legislation has circumscribed political appointments even more severely than before.

The United States[8]

The United States presents a case of a bureaucracy whose former control by politicians and party politics has subsequently declined, but which has not attained (and perhaps was not meant to attain) the partisan neutrality of its British and Australian counterparts.

When the American public administration was created in 1789-92, its penetration by party politics was not as deep as in Britain at the time, but political neutrality was not institutionalized. In the 1790s politicians showed a growing tendency to reserve places in the administration for their partisans; Presidents George Washington and John Adams often required the proper political opinion as a precondition for appointment. President Thomas Jefferson, elected in 1801, upheld the freedom of federal employees from party obligations. But he also began the practice of removing his political opponents from the public service. Although he did so in modest dimensions 'he proscribed enough public employees so that he, certainly as much as Andrew Jackson, is entitled to be considered the founder of the spoils system in American national politics' (Van Riper, 1958, p. 23). From then on, party service was considered as a legitimate prerequisite for appointment to office and party dissent as a cause for dismissal.

President Jackson, who took office in 1829, thus was not the first to use the spoils system, but according to Van Riper he must take credit for consolidating its principles into a systematic political doctrine. Also, he increased its dimensions and turned it from a local practice to a national phenomenon. From then on, 'For a full half century the tide of patronage and spoils rose higher and higher, submerging one effort after another to build a dyke around at least part of the public service' (White, 1935, p. 3). The system reached its peak under President Abraham Lincoln in 1860, when occupants of some 1,457 of the 1,639 available posts were replaced by party faithfuls (Fish, 1900 and 1905).

Under the spoils system, great portions of the public servants' efforts were devoted to partisan (rather than to administrative) purposes, including electioneering. Civil servants' financial contributions to their parties were also expected as a quasi-official part of the system. Thus, the civil service became more and more intricately tied in with party politics, and by 1860 'the two were almost inextricably entangled' (Van Riper, 1958, p. 50).

Some reforms were attempted at the time of the Civil War and gained momentum in the two decades following it. Acts of 1853 and 1855 had already established 'pass' examinations for offices, but these were non-competitive and unstandardized, hence of little significance. The Pendleton Act of 1883, termed by Ostrogorski (1902, vol. 2, p. 491) 'the Magna Charta of civil service reform', provided for competitive examinations for federal employees and for a civil service commission with some authority over recruitment. Coercion for political activity and discrimination on political grounds were prohibited. But certain categories of posts were exempted from the new merit system and the president's power to hire and fire was only slightly impeded. Almost all presidents after 1883 enlarged the merit, or 'classified' system, but large numbers of non-classified places remained. Civil service reform was thus left incomplete and patronage in the service was not eradicated.

Indeed, the patronage and spoils system reached new heights at the beginning of the twentieth century, most notably in local government. For instance, Gosnell (1937) reported that 60 per cent of the party precinct captains in Chicago held municipal jobs in 1928 and almost 50 per cent did so in 1936. This situation was not peculiar to Chicago; Gosnell cites comparable data for Philadelphia and Key (1958) cites studies reporting similar situations for Pittsburgh, Albany, Syracuse and Auburn. In New York City in the 1930s the annual pay for posts exempt from civil service regulations — that is for political appointments — exceeded 7 million dollars.

The federal civil service, too, was still heavily stamped with a partisan political imprint and the interference of politicians in administrative appointments was widely institutionalized. Ordinarily the chairman of the national committee of the president's party controlled the distribution of patronage. Certain types of patronage have customarily been controlled by senators in their States and representatives in the districts. Top level jobs have usually been under the discretion of the President himself, although presidents have differed in the manner in which they have exercised this discretion.

According to White (1945) President Franklin D. Roosevelt's role in this respect, for instance, was rather ambiguous. His public statements continuously upheld the necessity of public service reform, and these declarations were more than just lip-service: in his second term, he was responsible for visible progress in public personnel administration. Yet Roosevelt did not hesitate to use patronage extensively whenever necessary to further his own political aims.

In the meantime the patronage and spoils system met increasing opposition from public opinion and was gradually losing its respectability. Consequently, the civil service reforms, begun in the later part of the nineteenth century, were expanded by legislative acts of 1907, 1939 and 1940. Under these new reforms, the selection of employees was to be conducted largely by the departments, subject to uniform employment standards to be determined by the civil service commission. In practice, too, the competitive merit system made gradual headway. In 1883, only 10.5 per cent of all federal executive employees had been included in the classified service; by 1940 some 72 per cent were covered.

But at the time, politicians derived great benefit from patronage in the bureaucracy and had a strong vested interest in the preservation of the system. Hence, according to Van Riper, under President Truman, some 70,000 civil service posts were still open to patronage appointment, nearly half of them within the middle and upper levels of the civil service (even though they were subject to tenure restrictions). And according to Mills (1959, ch. 10) the Eisenhower administration declassified about 134,000 civil service positions and forced many thousands of other position-holders to resign on the grounds that they were 'security risks' – thus opening new vistas for partisan rewards.

Also, Sorauf (1956, 1960) reports, that at the beginning of the 1950s the Pennsylvania State civil service system covered only 20 per cent or so of its employees, while the majority were still politically employed. Similarly, Moynihan and Wilson (1966) report that in the New York State administration, in the years 1955-9, 62 per cent of all appointments were sponsored by the Democratic Party and another 12 per cent were cleared by it. Around that time, only about half of the States had attained merit systems applying to most employees and only in a few States were all employees covered by a merit system.

In the 1960s the situation still differed widely among States and localities. In Chicago, politicians still had some 15,000 city and county jobs at their disposal and another 13,000 to 17,000 State jobs. Pennsylvania still had 50,000 patronage positions as late as 1962 (Epstein, 1967, ch. 5). In a few cities and States, on the other hand, the number of patronage employees was very small.

In recent years, the merit system has made further inroads, especially in the well paid, specialized positions where the needs for expertise and training are greatest. A certain segment at the top of the American Federal bureaucracy is still legitimately filled by political appointments. But in general, the proportion of political appointments in relation to non-political appointments has been decreasing.

Yet the role of the American civil service with regard to immunity from party politics has not been as unequivocally clear as that of the British one. As Lukas (1976, p. 19) noted:

> Although the Hatch Act prohibits federal civil service employees from taking part in partisan political efforts, all presidents have tried to make bureaucrats march to their political tune. But the Nixon effort was unusual both in its scope and in the fierce determination with which it was enforced.

This statement has been corroborated by Mosher *et al.* (1974) who reported that the months before the 1972 election were characterized by an obsessive drive for re-election of the president. This seems to have affected government decisions even in fields of activity that were supposedly politically neutral: administration of revenue laws, antitrust prosecutions and the like (see also Lukas, 1976, ch. 2). In addition, President Nixon gained some political control over the bureaucracy by seeing to it that Republicans and people sympathetic to his views were likely to be selected, and those not sympathetic to his views were likely to be eased out of top, influential career civil service positions (which formally, were politically neutral) (Cole and Caputo, 1979; Randall, 1979).

President Carter followed a different path. He concentrated as many decisions as possible in the White House, but he did not make any blatant attempts to utilize the civil service as such, for party political purposes. He even attempted to protect it from such utilization. In 1978 he introduced a civil service reform designed mainly to reward initiative and creativity among top level officials and to shield them from party politics. For this purpose an elite cadre of top officials (the Senior Executive Service or SES) was created, the existent civil service commission was abolished and in its place, the Office of Personnel Management and the Merit System Protection Board were established.

The reform, apparently, was not a resounding success. As Lanouette (1981, p. 1296) indicates: 'Morale within the SES is low and getting lower, with its members complaining of low pay, inadequate bonuses and the potential for intimidation by their political bosses.' The author adds, however, that so far there is no evidence that under the Reagan administration, the dreaded political misdeeds have materialized.

Israel[9]

Israel supplies an example of a bureaucracy that has been pervaded by politicians and party politics from its inception and whose politicization has only partly declined in recent years. The roots of this politicization are to be sought in the pre-independence or *Yishuv*[10] era. Specifically it has its origins in the political institutions set up by the budding Jewish community under British Mandatory rule.[11] These included the *Histadrut* (the federation of labour unions) and a Jewish authority for self-government which was eventually recognized as such by the British authorities.

Shapiro (1975) shows that in the *Histadrut* party-political and administrative roles came to intermesh to such an extent that they were practically indistinguishable. At the head of the *Histadrut* stood representatives of various parties, chief among them *Ahdut Ha-Avoda*,[12] in elected political roles. Since the parties lacked the funds to pay these politicians' salaries, they found jobs in the growing *Histadrut* administration, so they held elected and appointed positions at one and the same time. Other positions in the *Histadrut* were also allocated as rewards for political adherence, and their incumbents geared their administrative work to the demands of their political bosses (who were also their administrative superiors).

This pattern was also established in the authority of self-government[13] whose bureaucracy had no system of entry based on objective qualifications. Appointments were made by the party-key — that is, all parties that co-operated with the national authority were allocated positions according to their electoral size.

The intermingling of political with administrative posts, and of political with administrative consideration was perpetuated after statehood. With the establishment of the state in 1948, the civil service expanded greatly, to staff the newly created government departments as well as those relinquished by the Mandatory authorities. As Medding (1972, ch. 11) points out, the political party bosses were called upon to fill the new positions. Whole ministries soon became staffed with party faithfuls. *Mapai*[14] (formerly *Ahdut Ha-Avoda*) as the dominant party, received the most important key ministries, which it staffed with its own supporters.

Not only appointments, but working procedures, too, were politicized. A sizeable proportion of the posts in the state administration was filled by persons who had previously held posts in the *Histadrut* and in the *Yishuv*'s authority of self-government. Not surprisingly, they perpetuated the work patterns to which they had been accustomed there. These included loyalty to partisan political leaders, obedience to their directives and precedence for party over state interests.

Eventually, new civil service regulations were introduced; these called for appointment by merit, public advertising of vacancies and the use of independent experts and representatives of the public in making selections. But as Medding (1972) notes, these regulations did not put an end to politicization. For one thing, the hiring regulations had little effect on appointments made earlier. Also, senior posts were left as political appointments which the ministers could fill almost at their discretion. In fact, 31 per cent of the senior appointments throughout the years 1960-6 were made without the public announcement of a vacancy (Globerson, 1970, p. 57). When there were such announcements, writes Medding, the more qualified candidates were more likely to get the jobs, but even then partisan considerations were still important in drawing up the precise qualifications being sought (so as to fit a party candidate already in mind) and in deciding between otherwise evenly matched candidates.

Promotions, too, were still based on the criterion of service to the party more than on objective criteria of talent, efficiency or initiative. Not surprisingly, a study by Akzin and Dror (1966) demonstrated that Israeli politicians continued to take a more active role in determining administrative policy than do those in most Western countries. As a result, de-politicization was slow and only partly effective. By the end of the 1960s and the beginning of the 1970s the penetration of politicians and their parties – especially the Israel Labour Party (ILP – formerly *Mapai*) and its coalition partners into Israel's major bureaucratic structures had not been eliminated, and several departments were still maintained as those parties' feudal estates.

Apparently, no fundamental change in these patterns occurred with the advent to office of the right-wing *Likud*[15] following the 1977 and the 1981 elections. When still in opposition, this party had advocated greater stress on statehood over partisanship and therefore the depoliticization of the public service. Accordingly, when it took office, the new government retained the bulk of the previous senior public servants, making only few political appointments. Subsequently, however, the party's leaders privately criticized the government for being 'imprisoned' by the public servants inherited from its Labour predecessors, these being persons who allegedly undermined its policy. They did not demand the dismissal of such (tenured) officials but insisted on increasing party representation through the filling of vacancies.

The fact that the Israeli bureaucracy is still beset by political partisanship at least to some extent is illustrated by recent occurrences in the religious affairs and absorption ministries. Traditionally, the former has been the fiefdom of the National Religious Party (NRP). Before the last (1981) election, however, the Minister for Religious Affairs left the NRP and founded his own party – *Tami*.[16] This political split left its imprint on the ministry: as the election approached, the public servants in some of the ministry's divisions were busily working for the NRP, while in others energetic work for *Tami* was in progress – all during working hours. Some of the ministry's officers were even observed at their respective parties' headquarters during working hours. This partisan split also left its imprint in daily struggles between supporters of the two parties within the ministry, which resulted in almost daily mutual accusations made to the press. Also, after the election the Absorption Ministry passed from *Likud* to *Tami* control. Subsequently there have been reports of *Tami* systematically ridding the ministry of all previously introduced *Likud* personnel.[17]

Italy[18]

Party politicization of the bureaucracy and its domination by the politicians of the party in power has long been one of the most fundamental features of Italian government. Whereas in many other democratic countries this tendency has been mitigated (or at least rendered less unfair to opposition parties) by the periodical replacement of the ruling party, this has not been the case in Italy. The Christian Democratic Party (DC) has maintained itself in power for over thirty-five years.[19] When this party has had to rely on the collaboration of smaller parties, their leaders have also gained influence over the bureaucracy. But the main power over the bureaucracy has remained with the DC leadership.

The DC's power over the bureaucracy is expressed not so much in general policy issues as it is in the area of bureaucratic positions. The DC leadership exerts an influence not merely on the use of existent jobs for partisan aims but also on the creation of new ones for such purposes. Thereby it has indirectly contributed to the enormous inflation and unruly size of the Italian bureaucracy. Newly created or existent positions have come under DC influence with regard to appointments and promotions. Thereby the DC exerts great power over bureaucratic careers. It has used that power to intervene with the bureaucracy in favour of its friends, clients and related interest groups,[20] chief among them the Catholic Action Group.[21]

La Palombara (1964), on the basis of interviews with senior Italian bureaucrats, reasons that those bureaucrats are not in a position to defend the bureaucracy against this *second* type of interference (which he terms *parentela*) because they are so vulnerable to the party's *first* type of interference, namely its ability to meddle with those bureaucrats' own careers. La Palombara adds:

> Bureaucrats who respond to the stimulus of *parentela*, and few of them do not, even though they claim immunity, are prone to take certain presumed rewards and punishments into consideration. The most apparent of these involves the Party's perceived willingness and ability to have an impact on bureaucratic careers. It is far from my intention . . . to suggest that the Italian bureaucracy is a limp instrument to be used by the DC. I do mean to say, however, that the Party can and does interfere in the careers of public administrators and that the presence of this fear is an important reason why the *parentela* pattern is possible at all. (p. 325)

La Palombara's respondents usually corroborate each other's evidence in reporting that DC supporters have much better chances than others of making a career, and vice versa. As one senior official put it 'the Christian Democrats . . . have the means for taking certain kinds of reprisals against those elements of public administration who create difficulties' (p. 321). Hence, not surprisingly, significant numbers of bureaucrats join the party and accept the authority of its leaders for purely opportunistic reasons. Interestingly, it is not only the leadership of the party itself, but the groups closely related to it which take part directly in controlling the career of bureaucrats. Among the groups most frequently mentioned by respondents in this respect is Catholic Action Group, which is reported to have a decisive say in promotions, transfers and the like.

Politicization has penetrated all *levels* of the Italian bureaucracy. It has not been confined to top positions, but involves lower levels which formally are supposed to be staffed strictly on the basis of merit and seniority. It has also penetrated all *parts* of the Italian bureaucracy. In particular the Ministry of Bureaucratic Reform has been designated as 'a striking example of the very patterns of public administration that the Ministry's creation was expected to drive out of existence' (La Palombara, 1964, p. 329).

Politicization, moreover, has also penetrated the two different *types* of the Italian bureaucracy: the state's central administration and the quasi-public administration of all sorts of agencies which have sprung up to foster economic development, especially in the South. According to Passigli (1975) both administrations are marked by strong politicization, although the agencies are more politicized than the central administration.

For instance the *Cassa per il Mezzogiorno* (Fund for the development of the South) has become a gigantic patronage organization which employs people and awards contracts strictly on the basis of political considerations. In Rome alone, in recent years, there are thought to be forty thousand such agencies, although not necessarily of similar size. Originally they were set up to put into effect temporary programs, but they have remained in existence as sources of political patronage. A recent study of a town in Sicily traces the growth of politicization in such agencies. In 1950 there were seventeen Christian Democrats in senior posts in local public agencies; by 1974 the number had grown to 98 (Caciagli, 1977).

A no less politicized element of the Italian bureaucracy are the prefects. These are the representatives of central government in the provinces. According to Fried (1963), in actual fact, prefects not only further the interests of the government but the interest of the government parties as well. Thus, the typical prefect organizes these parties' election campaigns in conjunction with the province's party secretary and provides information to government candidates on the activity of the opposition. He has considerable leverage in controlling local government authorities, and uses it in a partisan fashion — to aid authorities that support the government and harass the opposition in every possible way. In this fashion, the prefects have aided the DC in maintaining its hold over the bureaucracy during its thirty-odd years in power.

Italy has thus been endowed with what DiPalma (1979) refers to as an 'available state'; available, that is, first and foremost to the dominant party, the DC. Concomitantly DiPalma shows that the Italian state bureaucracy has been available to other parties (particularly from the left) as well, and that this availability, far from decreasing, has in fact become more pronounced in recent years (see also Pasquino, 1979).

France[22]

The French bureaucracy is renowned for its potentially powerful position in government and society; it is usually thought to occupy a more influential position than its counterparts in many other Western countries. It is of special interest, therefore, to explore the manner in which it has itself been influenced by politicians and party-politics.

It has been a long-standing tradition in France, for ministers to be supported by small staffs of political advisers – the ministerial cabinets. Here, ministers have full discretion over appointments and have legitimately used it to surround themselves with personal and political loyals. But even the regular (and formally neutral) bureaucracy has not been as clearly dissociated from the influence of politicians and party politics as its British and Australian counterparts. Partisan influence seems to have decreased to some extent after the Third Republic but, according to some observers, increased again in the early 1970s.

In the Third Republic, the government followed the tradition of previous regimes in removing political opponents from the bureaucracy and substituting them with its own supporters. In the 1930s officials' positions became more secure, and the most governments could do was to transfer their most outspoken opponents to less influential posts. Under Pétain, however, tenure was abolished and this increased the government's political influence over the bureaucracy: thousands of officials were purged.

Under the Fourth Republic political appointments diminished but were not eradicated. After the Second World War, the entire recruitment procedures into the civil service were modified. Before that, there had been numerous examinations – each ministry and each *corps* had administered its own, and set its own standards. After the war a reform came into effect whereby all civil servants were recruited by general, competitive entry examinations with uniform standards, and selection was centralized through the Central School of Administration – The Ecole Nationale d'Administration (ENA).[23] The admission to the school itself and its final examinations have been kept above suspicion of political influence and favouritism. Recruitment to medium and lower grades has also been unified by the institution of a national system of competitive examinations. According to Duverger (1958, p. 170), 'This has led to a decrease in political influence since it is more difficult to bring influence to bear on a national competitive examination than on the individual examinations of individual ministries.'

Despite all this, Meynaud asserts, there seems little doubt that during the Fourth Republic, high level administrative appointments were still politicized and posts were given to people who would not have been considered for them through normal channels. Observers generally agree, that even after the war, appointments were made with a view to party interests: senior officials were usually of the same party as the ministers, and departments were colonized by the major parties. Under *tripartisme* party influence on senior appointments became systematic when the three government parties[24] parcelled out the administration among them.

Gradually the administrative reforms began to further recruitment by merit. By 1947 open political patronage in the service was checked but according to Suleiman (1974), even then party politics could not be wholly excluded from appointments to policy-making posts. Rigid party spheres of influence were eliminated with the disappearance of *tripartisme*. But a looser allotment of ministries to partisan influence continued. The Departments of Interior and Education remained under Socialist and radical influence and the Foreign Office was monopolized by the MRP until 1954. In 1956, a more systematic partisan colonization of departments was revived 'when the Socialists, returning to office after five years without influence on appointments, set about making up for lost time' (Williams, 1964, p. 341).

During the Fifth Republic prime ministerial and presidential staff scrutinized all senior appointments. Hence, many higher civil servants, including about half of the directors of the central administration,[25] owed their positions largely to political collaboration with ministers and there were many cases where directors were forced out of their posts because of their political views. Partisan criteria were particularly important in staffing 'delicate' agencies such as the Foreign Ministry and the radio and television networks.

By the late 1960s the Gaullist party, the Union de Démocrats pour la République (UDR), had become France's dominant party. In the 1968 election it gained 45.6 per cent of the vote, reducing smaller rightist parties to satellites or to an insignificant opposition. This, Suleiman (1974, ch. 12) shows, was reflected in the party's control over the bureaucracy. Previously, various parties had influenced the bureaucracy but none had held exclusive sway over it. As the UDR gained political dominance, it was 'gradually coming to have a strong hold on the administration, which no political force had previously been able to secure. One important manifestation of this change is that the administration has become deeply engulfed in party politics' (p. 361).

Senior bureaucrats themselves preferred not to become politically involved. On the basis of a series of interviews with directors of the central administration, Suleiman (ch. 6) reports that most of those saw their own positions as separate from party politics and wished to keep things that way. At the same time, non-Gaullist directors tended to believe that many *others* in top positions were closely associated with the Gaullist regime and were there precisely for that reason. Outside observers, too, tend to concur that at the time political appointments reached scandalous dimensions.

From 1972 onwards the UDR began to decline, a process that was furthered by Pompidou's death in 1974 and the subsequent split in the right-wing camp. In 1977 an attempt was made to refurbish the Gaullist party (now named Rassemblement du Peuple pour la République — RPR). But in the 1978 election this party gained only 23.1 per cent of the vote and thus had unmistakably lost its pre-eminent position. At that time, the political colonization of the civil service continued, but apparently not with the same degree of forcefulness. By law, appointment to some 400 key posts of directors, prefects and ambassadors and about a quarter of appointments of the *grands corps* were at the discretion of the government, which did not hesitate to fill those posts with political sympathizers. None the less, not all top officials were rightists, many were sceptical or hostile to the government and some sympathized with the left — a tendency that was even more widespread amongst the lower ranks of the service (Wright, 1978, ch. 4; see also Stevens, 1978).

President Valéry Giscard d'Estaing used to reward members of his cabinet with posts in the Administration and many of the political activists who surrounded him had strong contacts within the Administration. But 'It is easy to exaggerate the links and hard to estimate the impact which they had' (Searls, 1981, p. 171).

François Mitterrand's election and the advent of a left-wing government at the beginning of 1981 precipitated only a moderate civil service purge. By the end of November 1981, less than a fifth of the vulnerable 400 had been removed from influential key posts and transferred to less sensitive spots (*The Economist*, 21 November 1981, pp. 62-5). Generally, it is still too early to tell whether and how the new regime will leave its imprint on the bureaucracy.

Belgium[26]

In Belgium party political control of the bureaucracy is widespread and intensive and has increased throughout the last century and a half. In the earlier part of the nineteenth century, there was political neutrality at least in the Departments of Foreign Affairs and Defence. (Except for these only a couple of other departments existed.) Since the middle of the century the party system developed, ministerial cabinets[27] were created and the traditional bureaucracy became politicized as well.

The system which grew up at that time was different for different ministries with no uniform criteria of appointment, service or promotion. Ministers and their political parties colonized the ministries, and political appointments were the norm. In the 1930s the civil service came under growing criticism and an attempt was made to reform it according to the British Northcote-Trevelyan tradition. Legislation to implement the reform and establish a merit system came into effect in 1937-9 but was delayed by the war and post-war upheavals, up to the 1950s.

Since then, formally the service has been run on the basis of objective rules and procedures. Officially, civil servants are recruited on the basis of examinations and promoted on the basis of merit. But in actual fact, breaches appeared in the system as soon as it was established. An article in the reform act has made it possible to recruit competent specialists outside normal procedures. This has served as a large gateway for patronage during the decades following the war, but is scarcely applied today. Rather, present-day politicization rests on the fact that the merit system for making appointments and promotions culminates in the presentation of a short-list of candidates to ministers who make the final selections. There are strong pressures on ministers to favour people from their own party or union background in making those selections.

Thus, recruitments and promotions are made chiefly by and through political parties and unions and (according to Moulin, 1975) around 60 per cent of all civil servants use party and union politics to promote their careers. Moreover, when the spoils are divided, hopeful aspirants must not only belong to the right political party or union but also to the right faction within it. Otherwise they stand in danger of being detoured in their careers or even stranded.

Overall, the partisan selection system is well organized. An apparatus for screening and selecting candidates for various offices has been set up in each of the larger political parties. Appointments, promotions and 'parachuting' are made so as to maintain the proportion and the equilibrium of power among the major political parties. This is attained through the change of ministers which enables different political groups to take their turn in staffing ministries. Alternatively, the less powerful parties can obtain a part (albeit a more modest part) of the spoils, by subtle scheming. For instance, the party may present a candidate, knowing he has no chance. But in return for its acceptance of the appointment of a candidate from another party, it can obtain assurance of some compensation price in the form of a lesser appointment. 'All this makes for a very subtle game . . . specialists, journalists and staff members take special pleasure in deciphering the obscure movements which accompany nominations and promotions' (Moulin, 1975, p. 171).

In view of this system of recruitment and promotion it is not astounding that civil servants introduce party political considerations into the performance of their official duties. Thus, many supply their parties with official information and adapt official policies to their parties' directives. Conversely (it is alleged) partisan civil servants tend to sabotage or delay the policies of ministers from other parties. Also, they frequently use information, time, skills and materials made available to them through their official positions, in the service of their parties' election campaigns.

As a result of all this, the apex of power in the Belgian political system is reached by combining power within the party with power within the government bureaucracy. An amalgamation of political and administrative power ensues. Thus 'The politicization of public administration in Belgium, seems to have become so general and so acute that an equivalent situation can hardly be found elsewhere' (Moulin, 1975, p. 171). Indeed, according to Dogan (1975), Belgium has the most intense penetration of politics into the civil service of any country in Western Europe (see also Covell, 1981).

Chapter 12

Bureaucracy and electoral manipulation

At one time, politicians and party politics had a grip on the bureaucracies of all seven countries here reviewed. In some of these countries, this grip was maintained or strengthened over time, while in others it was loosened or relinquished. It will now be seen that where the political intrusion into the bureaucracy prevailed, elections were manipulated through an exchange of material benefits for votes; and where it declined or ceased, this form of manipulation went into a parallel decline.

To clarify the argument, it is necessary to order the use of material benefits in the political process from the macro- to the micro-level. On the macro-level this device concerns the creation of overall national — especially economic — policies (e.g. tax cuts) in accordance with the perceived wishes of the electorate. On the intermediate level it concerns the moulding of policies in line with the demands of various nation-wide interest groups. On the micro-level it entails benefits to communities, interest groups within communities, or, finally, to families and individuals. The attempt to win political support on the basis of policies that yield benefits to the whole electorate or to sizeable categories within it is considered legitimate by both observers and participants. Indeed, it is part of the previously presented definition of democracy (see chapter 7). But when material benefits are handed out to families and individuals in payment for support, electoral victory no longer depends solely on the general policies of politicians and parties, or even on their images (as per the above definition) but rather on the resources those politicians and parties can marshall and deploy for the personal benefit of their supporters. Hence, the practice is perceived to be increasingly illegitimate as one moves to the micro-level until finally, at the level of families and individuals, where it turns into an explicit exchange of benefits for votes, it is regarded as bribery and corruption and is usually outlawed. It is this latter practice (or malpractice) which concerns us in the present chapter.

This type of corruption may not seem particularly ominous to the reader for, as will be seen below, it has drastically declined and has practically disappeared in most English-speaking democracies. It is therefore peripheral to political or scholarly attention in the English-speaking world. But it will also be seen that it does persist and has become even more common in some other Western countries. And while these countries' electoral results cannot be explained solely in terms of this corruption, and while they are still designated as Western-style democracies, it is clear that their democratic processes are seriously flawed.

Malpractices similar to the ones considered here have been dealt with by various scholars under the headings of 'political patronage', 'clientelism', or 'machine politics'. Each of these terms, however, has a slightly more narrow connotation than the phenomenon discussed here.[1] Hence I prefer the phrase 'exchange of material benefits for political support' while those other terms are used wherever specifically relevant.

It may be argued that the connection between electoral manipulation of this type and party political intrusion into the government bureaucracy is self-evident, because it is mostly (though not exclusively) through the bureaucracy that political parties obtain the resources to be handed out to the public as political inducements. Hence, it might be added, this thesis needs no further elaboration or support through empirical evidence. However, Marxist and like-minded theories endeavour to account for this manipulation through factors other than the politicization of the bureaucracy, namely, through lower-class characteristics and/or upper-class interests. Hence the importance of showing that it is, in fact, this politicization (rather than the other factors) that accounts for the practice.

One theory (presented, for instance, by Scott, 1973) holds that material inducements in electoral politics persist and flourish where there is widespread social disorganization (that is, the presence of large numbers of immigrants, as yet disoriented in the new society) and poverty — amongst the lower classes of the electorate, and where those lower classes can therefore come to depend on such inducements. Conversely, material inducements decline where those conditions diminish and disappear.

Another theory (presented, for instance, by Graziano, 1977 and O'Connell, 1980) suggests that the practice develops and persists where there has been an incomplete development of the capitalist economy and where the hegemony of the bourgeoisie over the working class prevents the latter from organizing and developing class consciousness. In such cases, it is argued, material inducements represent one method whereby the process of class formation on part of the labour force can be resisted. It will be demonstrated below, that although such factors may account for the development and decline of electoral corruption within some societies,[2] they cannot do so in a comparative perspective. In other words, they cannot explain why the phenomenon developed and persisted, or conversely, declined, in some countries and not in others. Concomitantly it will be shown that political intrusion into the bureaucracy or its elimination can furnish such an explanation, at least with regard to the seven countries here considered and whose review once more begins with Britain.

Britain[3]

In certain periods of Britain's history the exchange of material inducements for political support was a rather well-established practice; since the end of the nineteenth century, however, it has all but disappeared.

In the eighteenth century and at the opening of the nineteenth century many electorates were controlled by large landowning families or other large-scale employers. In such electorates, the votes were practically predetermined and not much direct bribery was going on. In other electorates (especially boroughs) where electors were more independent, bribery was rampant. There were constituencies in which a majority of the voters were bribed. Payment for votes took on a variety of forms: free meals and drinks ('treating') entertainment, hiring of large numbers of non-working committee-men and direct cash handouts. In some elections, considerable sums of the candidates' (and their friends') money were spent in this manner.

The Reform Act of 1832 greatly reduced the number of 'pocket boroughs' as the control of the landed oligarchy declined and new urban voters gained the franchise. It was thought that this would eliminate venal elections, but it did not have this effect. Several of the boroughs that during the reform had rejected corruption later succumbed to it again. The new electors apparently were no less susceptible than the old. Indeed, the abolition of the many pocket boroughs gave new impetus to bribery since the new electors had to be won over individually. It has been estimated that during the first decade following the Reform Act as many as two-thirds of the electors accepted bribes (Scott, 1973, ch. 6).

Mostly the candidates themselves were not directly involved in these practices. Rather, candidates were aided by what would now be called local party organizations. Election to parliament was impossible without their assistance. But this assistance often proved a liability to the candidates, as the local politicians who staffed these organizations had to be bribed too.

Despite such local party organizations, no political machines proper[4] developed. Their development was blocked, among other things, by the fact that the resources available from government for the engineering of elections were rather meagre. Beyond a small amount of cash that might help win a few close races and a number of safe seats in seaports and garrison towns, the government had only marginal control over elections. Even such limited government resources gradually diminished with the decline of political patronage in the bureaucracy. Thus, electoral corruption took place to a large extent on an individual basis as an exchange between the individual candidate and the voter.

King (1970) reports that at the beginning of the nineteenth century cash bribery was more widespread than treating, but towards the latter part of the century, treating was displacing bribery as the more common form of manipulation. Also, outright bribery was increasingly substituted by the employment of voters (or their friends and relatives) in large numbers in election campaigns, with the purpose of influencing their votes. Another method of manipulation which became more prominent was that of nursing a borough through gifts to the constituency. Such gifts usually consisted of building a church or a school, subscriptions to charity and the like. Thus, as the nineteenth century progressed, there was a clear shift of emphasis from the more blatant types of manipulation to the more subtle ones: from cash bribery to treating and from that to even more sophisticated forms of rewarding voters.

After the middle of the century political leaders of both parties turned energetically against the practice, as did the royal commissions investigating it. But although more drastic solutions than before were now sought to the problem, it was not easily and immediately solved. Laws to prevent corrupt electoral practices were passed in 1854 and 1883. But party organizations and candidates (or their agents) were highly ingenious in circumventing them. Indeed, in the 1868 election, corrupt practices prevailed to a greater extent than at all elections of the preceding half-century (Ostrogorski, 1902, vol. 1, ch. 4).

In 1872 the secret ballot was introduced. It was designed to curb bribery by making bribers uncertain of a return on their money. But even after that, the more subtle forms of bribery continued.[5] It has been estimated that between 1865 and 1884, at least sixty-four English boroughs, returning 113 members, or nearly one-fifth of the House of Commons, were corrupt, and the expenses this entailed for politicians were exorbitant. However, from then onward, electoral corruption began to decline. A royal commission in 1906 found 500 venal votes in Worcester — but this was the last revelation of systematic electoral bribery (Lloyd, 1968, ch. 5; Fredman, 1968). Even after that, some small-scale treating and bribery may still have occurred, but an investigation carried out during those years was unable to discover such practices on a large scale.

The nursing of constituencies was apparently perpetuated much longer, and even today may not have entirely disappeared. But observers usually agree that handing material inducements to individuals no longer occurs in significant dimensions. This is not to say that British politics is entirely devoid of corruption. Milne (1976), for instance, gives a detailed description of apparent political corruption in the North-East of England up to the mid-1970s. Interestingly, however, he does not mention the type of electoral corruption here considered. Given his detailed follow-up of other types of corruption, the exchange of benefits for votes — had it occurred — is unlikely to have escaped his notice. The same holds for many other recent observers of British politics who make no reference to this malpractice, or else comment on its absence.

Australia[6]

In Australia the practice of handing out material inducements to individuals in return for electoral support has never been as widespread as it has been in eighteenth- or nineteenth-century Britain. Such malpractices as did occur in the nineteenth century have been progressively diminishing and as a rule no longer occur today.

Before the introduction of the secret ballot, bribery and treating had apparently reached sizeable dimensions. But the ballot was introduced fairly early so there was no lengthy period during which these malpractices could entrench themselves on a large scale: the first elections did not occur until the beginning of the 1840s, while the ballot was introduced in most States in the 1850s.

The secret ballot hindered the use of material inducements, and thus may have helped keep the practice from reaching the blatant dimensions of pre-reform Britain; it did not, however, eliminate the practice. This is illustrated by developments in New South Wales. Loveday and Martin (1966) explain that for more than thirty years after the introduction of responsible government in this State (1856) no political parties emerged and governments functioned through majorities organized around fluid parliamentary factions. To win the support of candidates or members of parliament, faction leaders had to meet their requests for administrative action in their electorates – often on behalf of interests they personally represented, or by finding posts in the civil service for them and their political friends. Other persons who were helpful to parliamentary leaders in election campaigns (such as local agents) were rewarded in a similar manner. In other States the situation was similar. In Victoria for instance, writes Serle (1971), leading politicians, trying to create a faction around themselves, would 'promise bounty' to potential supporters.

Occasionally politicians accused each other of using outright bribery to gain electoral support. Such accusations are illustrated for instance by a collection of letters from politicians presented by Dickey (1969), of which the following are excerpts:

when I calmly reflect upon the influence with which I had to contend, I cannot imagine how we polled so many votes. Bags of flour sent to poor families, men who had not been able to pay rent for weeks past can now pay off the landlord and a little to spare. Is it not discreditable that our Attorney General should obtain his seat by such means, God forbid – that I should ever be a party to such vile practices.

As Mr Burley's hotel is almost opposite the Court House where the polling took place we had an excellent opportunity of seeing how faithfully he, Burke, and many other hirelings acted during the day in fulfilment of the bribery arrangement. From 8 to 4 there was one incessant stream of half muddled creatures led like sheep to the slaughter between two or more agents over to the booth, and on entering which, a printed paper (copy annexed) was placed in their hand . . .[7]

We shall have a great contest in East Maitland. Money and the damd grog his already at work [*sic*] but I shall beat Dodds.[8] (See also Martin, 1958.)

Similar practices are reported from other States. For instance, Bernays (n.d.) reports that in the Queensland elections of 1874 one candidate, by the name of Perkins, secured a seat in the lower house by the aid of a helpful friend. This friend loaded half a dozen trucks with Perkins's ale and toured the electorate, recording an uncountable number of votes in each little polling booth for the owner of the beer (p. 83).[9]

Eventually, towards the end of the nineteenth century, parties began to take shape, and successive legislation put increasingly stringent controls on electoral corruption. Thus, from 1890 onwards, electoral malpractices diminished and in the twentieth century they gradually disappeared. Nowadays, observers generally agree, they are largely absent from the Australian political scene. Occasionally, allegations of corruption have been levelled at certain aspects of State politics. But these are not, generally, the types of corruption dealt with here.

National elections were introduced in Australia at the beginning of this century, when reforms in the States' electoral systems were well under way. They have never been subject to the malpractices of material inducements on the micro-level to any sizeable extent, and are not subject to such malpractices today. While members of parliament occasionally build up their personal following by looking after the needs of their constituents, this does not take the form of political bribery. The assistance (when given) is more in the nature of representing the interests of constituents before the authorities. Its achievement consists mainly in expediting procedures that would have occurred (albeit more slowly) in any event. For the most part, parliamentarians who choose this path fulfil the function of an ombudsman, obtaining for their constituents what they were entitled to, to begin with. Only in a minority of cases (as far as this can be ascertained) do parliamentarians obtain for their supporters favours which are on the borderline of legality. In any case, such favours are usually trifling. Even if politicians had a desire to hand out material benefits on a large scale they would be unable to do so – they would have little chance of obtaining them from the bureaucracy, and neither they nor their respective parties would have sufficient funds for this purpose.[10]

The United States[11]

In the United States the practice of handing out material inducements to individuals in return for electoral support has been perpetuated mainly by political machines. Perhaps for that reason the practice has been more resilient in this country; even so it has drastically declined or even disappeared in recent years.

The classic American political machine has been a hierarchy headed by a 'boss' and held together by benefits it has handed out to its own workers and its clients. A large proportion of the machine's workers have simultaneously held office in the public administration, and this amalgamation of political with administrative tasks has been another important factor in building up and sustaining the machine. An especially prominent figure in the political machine (besides the 'boss') has been the precinct captain — because he has formed the link between the machine and the voters. Through him, the political machine has traditionally built up its power basis in the electorate by handing out cash, gifts, loans, jobs, welfare payments above formal entitlement and help or 'pull' in dealing with the authorities. All these benefits have traditionally been handed out on a personal basis and, as Merton (1957a) has pointed out, this personalization of benefits has been one of the machine's main attractions. The combination between its tight organizational structure and the personalization of its services has enabled the machine to wield enormous power in American politics and to exert a mighty influence on elections (see, for instance, Ostrogorski, 1902, vol. 2, chs 4-7).

The American political machine came into being in the 1820s and 1830s as soon as large numbers of Americans had the vote. At that time, candidates for office were required to pay the party to get their names on the ballots, and these receipts as well as party and public funds were then used by the machine to bribe the voters. Such bribing occurred when precinct captains paid voters at the polls. Also, generous provisions were made for party workers on election day: in some districts as many as 20 per cent of the voters were paid.

As Ostrogorski shows, since the introduction of patronage and spoils into the government administration the parties' political machines pressed heavily on the government executive to perpetuate the practice and employ it in their favour; they gained enormous influence in this respect especially after the Civil War. This pressure enabled large numbers of party leaders and machine workers to obtain jobs on the public payroll, thus further increasing the machines' power. But the machine activists would not have been able to do so, had not party politicization of the bureaucracy been part of the American political system almost since its inception, and had it not been institutionalized in the early stages of this system's development (see previous chapter).

In White's (1954) words: 'Certain it was that patronage greatly increased the power of local party organizations, in a vicious circle that gave them constantly greater standing to demand more and more in return for services rendered.'

The strongest political machines and the widest spread of corrupt practices occurred in the big cities, where there were concentrations of poor people and recent immigrants unused to the franchise. But these practices were not absent from rural areas either. 'The most shameless venality is often met with in the country districts. . . . Votes are sold there openly like an article of commerce' (Ostrogorski, 1902, vol. 2, p. 345).

By the 1870s, many people were aware and highly critical of the abuses with which the elections were beset. In response, the States began adopting the secret ballot from 1880 onwards; by 1910, it was being used in all States except Georgia and South Carolina. Despite this, the machines were not weakened and reached unprecedented dimensions around the turn of the century.[12] Hence, the extent of bribery became quite alarming. For instance, McCook (1892) estimated that 16 per cent of the voters of Connecticut were for sale and Speed (1970), on the basis of interviews with contemporary politicians,[13] estimated that in New York City around 1905, between a third and a quarter of the voters were venal.[14] Clearly, Speed concluded, in many elections such paid votes tipped the scale.

Despite widespread criticism of the system, reform movements did poorly and political machines reasserted themselves in all major urban centres during the first decades of the twentieth century. According to several observers, bossism did not fade away with the depression and the New Deal either. The erstwhile machine practices of distributing food baskets and shoddy clothes to the needy as a means of buying their votes was antiquated by the millions of dollars in new federal relief programs and welfare funds. But most machines became even stronger because their bosses had a say in the distribution of these funds. One of the most powerful machine systems was in Chicago, where bribery and other material inducements continued to be the accepted practice. The Republican machine collapsed in the depression, but this merely marked a changeover to a Democratic one; the basic machine model persisted. Other American machines resembled Chicago's in most important respects, except that not many of them were so successful for so long.

Although the New Deal did not eradicate political machines, other developments of that time had an adverse effect on these organizations.

Posts and other benefits from the public administration diminished; after the First World War immigration was limited and previous immigrants had become somewhat acculturated. When the depression ended, the standard of living rose, as did the level of education, although pockets of poverty (especially among blacks) remained.

Consequently, a certain weakening of party machines became evident in the 1940s. In 1948, 357 counties had no Republican chairman or vice chairman and almost one-fourth of the precincts had no Republican leadership. In the same year in Oregon, the Democrats had operating organizations in only 13 of 36 counties (Morlan, 1949). In the 1950s, the Survey Research Centre found that only 10 per cent of a cross-section of US citizens said that they had been contacted personally by party workers during the 1956 presidential campaign. But national statistics concealed quite a bit of local variation. A survey of Detroit voters found that only 6 per cent had been approached by party workers. On the other hand, 60 per cent of the voters interviewed in a 1959 survey in New Haven, Connecticut, said they had been contacted by party workers, most of whom belonged to an old-time party organization (Greenstein, 1966). According to Reichley (1966), Philadelphia's old-style machine also showed continuing vitality, as evident in its ability to control a minimum of 90,000 to 100,000 votes. In a primary election such a base would obviously be decisive; in a general election it need not necessarily – but could easily – be so.

In the 1960s, it has been claimed, most traditional machines no longer tipped the scales in elections. An analysis prepared by the Republican National Committee showed that the Democratic vote in elections was not appreciably greater in those cities in which the party was more highly organized (Rourke, 1970). Nevertheless, a few effective organizations continued to survive, notably that of Mayor Daley in Chicago. Daley's machine penetrated into all of Chicago's neighbourhoods by means of traditional machine methods, and delivered large numbers of votes to him and his chosen candidates. Indeed, candidates for governor and president could not hope to gain Chicago's (and to a large extent Illinois's) votes without his machine's support. Daley's machine proved its effectiveness in 1960, when it was a crucial factor in the close presidential contest. Daley made sure that the Democrats carried the State by 8,000 votes. This, in turn, was crucial for John Kennedy's election: it was reported that Kennedy had to wait for the results in Illinois, before being sure of victory.

Despite the general deterioration of political machines the exchange of benefits for votes was not yet defunct in the early 1970s. Describing the elections to city councils, Schlesinger (1975) reports that the candidates still had to pay off their supporters. And in the 1976 presidential election campaign, money was still being passed to voters, even though machines continued to decline.

In 1976 Mayor Daley attached his prestige to a Carter victory, but could not deliver Illinois's votes to him. Daley could still turn out the vote: of Chicago's 1.6 million registered voters, 79 per cent went to the poll. But because of the city's loss of residents to its Republican suburbs, the Daley organization could no longer guarantee a Democratic victory in the State. With the death of Mayor Daley shortly after the election, many claim, the era of American bossism and effective machine politics has come to an end.

This claim is supported by a study in New Haven which shows that although machine politics has not disappeared, it has become largely ineffective in gathering votes (Johnstone, 1979). The claim is also supported by a study in Chicago which shows that recently urban services have no longer been used by the machine to reward political supporters and punish enemies and indeed, are no longer affected by voters' choices (Mladenka, 1980). This, and similar studies reveal that distributional decisions in many large cities are now no longer made on the basis of political-electoral criteria, but rather on the basis of past decisions, population shifts, technological changes and technocratic-rational criteria.[15]

Israel[16]

Israel supplies an example of a country in which electoral manipulation through material inducements has been widely institutionalized and has only partly declined in recent years. The practice had its beginnings with the development of political institutions of the Jewish community in the pre-independence (or *Yishuv*)[17] era, especially under the British Mandate. These included a variety of political movements and parties among which the Labour movement and its parties were the most prominent. Most of these parties participated in the *Histadrut* and in the Yishuv's self-governing authority. This authority financed the party machines, and these in turn, utilized those funds to acquire and retain political support for themselves.

Although all parties had ideologies to which their faithful were intensely committed, they did not rely on ideological persuasion alone to obtain political support. They also sought to bind individuals firmly to themselves by the establishment and use of impressive networks of banks, housing construction companies, loan societies, economic concerns, labour exchanges, health services and the like, for both new and veteran settlers. Also, land was allocated to new immigrants through political organizations – so that land settlement served as another device for mobilizing support (Eisenstadt, 1967, ch. 9).

While all major parties employed these devices, the Labour movement headed by *Ahdut Ha'Avoda* was most prominent in turning them into a fine art. According to Shapiro (1977, ch. 5) this party developed an elaborate political machine which set the pattern for all subsequent ones, even though none of these could ever hope to equal its effectiveness. A large part of the *Ahdut Ha'Avoda* machine's activity took place within the *Histadrut*. The major activity of its functionaries (who were also *Histadrut* employees) concerned the handing out of material benefits as political inducements to rank and file members. These benefits included employment in the Histadrut itself or in one of the many concerns controlled by or related to it[18] as well as grants or loans on easy terms (e.g. for housing) from the *Histadrut* or party-related financial and welfare institutions.

In 1930, *Ahdut Ha'Avoda* united with another labour party to form *Mapai* which gained hegemony not only in the *Histadrut* but also in the *Yishuv*'s authority of self-government. Thereafter, the practices which had proved to be so effective in the *Histadrut* were stepped up and utilized for the advantage of the labour movement in the national authority as well.

The attainment of statehood did not basically alter the party composition and the political practices prevalent before – including those of handing out material benefits to service political goals. Indeed, the massive influx of new immigrants which occurred with the establishment of the state opened new vistas for these practices. A large number of these immigrants originated from traditional (mainly Middle Eastern) countries and both the culture of democratic elections and the ideologies of the Israeli parties were entirely alien to them. At the same time, most of them had neither the financial means nor the professional skills necessary for making their way in a relatively more modern occupational structure. So they were greatly dependent on the representatives of the absorbing society for their livelihood.

The parties did not hesitate to take full advantage of the situation. Public bodies and government departments in charge of immigrant absorption were highly politicized; hence absorption activities remained indirectly under party control. This made it possible for the parties to try to incorporate the immigrants into their own frameworks by a network of economic aid. Such aid was extended through banks, housing companies, economic concerns, labour exchanges and the like, just as it had been in the *Yishuv* era.

The handing out of material inducements flourished especially in development towns where new immigrants came to be concentrated, and where employment and housing were under the control of veteran Israeli functionaries. A large proportion of the population in these development towns became dependent on these functionaries not only economically, but psychologically as well. Many of them acquired the habit of moving from office to office and presenting their demands for employment, housing and welfare. Those in charge of the resources needed the immigrants' political support, hence could not afford to be unresponsive to their demands.

The labour movement headed by *Mapai* (which later became the Israel Labour Party − or ILP) had an obvious advantage in the use of these practices as it controlled the major public bodies and ministries and hence had access to the state's major resources. But the other major coalition parties did not refrain from such practices either. Thus, in his study of the 1965 and 1969 election campaigns in a development town, Deshen (1970 and 1972) tells of an intricate combination of symbolic devices and concrete benefits employed by the coalition parties to increase electoral support. The benefits consisted of religious articles donated to the congregations, and more tangible benefits such as jobs, housing, loans or other financial aid, provided directly to individuals.

The political use of material benefits was most conspicuous in, but not confined to new immigrants and development towns. Similar devices were used in urban areas (where the majority of the Israeli population resides) and *vis à vis* the veteran population as well. Thus, we learn from Medding (1972) that in Tel Aviv and in Haifa, ILP functionaries awarded large numbers of positions to both immigrants and veterans, thus producing significant benefits in terms of party membership and support. For instance, the Haifa Labour Council (which is part of the *Histadrut*) was generally staffed by ILP functionaries. These provided a following for the party by taking care of rank and file *Histadrut* members. They assisted them with employment, housing, educational facilities for their children and even helped place their relatives in *Histadrut* institutions for the aged.

Has this system changed significantly in recent years? As the waves of new immigrants in the early years of statehood became absorbed,[19] they should have become less dependent on the various official agencies for their livelihood, and hence should have become less susceptible to their material-political inducements. But the practice of allocating such benefits by political criteria is inherent in deeply engrained features of the Israeli socio-political system, rooted in a period which long preceded the mass immigration of the early state era. Hence, its perpetuation was by no means dependent on the existence of a mass of new immigrants.

Moreover, some immigrants came to be so effectively socialized into the system that they were most reluctant to relinquish it in later years. Thus U. Benziman writes that in recent years a distinct subculture has developed in a large number of development towns and urban neighbourhoods — comprising no less than one-sixth of the Jewish population of Israel. There, inhabitants tend to base their livelihood at least partly on the public bounty. The functionaries have got into the habit of channelling large sums of money into these localities, for various (not always warranted) welfare benefits. In return, the inhabitants employ a line of minimum interference, and are willing to close an eye (or even both) to whatever is happening on the local political scene. Political bosses are therefore free to do whatever they wish in their domains. Most inhabitants of these areas have reached the country soon after independence. By now, with the aid of the authorities, they have succeeded in educating a second generation to this way of life — a generation which is currently in the process of initiating a third generation into the same pattern (*Ha'aretz*, 12 and 13 November 1976).

Most recently, in the trial of the minister for religious affairs, A. Abuhatzeira,[20] a witness testified to the fact that there exist hundreds of public funds that are being channelled through the Ministry of the Interior and local councils. The witness, a former mayor and active participant in the deployment of such funds, admitted that the funds were used to educate and support the needy, with the tacit aim of bringing them closer to one of the factions within the National Religious Party (NRP) and thus increasing this faction's power in the party. The judge subsequently declared this evidence to be 'very important'.[21]

Thus, although the practice of handing out material inducements in return for political support in Israel may have diminished recently, there is indirect evidence to show that it is still institutionalized in some sectors of Israeli society and has by no means disappeared.

Italy[22]

Patronage — and political patronage in particular — has long been one of the most basic features, extending from the upper reaches of the Italian government down to the grassroots of Italian society; it has still been very much in evidence in recent years. As Zuckerman (1975) explains, in the early days of the Italian Republic this took the form of association between local notables and their retainers based on economic, quasifamilial and political ties. This has been most fully documented for the villages of the South. The patron used to provide favours based on the ownership of land and influence over government resources. The clients' obligations included deference, donating a portion of their produce to the patron and voting with or for him. Getting ahead in schools, courts, banks, local government, etc. was basically a game of patronage or protection. As the historian G. Sawemini (writing in 1911) put it: 'Merit consist[ed] in having a powerful protector.'[23]

After the Second World War, this type of patronage persisted. According to Boissevain's (1970) account, in Sicily, for instance, in recent years, civil servants who are usually from the more privileged classes have accorded preferential treatment to their relatives. Since most of the relatives are from the privileged classes too, these classes receive favoured treatment from the authorities. Sicilians of lower social classes thus face the problem of finding some inroads of influence on public agencies. They can do so by attaching themselves to a strategically placed patron, for instance by making him godfather of their child. In return for favours from the patron, clients must perform various services for him, including reporting on his (political and other) enemies and making electoral propaganda for him, should he happen to stand for election. Many people are both patrons and clients; thus a patronage hierarchy (based on personal and political favours and services) is created. A similar system persists in Sardinia as well (see Weingrod, 1968).

However, the old system of patronage of the notable is gradually being replaced by, or fused with, one based on the mass exchange of benefits for votes by the dominant political party — the DC. During the long rule of the DC, this system has been developed to levels unknown in most other countries. This takes the form of the manipulation of blocks of voters, through the allocation of economic development projects by the state, projects which supply large numbers of jobs. This has replaced the earlier attempts — rampant for instance in the 1958 election — to exchange votes for food and money. Now, positions, rather than immediate payouts, are to be obtained, and success in obtaining such positions is still dependent on the recommendations one can get from one's political patron – in exchange for electoral support. Observers concur with each other that a mass of DC adherents have been satisfied in this manner.

The system of exchange has also served to amass preference votes for patrons within the party. Under the Italian electoral system, voters choose party lists, and can then mark preferences for the candidates they favour. Candidates with the highest number of preferences are elected. Thus, the political activists' ability to rise within the party rests to a large extent on their preference vote, which, in turn, rests to a large extent on their ability to provide positions for their clients.

It is widely believed that practices such as these are more widespread in the South. According to Zuckerman (1975), 'there is reason to believe, however, that there exist strong similarities throughout Italy in regard to general norms and behaviour concerning [political] competition and authority' (p. 19). This has been corroborated by field studies that have located similar practices in the centre and the north (e.g. Bailey, 1971).

Similarity of practices all over Italy is also brought out by Zuckerman's own study of decision-making bodies in the DC in 1968-9 and 1972. He found several factions within the party clustered around political leaders; their primary goal was to control political offices. Each faction leader was supported by two sets of followers. The first was located in the leader's home province and was composed of his local political clients and those client's clients. The second set was composed of the political clienteles of other patrons, in other localities, who, in turn, had tied themselves as clients to that faction leader. Both were mobilized so as to supply the faction leader with preference votes. This practice was found to be common to all areas of Italy.

All over the country, then, DC factions were found to be political clienteles, whose leaders ruled their fiefdoms through the control of jobs for the benefit of the variety of their clients and the multitude of their clients' clients, thereby promoting themselves to positions of control in the party and the government. This system has introduced an element of weakness into the DC, as it provokes an incessant internal struggle over the allocation of resources and thereby slows down decision-making processes (Parisi and Pasquino, 1979). At the same time there is no doubt that on the whole, the DC has been greatly aided by, and owes much of its political power to the exchange of benefits for political support.

This has been conspicuous for instance, in the favoured treatment the DC has been able to elicit from the bureaucracy for its allies, the Catholic groups and especially Catholic Action. Because these DC allies have direct access to the ministers — they can get all they wish from the ministries. As a result, as a well-known Italian writer put it,

> it is not an exaggeration to argue that today in Italy very few jobs are awarded and very few careers are made if the individuals who are hoping to get the jobs or make the careers find themselves clearly at odds with the Italian clergy.[24]

Catholic organizations and their members, in turn, are favoured by the DC (and its representatives in the bureaucracy) because they are in key positions to influence elections. Catholic Action, in particular, does so through its vast organizational apparatus — spearheaded by the civil committees. Through these, it controls especially women's votes and delivers them to the party.

The exchange of benefits for votes has been perpetuated mainly by (and has worked mainly in favour of), the DC and its coalition partners, although it is not totally monopolized by them. For many years, the Italian Communist Party (PCI) had presented itself as (and was widely believed to be) a party 'with clean hands'. According to Ledeem (1977), this slogan was dropped in the 1976 elections, when the PCI was so widely involved in regional and city government, that its participation in the patronage system could no longer be denied. According to Pasquino (1979), however, the PCI showed itself as unable to 'deliver the goods' and this has led to a flow of votes away from the party in subsequent elections (see also White, 1980).

France[25]

In France the exchange of benefits for votes has been based largely, though not exclusively, on the intervention of the government party's deputies with the bureaucracy on behalf of their constituents; this practice may have declined somewhat under the Fourth Republic but has, once more, been very much in evidence in recent years.

After the restoration and under Napoleon III the administration itself played an active and formidable part in ensuring the election of government candidates and the defeat of their opponents. In the Third Republic, the bureaucracy still largely controlled the rural vote. At that time, it was also the practice for ministers to aid their parties' election by ensuring that their own ministries were favourably disposed toward those parties' deputies and the requests they made for their constituents. At the same time, letters from opposition deputies frequently did not even get replies.

In the Fourth Republic, after the Second World War, the tradition of parliamentary intervention with the bureaucracy to obtain minor favours for constituents continued. In 1949 a minister of justice received in nine months 11,700 requests from deputies for pardons or promotions for their clients. In 1957 a Minister of the Interior found that of 800 candidates for twenty posts of police commissioners, 600 had the support of a member of parliament. 'Yet this pressure was a nuisance rather than a menace; deputies often forwarded requests which they hardly pretended to support, and officials treated these in the spirit in which they were sent' (Williams, 1964, p. 340).

Ehrmann (1961) writes in a similar vein that many French functionaries mentioned that under the Fourth Republic they were perfectly well able to defend themselves against parliamentary pressures. At the same time, during the post-war years, many minor posts, especially for auxiliaries, which did not have the legal status of the civil service, were filled through the exertion of political influence. This turned out to be 'a way in which members of Parliament can dispose of some patronage in their constituency' (Duverger, 1958, p. 171).

During the Fifth Republic, the deputies of the majority parties have gained direct access to the administration, which became more responsive to their wishes than to the wishes of opposition parties' deputies. In the interviews conducted by Suleiman (1974), most senior administrators showed themselves to be ill-disposed towards deputies. Many said they tried to minimize contact with such deputies who always came to ask for favours on behalf of particular persons. Around 75 per cent of the senior bureaucrats interviewed expressed the belief that deputies were concerned only in making demands on behalf of their constituents. The senior bureaucrats said they would much prefer not to be approached on these matters. They saw the particularistic demands that the deputies made on them as natural enemies of the general interest of which they themselves were the guardians. As one civil servant put it; 'I try to have as little contact with deputies as possible. They always come to ask this for this person and that for that person. We do not speak the same language' (Suleiman, 1974, p. 292).

But deputies did not seem to be deterred by such attitudes. A multitude of individuals turn to deputies for assistance. According to

Suleiman, about one-third of citizens with demands on the administration do not turn to it directly but ask deputies to intervene on their behalf. The deputies tend to oblige, thus turning into intermediaries between citizens and the bureaucracy.

For their part, senior administrators have no choice but to enter into a relationship with deputies even against their own preferences. Ostensibly, ministers have sought to purify the administration from politics. But, according to Suleiman, in this instance, politics means no more than political opposition. For the ministers expect bureaucrats to treat deputies of the majority parties in a manner usually denied to the opposition. In several ministries, contact between the administration and deputies is restricted, by orders from the minister, to the deputies of the parties in office. Indeed, the administration as a whole is much more open to deputies of the majority parties, as can be seen from Table 12.1.

Table 12.1 *Proportion of directors' contact with majority and opposition deputies – (per cent)*

	Majority parties	Opposition parties
All	13.6	0
¾	46.9	1.2
½	35.8	38.3
¼	0	16.0
0	3.7	34.5
	100.0	100.0

Source: Suleiman (1974, p. 361).

Mere contact with deputies does not indicate the degree of responsiveness to their wishes. Here again, however, deputies of majority parties are far better off: through ministerial pressure on the administration, they have usually been able to obtain what they want. Thus, although in principle administrators would have liked to minimize contact with deputies, they have nevertheless been forced to give great advantages to the deputies of the majority parties. Hence, these deputies have been able to fulfil the needs of constituents better than their political adversaries.

This partisan use of the administration is particularly emphasized during election and referenda times. 'At such times the administration['s]

... attention is directed towards satisfying claims of groups that have long been denied, toward being open and receptive, making promises, insuring funds for projects, and being less zealous about adherence to the law' (Suleiman, 1974, p. 363).

In the presidential election of 1969 the government gave orders to its tax collectors not to push the collection of taxes. Civil servants in the ministry of finance cited this as one example of the kind of service they had to perform on behalf of the government at election time. This is only one example of a variety of practices which under the Fifth Republic has been normal and has had to be accepted by civil servants even though it has placed them in an uncomfortable position.

These practices were not new in the Fifth Republic. But under the Third and Fourth Republics, there was, according to Suleiman, a greater fairness to the game because no government was controlled by one party. Under the Fifth Republic, however, the UDR, as the dominant party, has been in a particularly advantageous position in using the administration to attend to its constituents and to perform political favours for them − thus giving itself a greater electoral advantage than any other party has gained from the bureaucracy before.

Among other things, UDR deputies were able to elicit favours from the bureaucracy on behalf of large business enterprises (and sometimes enterprises in which they themselves had direct financial interests). Consequently, charges of corruption and scandals have followed each other in rapid succession. The Ministry of Equipment and Housing, for instance, because of its wide responsibilities for housing, highway construction, parks and public works, was constantly bombarded by political pressures.

Given the predominant position of the UDR, almost all economic groups seeking licences, contracts and so forth from the state, preferred to work through it. If a group frequently worked through the UDR, the party for its part came to rely on its support and resources. It therefore gave that group as much satisfaction as possible by ensuring that the administration was open to its demands (see also Percival, 1974).

In part, the situation described by Suleiman was found to persist more recently as well. In a study conducted in 1977 Schonfeld (1981) found that Gaullist politicians still had significantly more contact with high civil servants than their socialist counterparts.

Belgium[26]

Various observers concur that Belgium's political parties and related associations have become social service agencies, running child-care centres, clinics, sanitariums, maternity and rest homes, vacation centres, mutual funds, insurance agencies and the like. Substantial benefits, deriving largely from state resources, have thus been distributed to the citizens by various politically significant bodies, which have thereby turned into gold mines for their adherents. In line with this, Billiet *et al.* (1978) report that the gradual secularization of Belgian society has not been followed by the weakening of Catholic 'pillar' organizations, that lend support, job security and possibilities for advancement to their loyal members — such as the Catholic school system and the Christian hospitals. These, in turn, maintain informal ties with the Christian Democrat Party.

The situation can best be summarized in Fox's (1978) words:

The family, the community, the region, the social class . . . the ethnic-linguistic group to which one belongs . . . and the political party with which one identifies . . . not only affect one's existence in Belgium, but determine it in many, inescapable, immutable ways. . . . These particularistic categories and constellation of categories ascriptively influence the type of hospital in which one is born, the schools one attends, the occupations for which one is eligible, the jobs and positions one can hope to obtain, the sick fund, mutuality, and syndicate in which one is enrolled . . . (pp. 208-9)

the national government is the major banker, directly and indirectly supporting these nets through a maze of intricately interconnected ministries, foundations, organizations, etc. (p. 213)

It is this network of support organizations and benefits, more than ideological commitment which, in Belgium, determines lifelong political allegiances. According to Moulin (1975, p. 172), it has created:

an extremely dense network of allegiances which encloses the life of a Belgian citizen from his birth to his death and from which, supposing he would wish to do so, he would have a hard time escaping. . . . Nine tenths of Belgian citizens are instantly labelled. They are hardly disposed, aside from badly looked upon exceptions, to deviate from the line traced for them since childhood.

Thus, Belgium has reached unparalleled heights not only in the parties' intrusion into the bureaucracy, but also in those parties' manipulation of citizens through a set of institutionalized material inducements.

Electoral manipulation: an explanation

This overview of electoral manipulation in seven Western-style democracies leads back to the question of how the similarities and the differences among them may be explained. Could it be that disorganization, i.e. the presence of large numbers of immigrants as yet disoriented in a new society, or poverty amongst the lower classes might furnish the explanation, as Scott (1973), for instance, has suggested?

The diminution of immigration to the United States after the First World War may be held to explain the partial decline of the party machines there, from the 1940s onward. The partial decline of immigration to Israel after the early 1950s may help explain whatever partial decline in electoral corruption has taken place in that country in recent years. But recently immigration (including illegal immigration) to the United States has soared again, apparently without leading to a large-scale revival of political machines. And immigration has even less explanatory power when the various countries are compared to one another. The United States, Britain and Israel have had an inflow of immigration in recent years and Australia has been a country of massive immigration since the Second World War. Yet in Britain and Australia electoral corruption of the kind discussed here has declined in recent years, and in Israel it has declined only in part. Italy, France and Belgium have not been countries of large-scale immigration, yet they are the countries in which the practice has been most persistent in recent years. Trends of immigration and trends of electoral corruption thus do not follow the same lines.

The same holds for poverty. In the United States there have certainly been pockets of dire poverty around the turn of the century. Also, it has been estimated that in 1959 some 24 per cent of the population lived in poverty. Since then, and especially in the 1960s, the proportion of impoverished persons has diminished and it has been estimated that in 1976, 12 per cent (or half of the 1959 percentage) lived in poverty — a decline that may conceivably have contributed to the decline of party machines there.

But here again, the comparative perspective sheds a different light on the problem: Britain does not stand out as a country devoid of poverty – but it does stand out for propriety of electoral practices. Italy, France and Belgium are not noted as having especially large dimensions of poverty but they are noted for political inducements through material benefits.

Could it be, as Graziano (1977) and O'Connell (1980) have argued, that electoral corruption of the type here reviewed appears and persists where the development of a capitalist economy and of working-class formation and consciousness have been wholly or partly arrested? This theory was originally applied to Ireland, and southern Italy (where industrialization and capitalist development have lagged behind those in the central and northern parts of the country) and may well be appropriate for these areas. However, the preceding overview has shown that in Italy the practice has by no means been confined to the South: all areas of Italy have had their share in it. And Italy, which has one of the strongest Communist parties in Western Europe, certainly cannot be designated as a country in which the development of class consciousness has been arrested. The latter argument holds for France as well.

The United States stands out among Western democracies in the lack of a large-scale labour party within it. This absence could be taken to indicate underdevelopment of working-class consciousness, and in line with O'Connell's reasoning could conceivably be used to explain the extraordinary development and tenacious persistence of machine politics in that country, for many years. However, a working-class consciousness (as indicated by the large-scale organization of labour) has not been more evident in this country in recent years than it was in previous years, and yet the practice of machine politics has recently declined.

To clinch the argument it must be pointed out that in Israel (both before and after independence) the capitalist class has been relatively weak and subdued. On the other hand, a working-class consciousness has been well developed, the working class has been highly organized, and its leaders and representatives have had a virtual monopoly over political power for close to half a century. Yet, throughout all of this period, material inducements in Israel's elections have flourished. Indeed, it has been the (fully class conscious) labour movement and its leadership, which has been most prominent in the perpetration of this practice (though ably assisted by its coalition partners, most notably the National Religious Party). Thus, the comparative perspective shows that a working-class consciousness and the development of material inducements in elections have little, if anything, to do with each other.

In contrast, the suggested explanation concerning the penetration of politicians and party politics into the bureaucracy works for every one of the countries reviewed: Britain and Australia are the countries in which such intrusion has declined earliest and most thoroughly, and electoral manipulation through material benefits has done likewise. In the United States political intrusion into the bureaucracy has declined and has recently been confined to a limited number of appointments at the top. In line with this, recent research has documented the widespread decline of machine politics in that country. In Israel, both political intrusion into the bureaucracy and electoral manipulation through material inducements have declined but only in part, and in Italy, France and Belgium both practices have persisted or gained strength in recent years.

It must be concluded, then, that the use of material benefits in elections depends not on class characteristics and interests but on the intrusion of politicians and party politics into the bureaucracy, on the consequent availability of bureaucratic resources for partisan-electoral purposes and on an elite political culture that treats the deployment of bureaucratic resources in such a manner as (at least unofficially) acceptable. Conversely, the elimination of material inducements from elections and the development of (in this sense) proper democratic procedures hinges on a certain change in the bureaucratic-political rules of the game; on the bureaucracy's becoming independent from the intrusion of politicians and party politics, at least in its grossest and most blatant forms, and on the consequent withdrawal of bureaucratic resources from the party political contest. Finally, it hinges on the restraint this sets upon the manner in which the political elites can conduct their struggles for power.

Chapter 13

Bureaucracy in a double bind – some case studies

In the preceding two chapters it could be seen that Western-style democracies differ widely with regard to the penetration of party politics into their bureaucracies: they range from countries whose bureaucracies have become largely non-partisan, to countries whose bureaucracies are largely party political in their appointments, promotions and loyalties. It could also be seen that only in countries of the first type can proper electoral, democratic procedures take place. The preceding chapters thus traced the implications of bureaucracy for democracy. In this chapter the question will be turned around and – to paraphrase John Kennedy's famous words – we will ask not what bureaucracy does to democracy but what democracy does to bureaucracy. From this vantage point it will be seen that the problem of party politics has not been solved, that it poses a dilemma, and daunts bureaucracies in countries of both types.

For in countries of the first type bureaucracies are expected to be subject to the control of politicians (in policy matters) and free from such control (in partisan matters); they are also expected to be political (in the policy sense) and non-political (in the partisan sense) at one and the same time. However, policies frequently have implications for party politics, and the boundaries between the two are by no means clear. Hence, even bureaucracies which are basically non-partisan become occasionally entangled on the edges or outskirts of party politics. Bureaucracies of the second type are (obviously) also expected to be under the control of politicians and to be political in policy matters. In addition, they are likely to be under great pressure from their political superiors (and those superiors' faithful within the administration) to take account of partisan considerations in all their activities. On the other hand, even such politicized bureaucracies are frequently expected by public opinion and the media to be party-neutral and must formally present themselves as such. Moreover, some senior bureaucrats may well harbour such neutrality and cherish it as part of proper administrative and democratic procedures. Hence, such bureaucracies, too, face a dilemma. In both types of countries, inconsistent democratic rules thus put bureaucracy in a double bind. This, in turn, creates various degrees of strain, controversy and conflict for bureaucracy and for the political arena of which it is part.

Strain and conflict, of course, are part and parcel of political and bureaucratic life in general. But the strain and conflict created by the verging of bureaucracy on party politics is especially disruptive and frequently involves the abolition of bureaucratic agencies, the dismissal of senior bureaucrats or the electoral defeat of governments and senior politicians. This will be illustrated through an account of three case studies from three Western-style democracies.

In this context, too, the argument with Marxist tenets must be resumed. Marxists have argued that in capitalist countries bureaucracies are in any case politicized, in that their members tend to have conservative inclinations, and to advocate the maintenance of the *status quo*. If bureaucracies seem to be party-neutral this is because parties in power resemble each other: none have tried to implement policies that are at variance with the *status quo* and with conservative interests. The following case studies, however, show that bureaucracies are not invariably conservative and that policy differences between parties are at times still large enough to place bureaucracies in a double bind as far as party politics is concerned.

The war over poverty (USA)

The first case concerns the US Office of Economic Opportunity (OEO), established in 1964 to carry out President Lyndon Johnson's war against poverty. Headed by Sargent Shriver, the OEO initiated several programs for this purpose. The heart of its campaign was the Community Action Program, which was to grant federal moneys to local or State organizations for their own schemes to battle poverty. The funds for this program were not to sift down through the existing governmental structures but rather were to be channelled through new policy-controlling boards. On these boards, three elements were to be represented: the governmental bodies concerned, the welfare agencies, and the poor themselves – to the maximum extent feasible.

In addition there was the Job Corps – a scheme for the establishment of residential work camps to educate disadvantaged youngsters and train them for employment. Another scheme was project Head Start, whereby it was hoped that the cycle of social backwardness might be broken by giving pre-school children an early start. Another program was VISTA (Volunteers in Service to America), modelled after the Peace Corps but domestic in its focus. It provided volunteers to work in developing communities and emphasized person-to-person relations. Yet another program was that of free legal aid to the poor.

Initially, Congress was quite encouraging towards the new office and its program. It was at the time dominated by liberal Democrats who were anxious to support it and force the Republican opposition into an 'anti-poor' position. Thus it authorized $784.2 million to be allocated to the poverty program in 1964 and this sum was more than doubled in 1965. But from the outset the agency's Community Action Program was controversial and riddled with tension. In the first place, bureaucratic infighting began. Established agencies sought to promote themselves by gaining charge of the program. The president had to back the office personally, to protect it from these attacks (Rehfus, 1973, ch. 1).

Also, the OEO was sensitive to the insistent urgings of civil rights movements and was determined that the poor themselves, the residents of the program's target areas, should share control of the new resources, and that a majority on the project boards should be their representatives. This triggered tension and power contests within local government, which felt itself threatened and set out to defend its jurisdiction. Many mayors and other local politicians were concerned over who should define the boundaries of the target areas, represent those areas, pass out the jobs. The program's opponents claimed that it did more for politicians and their parties than it did for the poor and spoke of the revival of political bossism. The program's supporters saw it as the realization of true democracy, the stirring to political participation of people previously left out. Some office-holders feared that it was their political rivals' instrument for their ouster. Those close to the OEO retorted that a basic change in local political power was precisely what was needed to shake political decision-making out of its inertia. From one side it was charged that extremes of participation by the poor would put irresponsible people in charge of government resources. From the other side it was countered that traditional welfare programs were poorly designed and that recipients were best qualified to know what they needed (Sharkansky and Van Meter, 1975, p. 141). Thus the war on poverty became the war over poverty.

In addition, criticism of the program made itself felt among

Republicans in Congress. In August 1965 Senator S. Thurmond stated that the program's history 'provides a catalog of futility, abuses, political partisanship, wastefulness, shipshod administration and scandal'[1] and Senator Scott proclaimed that 'The war on poverty, as administered from Washington by the Office of Economic Opportunity is distinguished today not for its accomplishments, but for its failures. The war on poverty has degenerated into a nightmare of bureaucratic bungling, overly paid administrators, poorly organized fieldworkers, and partisan politics.'[2]

The degree to which the Community Action Program was actually utilized for partisan politics varied from one locality to another. In Chicago the program was quickly assimilated into Mayor Daley's Democratic machine and kept under its control. To direct the program, Mayor Daley set up a Mayor's Committee, calling it the Committee on Urban Opportunity. To represent the poor, five blacks were appointed, and these were part of Mayor Daley's machine, as were the assorted welfare officials who participated. Local politicians were actively rounding up people to seek aid under the various projects and 'Mayor Daley [saw] nothing wrong in a democratic ward official sending a deserving man or woman along to the committee. After all, the political workers know their neighbourhood, and it is the committee which makes the final decision' (*The Economist*, 1 May 1965, p. 526).

A similar, though less successful, attempt to utilize the program for party political purposes was made in New York. Harlem's anti-poverty project had charges of political patronage levelled at it and as a consequence federal aid in the amount of $2.2 million was frozen, until the director, a friend of black congressman Adam Clayton Powell, was suspended.

On the other extreme was Atlanta, Georgia. Atlanta was one of the few cities in the US where the war on poverty was not overcome by political wars and where there were tangible signs of success. The city's anti-poverty war was run by the Atlanta-Fulton County Economic Opportunity Authority. For the most part, it represented the view of the white business community, but there were blacks involved in the effort as well.

Less clear-cut and more tension-ridden situations developed in California. In several Californian cities the political struggles over who would choose the representatives of the poor was waged quite openly and fiercely. Since in California the majority of the poor were Democrats (if they voted at all) these struggles came to be intermingled with partisan friction. As a result, there were delays in implementing the program. In some cases (such as Oakland and Sacramento) representatives of the poor were duly included and the funds to run the program were obtained. In other cases (such as San Francisco and San Diego) funds were withheld until the OEO was satisfied with local arrangements.

In San Francisco, for instance, the mayor's Economic Opportunity Council (a corporation created to receive poverty funds) had by May 1965 prepared a four and a half million dollar program. But the neighbourhood groups would not approve it, so long as the council was dominated by whites. The OEO, for its part, would not accept any program without their approval. The mayor attempted a compromise, which the neighbourhood leaders treated as an evasion. Eventually, the mayor had no choice but to give way. Sixteen new neighbourhood representatives were elected to the full committee of the council, giving them a majority of one, before the OEO released the first two millions of its grant (Marris and Rein, 1972, ch. 9).

In Los Angeles, large sums of money (totalling $8.5 million) were allocated to Watts, one of Los Angeles's black neighbourhoods and the scene of the previous year's riots. The aim was to create as many jobs as possible for young people. 'Not surprisingly, these projects have been popular and quickly organised — although with some complaints that politicians' nieces have driven to their poverty-project jobs in red convertibles.' However, Los Angeles Mayor Yorty, although a Democrat, clearly did not welcome the build-up of State and federal patronage in his city. Consequently he engaged in an extended dispute to gain control of the program (*The Economist*, 4 December 1965, p. 1076).

Other mayors (many of them Democrats) were similarly annoyed at the community action groups. In many cities the poor actually began to organize, developing into militant lobbies in city hall. Much of the activity was a struggle for power between their spokesmen and the mayors — in several cases pitting two elements of the Democratic party against each other. Hence, some mayors protested that their political base (which often was the same as President Johnson's) was threatened (Rehfus, 1973, p. 33). The OEO countered the mayors' protests by announcing that where a community project did not offer enough control to the poor, the office would fund an independent program which better represented them. Thereby local agencies were to be bypassed altogether and this posed a new threat to the mayors. The OEO did, in fact, fund such independent projects in some cities (e.g. Syracuse) thus enraging those cities' mayors more than ever. In some cases 'the struggle evolved into almost warlike confrontation between proponents of community action and city hall . . . [and] led to intense and occasionally violent confrontations' (Sharkansky and Van Meter, 1975, p. 140; see also Marris and Rein, 1972, ch. 9). Protests from city governments about the new Community Action Program began to pour into Washington.

Perhaps partly for this reason, opposition to the program in its existing form began to emanate from Washington as well. Neither Congress, nor President Johnson, nor yet the executive had envisaged the extent to which the poor themselves were to become involved, and the problems this was to create. The Budget Bureau now believed that the war on poverty would move faster if the insistence on involving the poor themselves in its administration were dropped. Accordingly, it pressured the OEO for less participation of the poor by withholding $35 million from its budget.

The OEO administrators, however, continued to insist that the poor ought to be aided in obtaining not merely money, but power as well. Hence, they fought back by taking the story to the public and by concealing their moves from their superiors and other parts of the bureaucracy. It is unlikely that they deliberately wanted to cause political problems. But they were willing to take this risk in order to activate the poor (Rehfus, 1973, ch. 1; Marris and Rein, 1972, ch. 9). Shriver publicly rebutted the attacks against the participation of the poor. He argued that the struggle on how the poor should be represented could not be defused by dropping them — the poor — altogether. Instead he decided to stage an election among them,[3] in a few cities, including Los Angeles:

> The struggle was to determine whose poor should be seated — those owing allegiance to members of Congress representing the most impoverished districts, or those supporting the Mayor, Mr. Yorty. Under federal prodding, agreement was reached to stage an election. (*The Economist*, 5 March 1966, p. 900)

The OEO promoted interest in the election by sending vans with loudspeakers through the streets, calling on people to vote and issuing the biographies and campaign pledges of all candidates. But disappointingly, only 0.7 per cent of the poor turned out to vote. In similar elections in other cities the turnout was somewhat, but not much, greater. In Philadelphia, 2.7 per cent, in Boston 2.4 per cent, in Cleveland 4.2 per cent and in Kansas City Mo 5.0 per cent cast their ballots. 'Smaller communities sometimes got larger turnouts, but never

anything nearly approaching that of a listless off-year election'
(Moynihan, 1969, p. 137). Moreover, according to Moynihan, once
elected, the representatives of the poor were not greatly effective; the
boards were beset by constant quarrels and by struggles for executive
places.

In the meantime the program got into more trouble in Congress.
There were many Republican and conservative Democrat members of
Congress who argued that with the mounting costs of the Vietnam War,
America could not afford to spend so much on problems at home. The
program's fate was also affected by riots of the poor in various cities
across the country. The program's opponents in Congress now argued
that instead of increasing satisfaction, it seemed to foster discontent
among the poor. Accordingly, these people were 'sharpening their
knives for an assault on the Office of Economic Opportunity' (*The
Economist*, 31 December 1966, p. 1394). They did so by attempting to
restrict the funds available to the program and the freedom of action of
its administrators. In November 1967 Congress authorized $460 million
less than requested by the president. The program was saved in the
closing hours of Congress, and the total appropriations were not seriously
reduced. But the funds were increasingly earmarked for specific purposes so that stricter limits on administrative discretion were imposed.

In the 1967 elections the Republicans gained 45 seats in the House
of Representatives, all of them from liberal Democrats. Thereby, the
Johnson administration lost the near-automatic majority for liberal
programs which had persisted for almost three years. The Republican
conservatives (with the aid of their Democratic sympathizers) were now
strong enough to shelve most of the president's new and controversial
projects. In addition they initiated a drive to abolish the OEO altogether
and transfer its more popular programs (such as Head Start) to established departments (Marris and Rein, 1972, ch. 9).

The office had gained support as well. Protest against its proposed
dismantling was heard around the country and in the end it survived.
But opposition to its program was apparently more widespread than the
support it had marshalled, and hence its popularity among politicians
began to wane: 'the antipoverty program was becoming a political
liability. It patently had few friends among mayors, few among congressmen, and . . . few among the poor' (Moynihan, 1969, p. 142).

All this had an impact on the president as well. 'While Johnson
regarded anti-poverty programs as economically beneficial to poor
people, he had to obtain political benefits [through them]' (Rehfus,
1973, p. 16). When these benefits seemed to diminish even the

president's own support became less adamant. According to Moynihan (1969, ch. 1), in 1967, the president told a leading member of the Senate committee responsible for the anti-poverty legislation that although he was prepared to stick with it, this was hardly his favourite program. He made no move to dismantle the agency but the new programs he proposed were to be administered by departments with greater political support: the Department of Labor which was to launch a drive against unemployment, and the Department of Health, Education and Welfare which was to take responsibility for carrying project Head Start into the schools themselves. Also, the president announced a pilot scheme (previously advocated by conservative members of Congress) to interest businessmen in providing employment and job training in several poverty areas. This scheme was to be sponsored by the Department of Commerce (*The Economist*, 14 October, 1967, p. 155).

In the meantime the struggle over the OEO continued in Congress. The conservative Republicans continued their drive to turn over the bulk of the OEO existent programs to the older government agencies. Several liberal Democrats rallied to the agency's assistance. They elicited support from politicians in various parts of the country by giving them assurances that the controversial Community Action Program would be placed under the control of local elected officials and the municipal bureaucracies they headed. Local governments would now have the option of bringing their Community Action Programs under their control, provided a third of the representatives on its board were poor. Thereby, the liberal Democrats ensured a further two-year survival of the OEO and its programs.

But this meant that the poverty warriors of OEO were now forced to make concessions to appease their opponents. They did so by guaranteeing state governors, mayors, officials and business people a voice on local poverty boards. Although the poor were still to make up a third of these boards, politicians would no longer have to fear that they were being organized by outside agents, as federal poverty officials were strictly instructed to stay out of politics.

Also, the OEO was obliged to shift more and more of its emphasis from the local to the national level. National programs, involving, for instance, Head Start, accounted for more and more of the anti-poverty budget. Thus, the emphasis came to be more and more on conventional services (Marris and Rein, 1972, ch. 11). In this manner the OEO had to relinquish many of its original aims in order to obtain another lease on life.

After Richard Nixon's election in 1968 the OEO's future became even more uncertain. Under his administration the war against poverty was to continue but the previous impetus had clearly been lost. At the beginning of 1969 it became clear that the president was intent on dismantling the OEO. It was given at least another year of life, but it was to lose Head Start, its most successful program. Also, despite opposition from Democrats in Congress, the Jobs Corps (the youngsters' training camps for employment) were partly dismantled, and the number of youngsters involved in them were substantially cut. Instead, there was to be an expansion in JOBS (Jobs Opportunities in the Business Sector), a program whereby businessmen were to receive government subsidies for training the hardcore unemployed. Later in the year, the president decided to downgrade the agency even further to a mere unit of research and experimentation into social policy. Accordingly, its general budget was halved but its research budget was doubled.

In August 1969 President Nixon outlined new welfare programs, most prominent among them the establishment of something close to a negative income tax. According to this program, all families with dependent children below a certain income level would be entitled to payments from the government. Nixon's family assistance bill, designed to implement this program, delighted liberals but was not passed by Congress. In 1971, in the midst of an economic setback, the president himself asked Congress to defer the bill for another year. Two years later, in 1973, the Senate in effect rejected the bill and thus the program never eventuated.

In 1971 the struggle over OEO was revived. The Democrats in Congress (especially the liberals) wanted it to remain intact, albeit under the strict control of the federal government, while the Nixon administration and the conservatives in Congress wanted to dismantle it by parcelling out more of its programs to other departments and handing over more responsibilities and funds to States and local authorities. The Democrat majority in Congress refused to go along with these plans and voted to extend the OEO for another two years.

At the same time Congress went along with the Nixon administration in its vote to split off the controversial free legal services for the poor from the OEO. By that time the OEO was funding more than 900 neighbourhood law offices with a budget almost half as great as the cost of all the federal courts in the country, including the supreme court. Apparently lawyers in this program had frequently become involved in political issues, to the annoyance of State authorities (especially in California). The most controversial activities of these lawyers were attempts to change laws and regulations by test cases and class actions in order to make government more responsive to the needs of the poor. Controversy also rose from legal action on behalf of rent strikes (Fried, 1976, pp. 269-70). The service was now to continue as a separate corporation and the lawyers working for it would be expected to avoid politics.

In September 1972, Congress once more voted to extend OEO's life, this time until 30 June 1975. But in his budget speech in January 1973, President Nixon did not request funds for the agency for the 1973-4 fiscal year. In fact, in April 1973, the administration began dismembering OEO, an action that was temporarily brought to a halt by a federal court rule that the anti-poverty program be continued until Congress ordered otherwise (*The Economist*, 21 April 1973, pp. 47, 49). However, this was only a short-lived reprieve, and on 6 July 1973, the office was finally closed down.

In retrospect, its success had been rather meagre. Despite its many novel ideas and despite the fanfare of the war on poverty, little was achieved. Poverty declined substantially in the 1960s. But this decline was mainly the result of general economic growth rather than of deliberate administrative measures which turned out to be no more than 'a drop in the ghetto'. Moreover, during these years, black protest had been more widespread and violent than ever before, so that the crusade on poverty had done little good in this respect either.

Beyond this, however, the most outstanding fact about the Office of Economic Opportunity was the amount of political controversy, tension and outright political struggles it attracted; in the end the community action groups might better have been called 'community faction groups'. Part of the explanation for this controversial nature of OEO is to be found in the definition of its role. As Rehfus (1973, p. 14) put it, in effect it was 'designed to federally finance opposition to local political leaders'. In this manner, it posed a threat to people in established local power positions, predominantly to politicians at various state and local levels. At the same time it strengthened the power of other political leaders and even brought to the fore new political power-holders. Thus the OEO had become involved in power struggles, and these were partly channelled through political parties. In other words, the OEO had (perhaps inadvertently) become entangled on the edges of party politics. While it cannot be said that the OEO posed a threat to power-holders of one political party only and favoured the other party exclusively, it had nevertheless plunged into politics with partisan connotations and this in turn had led to strain, controversy and open conflict. This conflict was focused on, but by no means confined to, the local level. The threatened politicians responded by activating party political channels to pressure Congress. Thus the party political power struggle was fought out at the congressional level as well.

A second fact that stands out is that where OEO's program was wholly absorbed into the party political structure and utilized as part of the existent political machine (as happened in Chicago), it posed little or no threat and the tension it generated was minimal or non-existent. Similarly, where the OEO's program did not become involved in party politics at all (as in the case of Atlanta), tension did not eventuate either or was minimal. It is where OEO's programs verged on party politics but did not become absorbed into party political machines (as happened in some Californian cities) that tension was the greatest and the power struggles the most severe.

The final point to be made on this case is that OEO's programs overlapped with party politics not only in the power struggle but also in the ideological controversy they created. The programs clearly emanated from a liberal point of view, at least 'liberal' in the twentieth-century American sense of support for greater government intervention to effect social reforms. The OEO was clearly staffed with reform-oriented people. According to Moynihan (1969, ch. 5) the man in charge of the Community Action Program was clearly intent on arousing the poor for political action. And according to Marris and Rein (1972, p. 222) one of the main achievements of the war on poverty was that through it 'a new kind of public servant had become crucially important, at once more independent of established authority and more responsive to the people. . . . Of all the innovations of community action, this may prove the most important: it created the professional reformer.' This explains why the OEO and its programs were dear to the heart of the liberals in Congress and coldly received by conservatives. While obviously not all liberals were Democrats and not all conservatives were Republicans, there was a partial overlap between the two, which is why OEO could marshall more support among the Congressional Democrats than it could among their Republican counterparts.

This would also explain why a struggle over OEO developed between the Nixon administration and the Democrat-dominated Congress. Clearly, Nixon became intent on abolishing the agency not only because it had been established to carry out his predecessor's (rather than his own) pet project and not only because its success had been meagre, but also because its policies were not congenial to his conservative outlook. He accepted the Friedmanite idea that the poor could best be helped by giving them money or ensuring a minimum income for them – hence his alternative program for a negative income tax for the poor. But even on this program Nixon was less than adamant, he never succeeded in carrying it through and he generally did not share the previous administration's enthusiasm for social welfare. It is for precisely this reason that a more liberal-minded, Democrat-dominated Congress continued to wage a losing battle for the maintenance of the agency. On this level, too, the OEO's policies verged on party politics, and this overlap, too, created controversy and conflict.

The reluctant treasury (Australia)

The second case concerns the friction that developed in Australia in 1974-5 between the Labor government (headed by Gough Whitlam) and the Treasury. At that time the government had severe difficulties in dealing with the country's mounting economic problems, including rising inflation and unemployment. This gave the opposition-controlled Senate the grounds (some say the pretext) to block the government's budget. The blocking of supply resulted in the dismissal of the prime minister and his government by the Governor-General. In the subsequent general election held at the end of 1975 a Liberal-Country Party coalition (led by Malcolm Fraser) came to power. According to several observers, the friction between the Labor government and the Treasury contributed to the difficulties and eventually to the downfall of the government. As Freudenberg (1977, p. 281) put it 'hostility on the Government side and disloyalty within the Treasury . . . powerfully, perhaps decisively, would contribute to the destruction of the Whitlam Government'.

The disagreements between the government and the Treasury were that the latter urged an economic strategy of tough anti-inflationary measures – a tight monetary policy, a budgetary surplus, restraint on the public sector (especially cuts in government spending), higher interest rates, increased taxation and abandonment of the government's wage-indexation plan. The government, however, was committed to precisely the opposite tack, to an increase in government spending and to lowering taxation:

> By June [1974], Treasury was urging an austerity budget as the
> appropriate strategy against rising inflation. The alternative was a

large increase in taxation, . . . Whitlam argued that tax increases would go against the spirit of his undertakings and against the spirit of the mandate. (Freudenberg, 1977, p. 283)

In June and early July 1974 the Treasury strategy prevailed but opposition began to emerge. Some senior ministers felt that Treasury was aiming to reduce cost inflation by raising unemployment, and that it wished to raise unemployment as an instrument to dampen wage increases in the labour market. Both Labor ministers and members of parliament were unanimous in their rejection of these aims.

The June quarter figures showed a 4.1 per cent cost of living increase. Consequently, Treasury submitted a proposal for an economic package of a 'short, sharp shock' remedy along the above lines. Whitlam was almost alone in supporting the proposal on 20 July; most of the package was rejected by cabinet and the 1974 budget did not reflect Treasury advice.

Subsequently, the government raised interest rates, as Treasury had proposed. But it did so through an abrupt announcement rather than by allowing banks to push them up gradually. So the resulting money squeeze was more severe than had been envisaged by the Treasury.

On 12 November 1974 the prime minister unveiled a new 'mini-budget' in parliament which marked a change of the government's economic strategy. The package was an effort to woo the business community, which at the time was scaling down investments. It included cuts in company tax and personal income tax and increases in import duties in some industries. While the Treasury supported the cuts in company tax, it opposed the cuts in personal tax, claiming that they would only fan inflation. Also, Treasury argued that the continuation of the September budget policy and the recent devaluation, together with the provisions of the mini-budget, all added up to a substantial boost to the economy. Treasury worried that these moves would unleash a new round of inflation (Kelly, 1976, ch. 7).

Another disagreement between the government and the Treasury was over the now-famous loans affair, which eventually also contributed to the downfall of the government. The government's intention was to raise a substantial loan ($4,000 million) overseas. Treasury opposed the venture outright and set out to torpedo it, citing as reasons for its opposition the employment of irregular methods in seeking the loan and its concern with the repercussions of introducing such enormous funds into the Australian economy. Whitlam and his government, however, persisted with their plan, citing as their reason the need to finance a range of public projects.[4]

In 1975 the government started on an economic course which, but for the renewed flare-up of the loans affair, could have improved the Labor Party's electoral standing. The budget (delivered in August 1975) was based on the need to restrain the government sector and stimulate the private sector as the first step in a gradual economic recovery. It included scaling down in outlays to educational institutions, restraints on growth in pensions and a ceiling on public service growth. It also included increases in indirect taxes and reforms in the personal income tax system. Most commentators accepted, and the opposition privately admitted, that the budget had a stamp of responsibility. Presumably it was more palatable to the Treasury as well, but by that time the Labor government had only less than three months left, so it eventually made little difference (Freudenberg, 1977; Kelly, 1976, ch. 19).

As a consequence of the overall disagreements between the government and the Treasury, the relations between them deteriorated. When Treasury's advice on the 1974-5 budget was rejected, the relations reached a near breakdown. As Freudenberg (1977) sees it:

> Treasury weakened its own influence with the Labor Government not because its advice was often unpalatable but because it was always monolithic. Treasury refused to set out the economic options available to the politicians. It presented its advice on an all-or-nothing, take-it-or-leave-it basis. If its first advice was rejected, Treasury volunteered no other. If Cabinet persisted in rejecting the original advice, some Treasury officials then used their contacts with other departments, the press, business and Opposition spokesmen, to build support for its line. (pp. 281-2)

> The eclipse of Treasury in the last months of 1974 was to have a profound effect on the fate of the Labor Government. The first reaction of some of the senior officials to the rejection of their Budget advice was sullen resentment. They restricted their involvement in the preparation of the Budget to the minimum needed to carry out Cabinet's decisions. They refused to take part in the 'selling' of the Budget, the process of public relations . . . to secure better understanding . . . and hopefully, favourable press reaction to it. . . . [Frank] Crean's replacement [as Treasurer] by [James] Cairns transformed Treasury sulkiness to hostility. It was then that certain Treasury officials, known by the code name of 'Mr Williams',[5] began clandestine contact with some members of the

opposition. For the next six months, the Opposition was closely informed of the Government's intentions, particularly its overseas loan raising activities. . . . Some of the officials . . . were prepared to use their position and their knowledge to damage the elected Government and they did so. (pp. 307-8)

By November [1974], the relations between the Government and its Treasury had so degenerated that in some Ministers' eyes Treasury could be bracketed with anti-Labor State Governments and the Liberal-controlled Senate as a hostile force. (p. 349; see also Kelly, 1976, ch. 7)

In autumn 1975 the Treasury believed that inflation would fall to 10 per cent by the end of 1976 and that economic recovery would be under way by June 1976. Labor leaders were anxious to publish these optimistic forecasts. Treasury resisted publication on the ground that the current funds crisis had to be resolved before this forecast could be seen as valid. Thus Labor was deprived of a formidable campaign weapon:

Nothing has contributed so deeply to the Labor Government's decline as the fear of the middle class that inflation had taken an unbreakable hold and was beyond control. It was this fear which made the removal of Labor by any means acceptable to the conservative middle class. At the time of the greatest fear, the Government was deprived of its best means of allaying the fear. (Freudenberg, 1977, p. 404)

Why did this breakdown between the Labor government and the Treasury take place? Apparently it occurred because of successively worsening mutual suspicion. According to Patience and Head (1979), Whitlam's initial suspicion of the public service (that had served a Liberal-Country Party Government for so many years) led to his idea of a 'countervailing force' to the bureaucracy, that of the ministerial staff. According to Reid (1976) it led to the introduction of non-public service advisors on a scale not previously known in Australia. This, in turn, created suspicion on part of the bureaucracy, and as Freudenberg (1977, p. 281) put it: 'The new Government's tendency to look for different advice was the beginning of the mutual suspicion between the Labor Government and the Treasury.'

Senior people in the Treasury saw the government's tendency to seek outside advice as a threat to themselves. They saw the rejection of the Treasury's 1974 budget strategy as part of a concerted effort to diminish their power. At that time, too, the responsibility for preparing national wage-case submissions was shifted from the Treasury to the Labour Department, which Treasury people again saw as a threat to their position. This threat was emphasized even further by Whitlam's appointment of his former private secretary, John Menadue, as head of the Prime Minister's Department. Menadue intended to make the department an alternative source of economic advice as a counter to Treasury, and indeed, the new economic package announced by Whitlam in November was devised entirely in the Prime Minister's Department.

A similar threat was posed by the loans affair, since the sum was supposed to be raised by the Department of Minerals and Energy. The Treasury's opposition was on economic grounds but was also based on the fear that, once in possession of such huge funds, the Minerals and Energy Department would become a rival empire. Also, the government intended to establish a Department of Economic Planning. Treasury saw this as another threat to itself and bitterly resisted it (Freudenberg, 1977, chs 20-4).

In a way, the conflict between the government and the Treasury over policies was thus a struggle centred on the Treasury's own vested interests. But it also shaded over into a party political, ideological cleavage. From his earliest days, Whitlam had been a proponent of a federal role in services like health, education, roads, etc. It was a commitment that had endured and developed throughout his political life. His was an Australian brand of Fabian socialism. The Labor Government as a whole proceeded on similar lines. It was committed to a course in which economic issues played a secondary role to the great programs in housing, education, health, social services and wages (Edwards, 1974a).

On the other hand, Fraser, who came to power in December 1975, 'is essentially a supporter of stable government, gradual change, a strong private sector, a viable rural sector, and as small a role as possible for government, consistent with the demands of a welfare society' (Kelly, 1976, p. 153).[6] This inclination, too, was reflected in the Liberal government as it eventually took shape under Fraser's leadership.

It can by no means be said that Treasury was a party political instrumentality. But its own inclinations were clearly more closely akin to those of Fraser and the Liberals than they were to those of Whitlam and the ALP. Not surprisingly, various observers concur that the clash between the Labor government and Treasury was one between groups holding conflicting assumptions and values (Edwards, 1974b; Kelly,

1976, ch. 7). Evidently there was only a slim chance of an understanding between the Treasury and a Labor Treasurer (Crean) who, announcing the budget on 17 September 1974, said: 'Crucial as the fight against inflation is, it cannot be made the sole objective of government policy. This government is committed to the program of social reform to improve the position of the less privileged groups in our society and to maintain employment opportunities' (Kelly, 1976, p. 70). Nor was there a good chance of understanding between the Treasury and the next Labor Treasurer (Cairns), who said: 'What is needed is not just a way to control inflation but a way to reform society so that it may avoid inflation' (Freudenberg, 1977, p. 323). In view of these basic differences in outlook, it is not surprising that Labor ministers assumed 'that Treasury officers were following not just their profession, but also their class instincts' (Kelly, 1976, p. 167) and believed Treasury to be 'too rigid in its approach to economic problems as well as reflecting conservative viewpoints deeply ingrained during twenty-three years of Liberal rule' (Reid, 1976, p. 189).

Paradoxically, a recent occurrence has highlighted the fact that friction on similar lines can arise between Treasury and a Liberal government as well. Although the overall relations between the Liberal government and Treasury have been much smoother, there developed an area of disagreement. The Secretary to the Treasury, John Stone, seemed to favour a resource-rent tax[7] — also favoured by the Labor Party — a policy the Liberal government opposed. As a consequence, Paul Keating, then shadow minister for Minerals and Energy, was able to quote Treasury papers and officials to back his case for a resource-rent tax (*Australian Financial Review*, 11 March 1981, p. 6).

It is not too far-fetched to surmise that it is for that very reason that the then Treasurer, John Howard, displayed special sensitivity to the Secretary to the Treasury's statements on this issue before the Senate's Standing Committee on National Resources. The Treasurer reprimanded the Secretary and this reprimand became public knowledge despite the fact that the Secretary had merely admitted that a resource-rent tax was a policy option and had referred the Committee to a previous statement of his on this matter (*Australian Financial Review*, 9 March 1981, pp. 1 and 6).

This example, too (though in two opposition directions) shows that the demarcation line between formulation of policy and party politics is not unequivocally clear. It shows that even where the bureaucracy is not party politicized, the policies advocated by one of its agencies may have party political implications; and when the borderline between politics in the policy sense and politics in the partisan sense is approached or crossed, friction and even crises are likely to occur.

The Inspector-General (Israel)

The third case concerns the conflict that recently developed in Israel between the Minister for the Police and the Police Inspector-General. In December 1980, the Minister for the Interior and the Police, Yosef Burg, of the National Religious Party (NRP), dismissed the Inspector-General of the Police, Herzl Shafir. The alleged ground was that mistrust had developed between himself and Shafir because the latter did not accept ministerial control, and because the procedures he had introduced did not safeguard civil rights and were not suitable to a democratic country. In particular he referred to the fact that in its investigation into the alleged corruption of a government minister, Shafir's team had leaked false information to the press in order to persuade potential witnesses to come forward and testify against the said minister; that it had used illegal methods of questioning and had threatened the prospective state witness with imprisonment if he refused to testify. Shafir admitted that he had leaked false information to the press on the investigation of the government minister, but rejected all other allegations (*Jerusalem Post Weekly*, 14-20 December 1980).

The dismissal caused a furore in parliament and among the Israeli public. Representatives of various parties in parliament demanded a parliamentary inquiry committee into the dismissal. In Tel-Aviv, a citizens' organization led by high-ranking former military and police officers was established to back Shafir. This organisation, too, called for an official inquiry into the dismissal (Wallfish and Bar, 1981, p. 1).

The reason for these reactions was not only that Shafir, previously himself a senior military officer, was highly regarded and popular in Israel. It was also due to the fact that the minister whose alleged corruption Shafir's team investigated, Aharon Abu-Hatzeira,[8] happened to be the Minister for Religious Affairs and to belong to the NRP to which Burg, the Minister for the Police, also belonged. The allegations were that Burg had sacked Shafir not so much – or not only – because he had circumvented legitimate procedures but also because he had been over-zealous in his investigation of the Police Minister's own political colleague. Allegedly, the situation was complicated by the fact that Abu-Hatzeira was Burg's rival in the party. Initially, Burg had attempted to extricate himself from the difficult situation by preferring to know nothing about the police investigation. But thereby he had incurred the wrath of his own party colleagues. The solution he hit upon was the dismissal of the Inspector-General.

Immediately after the dismissal, a Labour member of parliament contributed to public indignation by alleging that the Interior and Police Minister had previously instructed the Inspector-General to discontinue investigation until after the election (which was to be held almost a year later) on a file by the code-name of 'Peach'. This file contained some preliminary leads on alleged corruption in the Minister's Department of the Interior and in his National Religious Party. According to these leads, the Department of the Interior (*via* local authorities) had allocated sums of money to various religious institutions that were either non-existent or closed and a certain percentage of the money allocated to (these and other) religious institutions eventually found its way to the NRP.[9]

In a cable to the Attorney General, the said member of parliament wrote that on 3 December 1980 Shafir had notified Burg that he had received information raising suspicion of criminal offences in the Interior Ministry. On 14 December, Shafir was called in to see Burg, who told him that the investigation must continue only after the election. Two days later Shafir gave a memorandum on this to a known public figure, to keep in case of unexpected developments (Wallfish and Bar, 1981, p. 1).

The Inspector-General subsequently reiterated those claims before the Parliamentary Interior Committee. Most committee members strongly criticized him for not turning initially to the Attorney General and informing him of the matter. They also criticized the reserve officers' organized support for him as a danger to democracy; they called on him to put a stop to the movement.

Shafir also turned to the prime minister, Menahem Begin, who apparently supported him. He called Burg with the ousted Inspector-General still in his office, and asked him to reconsider the dismissal. Burg refused, whereupon Begin informed Shafir that there was nothing more he could do.

Shafir laid his case before the public as well. At a press conference, at the beginning of January 1981, he claimed that the reason for his dismissal was 'Interior Minister Yosef Burg's desire for a good party (NRP) and not for a good police force' (Bar, 1981, p. 3). He claimed the minister's order to stop the 'Peach' investigation was illegal, called his motives political and charged the Interior Ministry with deliberate leaks to the press intended to besmirch him.

Interior Ministry officials, for their part, called the police action with regard to 'Peach' political, since the file was reportedly full of allegations but lacking in hard evidence (*Jerusalem Post Weekly*, 4-10 January 1981, p. 1).

The minister himself categorically denied the allegations that the Inspector-General's dismissal had occurred because of the investigation of the Religious Affairs Minister. He also claimed he had never heard of the 'Peach' file before the matter became public knowledge. He admitted, however, that he had been informed on rumours of irregularities in the Interior Ministry and that he had told Shafir that before an election matters of this nature had to be handled with the utmost care.

In a television interview, the Israel Defence Forces Ombudsman, Major General Haim Laskov, revealed that he was the public figure whom Shafir had previously entrusted with the memorandum of his meetings with Burg over 'Peach'. According to Laskov, Shafir had said he was willing to wait with the investigation, but there was no way of preventing leaks and keeping information secret. He said he was convinced of the truth of Shafir's version. Burg retorted that he objected to army generals setting themselves up as judges (*Jerusalem Post Weekly*, 17 January, 1981, p. 8).

Several interpretations of the affair in the Israeli press blamed party political considerations for the Inspector-General's dismissal. Thus, a leading article in *Ha'aretz*[10] (1 January 1981, p. 9) included the following comments: the motives for the dismissal are to be sought in the political arena; the dismissal is part of the battle to discredit the police in the eyes of the public, so as to curb the investigation of Abu-Hatzeira or, alternatively, influence the court in his favour. Shafir has proved himself as the best Inspector-General the police has ever had. Under his direction an unprecedented attempt has been made to establish the rule of law and exceptional success has been achieved in the investigation of various major crimes. There were several irregularities in his way of handling these cases; but these were not the causes that led to his dismissal. Burg has attributed the dismissal to the lack of trust between the Inspector-General and the Police Minister. And indeed, it is not easy to maintain such trust when that minister belongs to the party which has most to lose from police success – specifically, but not solely, in the Abu-Hatzeira case.

This was followed by another leading article in the same newspaper on the next day (2 January, p. 13) in which the following points were made: since the minister is responsible for police activities before parliament he has the right and duty to interfere in these. But there is only a thin line between such legitimate interference and interference for political purposes. The Inspector-General is obliged to accept the former but has the right and duty to insist that the minister not abuse his authority.

On the same day, another article in *Ha'aretz* came to the following conclusion: Shafir paid with his head because he investigated a case which brought shame on the NRP in an election year (Eldar, 2 January, 1981, p. 14). On 8 January M. Peled commented in the same newspaper (p. 9) that the case obviously entailed a contradiction between rules of proper administration and party interests.

J. Goell, in an article entitled 'No Job for Political Innocents' (*Jerusalem Post Weekly*, 11-17 January 1981, p. 8) attempted to summarize the affair. Burg (he wrote) had appointed Shafir in the hope that he would be an adept pupil in shaping up to the realities of civilian politics. 'Shafir had to go because he proved inept at that task.' He had to go because he lacked the political tact necessary to conduct an investigation of such an NRP stronghold as the Religious Affairs Ministry.

Soon after Shafir's dismissal Burg set out (rather successfully) to defuse political tension by speedily appointing a new Inspector-General for the Police. Approximately a year later, however, A. Eldar, in an article in *Ha'aretz* (1 January 1982, p. 15) criticized the appointment. According to some observers (he wrote), minister Burg had clearly drawn a lesson from the appointment of Shafir, an Inspector-General who was not among his political faithful. Shortly after dismissing Shafir, Burg appointed an Inspector-General whom he had previously passed over as insufficiently qualified, and who obviously is much inferior to Shafir in his talents. But by doing so, he managed to avoid further political embarrassments. Although the professional standard of the police force has consequently declined, Burg is happy, because he is no longer harassed with the troublesome 'Peach' file, which has largely been forgotten.

Since in Israel political crises quickly supersede one another, the Shafir Affair, too, was soon removed from the public agenda and has largely been forgotten. It does, however, raise several questions:

— Would the whole issue have arisen if the Interior and Religious Affairs Ministries had not been so closely connected with the Interior and Police Minister's party, the NRP?
— Could the issue have been avoided if the Inspector-General had been more clearly aware of the political implications of the police's action?

Under democratic 'Rules of the Game':
— Where does legitimate control of the elected politician (the Police
  Minister) over the appointed bureaucrat (the Inspector-General) end
  and illegitimate control for partisan purposes begin?
— What type of control from the political echelon is the bureaucrat
  obliged to submit to? What control can he legitimately reject and
  where is the limit between the two?
— Is the bureaucrat obliged to accept his own dismissal even if partisan
  considerations were at work?
— How is it that the Inspector-General tacitly accepted what he later
  on considered to have been the minister's party political interference
  in the manner in which the police carried out its duties, and how
  is it that he saw fit to raise the issue publicly only after his own
  dismissal?

Conclusion

Other, no less colourful, examples could be recounted. But even those
cited lend tentative support to the thesis that the boundaries between
the control politicians exert on the bureaucracy legitimately and the
control they exert for partisan purposes as well as the boundaries
between bureaucratic policies and party politics are hazy, that they are
at times approached or crossed (intentionally or unintentionally) and
when this happens it imposes a strain on the bureaucracies and ultimately on the democracies of which they are part. In all three countries
the bureaucratic agencies in question were working out policies within
their own respective areas of competence. Yet in all three cases these
policies impinged on partisan ideologies and/or on partisan interests,
and friction or outright conflict was the result. From this point of view
it matters little whether a country's bureaucracy is in fact party politicized or not. In Australia, the political partisanship of the bureaucracy
has declined extensively; in the US it has declined to a considerable
degree and in Israel only marginally (see chapter 11). Yet in all three
countries, bureaucratic actions with even indirect implications for
party politics have generated unusually pervasive controversy and
tension.

Marxists have argued that in capitalist countries, bureaucracies are
always politicized in that they are conservative and *status quo* oriented.
The foregoing account has shown that this is not invariably so. The
Australian Treasury can be presented as conservative by some standards;

the US Office of Economic Opportunity cannot be presented as conservative by any standard. According to M. Sexton (1979), the Whitlam government in Australia came into conflict with the bureaucracy because it was a reform-oriented government. But in the American case it was the reverse: strains emerged because the OEO was a reform-oriented bureaucratic agency. And in Israel's case, of course, the tension created was unrelated to the police force's leanings towards either conservatism or liberalism, even if it had such leanings — which is doubtful.

Marxists have argued that in capitalist countries, not only bureaucracies, but parties in power and the governments they form are conservative as well. If bureaucracies seem party-neutral, this is because the parties in power resemble each other; none have attempted to implement far-reaching reforms. It follows that the parties in power and the bureaucracies are all eminently compatible with each other, and no source of strain is evident. The foregoing account has shown that both in America and in Australia policy differences between the major parties alternating in power have still been large enough to make the bureaucracy's path more obstacle-ridden than Marxists would have envisaged. And in all three cases politicians and bureaucrats have stepped on each other's toes (while themselves tripping in the process) because their respective domains have verged on each other and they have therefore posed a threat to each other's bases of power. Thus, the Marxists, who are usually quick to point to the internal contradictions of capitalism, have, in this case, overlooked an important source of strain in the politics of capitalist societies.

Conclusion

A large number of partly overlapping, partly contradictory theories have addressed themselves to the relationship between bureaucracy and politics in Western democratic societies. The first part of this book was intended to serve as a minor guide for the perplexed through the maze of these theories. The review of theories was complemented by their critique and evaluation which, in turn, led up to the viewpoint here presented. The attempt to substantiate this viewpoint in the second part of the book, led to an overview of the development of bureaucracy and its relationship to politics in Western countries. It concluded with some case studies designed to bring into relief the problems and dilemmas of this relationship.

From among the theories reviewed, Marx's theory and that of his present-day followers was singled out especially for critical attention. This was done not because the Marxist school of thought has not made a considerable contribution to our understanding of modern society — for it obviously has. Rather, this was done to combat what I regard as an 'imperialist' tendency on its part, namely, its purporting to explain political life (as well as all other social phenomena) almost exclusively through economically based class interests.

For this purpose, Marxist analysis usually resorts to the assumption that ownership and the economic power that flows from it lies at the basis of political power and that economic exploitation is the crux of social inequality. In contrast, the present analysis has been based on the assumption that political power is not based on, and is no less crucial than, economic power, and that political domination may generate no less inequality and be no less repressive than economic exploitation. Marxist analysis works on the further assumption that despite some limited autonomy, state elites (or apparatuses) represent the economically dominant or ruling class's interests. In contrast, the present

225

analysis has been based on the assumption that state elites (sub-elites or elite persons) usually act in their own interests, specifically those of maintaining and augmenting their own power, and that they promote class (or other elites') interests only to the extent that they coincide with their own.

The assumption that political power is crucial and potentially repressive in its own right has led to the further assumption that democracy is worth promoting because it serves as the most effective known restraint on such power. In this context, it is a widely shared assumption that elections and the consequent threat of replacement as well as the codes of ethics or 'rules of the game' which elites in a democracy must be seen to adhere to in order to gain and maintain power (and which Marxists have, if not disregarded, at least greatly underplayed) are crucial in restraining power and power struggles. This assumption has been adopted for the purpose of this analysis as well. It has less frequently been pointed out, however, that the democratic rules are fragile, that they are easily circumvented when interests are at stake, and that they are not always clear-cut and definitive. And when the rules are hazy, inconsistent or controversial, the restraint they put on elite power and power struggles becomes even more fragile than it usually is; power is thus enhanced and power struggles are exacerbated. Under such circumstances power struggles may become especially disruptive and pose a threat to democracy. These assumptions too, are at the basis of the present analysis.

In a way this book may be seen as an attempt to show that this set of assumptions (clustering around elite interests, 'rule-conflict' and 'role-conflict') are more efficacious than the Marxist assumptions (clustering around class interests and class conflict) in helping explain the relationship between bureaucracy and politics. In particular it is an attempt to show that they are more efficacious than the Marxist ones in helping to explain the strains and conflicts between senior bureaucrats and politicians in Western democratic societies.

For if (as the Marxists have assumed) political struggles can be explained mainly through class interests and if (as Marxists have also assumed) state elites – including senior bureaucrats and politicians – all represent ruling-class interests, then they are all eminently compatible with each other and no source of strain is evident. Consequently the Marxists, who are usually quick to uncover the internal contradictions of capitalist societies, are in this case prevented from doing so in a meaningful manner. By being encapsulated in a theoretical framework whose main weight and contribution lies elsewhere, they are thus prevented from adequately analysing an important type of strain in the political arena of Western capitalist societies.

The assumptions of the present analysis, however, have led to a conception of a symbiotic though self-contradictory relationship between bureaucracy and democracy, leading to strains and tensions between senior bureaucrats and politicians. A brief historical overview has shown that bureaucracies in Western societies have been growing and proliferating and (despite some apparent counter-trends) have reached ominous proportions in recent years. It has also been argued, and anecdotal evidence has shown, that by sitting atop such ominous power bases, senior bureaucrats have been able to gain independence from, to promote their interests and pit their wills against those of duly elected politicians. Thus bureaucracy (whose principles are largely non-democratic) has been shown to pose a threat to democracy.

However, since politicians struggle for power through party-channelled elections, it is in their interest to promote their and their parties' electoral chances, and they must be sorely tempted to do so through any means at their disposal. Thus, as Mosca was the first to point out, unlimited democracy is apt to lead to illicit exchanges of favours, that is, to corruption, and ultimately to the negation of the democratic principle itself. And only bureaucracy (in which – it may be added – power struggles are independent from the partisan-electoral process) may serve as a bulwark against such corruption. In line with this argument, it has subsequently been shown that only in countries that have in fact developed bureaucracies with independence from party politics have proper democratic procedures developed. A bureaucracy that is independent from politicians is thus both a threat to and a requirement for democracy. To be sure, such a bureaucracy is not by itself sufficient to bring forth or safeguard democracy. It is thus by no means a sufficient condition for democracy, but it is certainly a necessary one.

The strains created by the relationship between bureaucracy and democracy have been exacerbated by the fact that it is precisely at the juncture between the two, that the codes or rules inevitably are unclear, inconsistent or even reach a breaking point. For in practically all Western countries the rules call for bureaucrats to be both subject to the control of politicians (with respect to devising and implementing policy) and free from such control (with respect to partisan interest). This, however, is hardly possible, as policies and partisan interests frequently verge on each other and at times become indistinguishable.

Given the tendency of both bureaucrats and politicians to promote their own interests, and given the inconsistency of the rules that govern the relationship between them and hence the promotion of these interests, it is not surprising that tensions between them occasionally mount. And as has been shown by means of some case studies, such tensions may erupt into especially vicious power struggles. Both sides would probably prefer to avoid such struggles. This is perhaps not so much because they pose a threat to the fragile institutional framework of democracy, but because, while victimizing others, both sides may themselves easily become those struggles' victims.

The problems which bureaucracy and democracy create for each other, do not seem open to any ready-made solution. Despite anti-statist movements and regimes, bureaucracy seems in the process of growing even bigger and more pervasive and this seems to aggravate even further the dilemmas which bureaucracy and democracy create for each other.

It has sometimes been suggested that the initiative for curbs on bureaucratic power would have to come from the public and the informal elites of voluntary associations rather than from the bureaucratic or political elites. This would not take the form of transferring bureaucratic services to private enterprise – as the New Right has suggested. Rather it would entail greater willingness on part of the public and its spontaneously created elites to take responsibility for the administration of their own welfare, thereby relieving bureaucracy of some of its ever-growing responsibilities which also spell its ever-growing power.

But it may well be asked whether the problems created by this solution would not be greater than the ones it was meant to solve, or, in other words, whether the cure would not be worse than the disease. For, in the first place, there is widespread (and well-documented) political apathy amongst the public of most Western countries. It is as if the people were expressing the spirit of the saying: 'Apathy is indeed a problem – but who cares?' This being the case, those few who would be willing to become activists in the areas to be relinquished by bureaucracy might not be representative of the public at large. They might well be more extremist (in various directions) than the silent majority. Indeed, the decisions they might reach and implement might well be less palatable to the majority of the community than those of the seemingly more distant bureaucracy.

Furthermore, even those willing to immerse themselves in voluntary public activity might have difficulty in reaching a consensus. Thus, the struggle over the allocation of resources, already taking place in the institutionalized political arena, would be duplicated in the voluntary political arena. It is questionable whether it is this that Western democracies most urgently need at the present time. This possibility may still be worth thinking about, but it does not seem to present the evident solution to the aforementioned set of problems.

What, then, is the solution? Disappointingly, all I can say is that if I had it, I would not content myself with being a political sociologist. Rather, I would make a bid to become a politician or a bureaucrat, perhaps even reaping some of the fruits of bureaucracy's growing power. As it is, I must settle for the hope that this book has made some contribution to people's awareness of the problems surrounding bureaucracy in a democracy, and for the further hope that awareness of these problems is in itself a first step towards their eventual solution.

Notes

Preface

1 As cited in Meier (1979, p. xv).

Introduction

1 For a definition of the terms 'democracy' and 'bureaucracy', see chapter 7.
2 See also Bennis and Slater (1968); Toffler (1970).
3 These and other theories are reviewed in the first part of this book.
4 In Malinski v. New York (1945), cited in Freedman (1978, p. 125).

1 Classical theories: Marx, Michels, Mosca

1 The analysis in this chapter has been aided by the interpretations of Albrow (1970), Krygier (1979a and c) and Miliband (1977).
2 Early Marxists, including Lenin and Trotsky, developed some ideas on this topic as well. They were intent, especially, on explaining why bureaucracy had not withered away but on the contrary had gained more power after the communist revolution. Here, however, we will be concerned only with more recent Marxist writings, since these are commonly regarded as part of the discipline of the social sciences proper. On this, see chapter 6.
3 A movement to secure ownership of industry by workers through 'direct action', especially strikes.
4 For instance by Machiavelli and later by Taine, with whose ideas Mosca was clearly familiar.

2 Classical theories: the Weberian framework

1 The analysis in this chapter has been aided by the interpretations of Albrow (1970); Krygier (1979d); and Mouzelis (1975).

2   This reference is to: *The Theory of Social and Economic Organization*. This is a translation of Part 1 of *Wirtschaft und Gesellschaft* which Weber wrote during the last years of his life, and was published posthumously in different editions.

3   This reference is to: *From Max Weber: Essays in Sociology*. The Essays quoted here have been translated from *Wirtschaft und Gesellschaft*.

4   For an explanation of what Weber meant by rationality, see below.

5   This reference is to *The Protestant Ethic and the Spirit of Capitalism*, first published in 1904-5.

6   This selection was translated from: *Gesammelte Aufsätze zur Soziologie und Sozialpolitik*, first published in 1924.

7   This is a translation of *Wirtschaft und Gesellschaft*, based on the 4th German edition (Tübingen, Mohr, 1956), pp. 1-550, 559-822.

8   Cited in Gerth and Mills (1958, p. 50).

9   On this school of thought see, for instance, Rose (1978).

10 As noted (p. 2) Bennis subsequently modified this forecast.

3   Modern theories: pluralism and government overload

1   Some of Thomson's ideas fit in with a pluralist perspective while others are more in line with the technocratic perspective (see next chapter).

2   As quoted in Domhoff (1978, p. 132).

3   As quoted by Knoke (1979, p. 58).

4   This is the title of one of Lindblom's articles (1979).

5   This is the title of one of Lindblom's books (1965).

6   It is of interest that Lindblom is part of the pluralist school, as seen above, and is also apart from it.

7   It has recently been conjectured that Stalin, for instance, considered to be one of the most absolute of absolute power-holders, was in fact murdered at the instigation of his subordinates.

4   Modern theories: the technocratic view

1   *Grand Larousse Encyclopédique*, Paris 1964 (as quoted by Bell, 1973, p. 348).

2   Here we shall be concerned only with their ideas on the rule of bureaucrats and not with their other ideas.

3   On Mosca and Michels, see chapter 1. On Pareto and for a brief review of elitist theories in general, see Etzioni-Halevy (1981, ch. 6).

4   Although the military and the scientific-technical elites are also included.

5   Quoted in Dogan (1975a, p. 7).

6   For a related theory see Bell (1973).

7   Quoted in Meynaud (1964, p. 145).

5 Modern theories: the corporatist view

1 There have also been some writings on corporatism in the early twentieth century (reviewed, for instance, by Schmitter 1979a) and in the 1960s (e.g. Beer, 1965; Shonfield, 1965; and Lowi, 1969). But it is in the 1970s that corporatist writings have become a popular 'growth industry' (see Panitch, 1980).

2 Despite some disagreement on details, this definition with minor variations, is propounded or accepted by a wide range of writers and may thus be seen as the mainstream definition of corporatism (see for instance Schmitter, 1979a, p. 13; Panitch, 1980, p. 173; and Diamant 1981). An alternative definition that is sometimes cited in the literature, but not as widely accepted, is that by Winkler (1976, p. 103) according to which 'corporatism is an economic system in which the state directs and controls predominantly privately-owned business . . . according to four principles: unity, order, nationalism and success'.

3 According to the corporatist view, the above definition characterizes an 'ideal type' which nowhere fully exists. But modern reality increasingly approaches it.

4 This article as well as several articles mentioned in this chapter have been published in Schmitter and Lehmbruch (eds) (1979). Many of the same articles have previously been published in *Comparative Political Studies* (vol. 10, no. 1, April 1977) of which the whole issue is devoted to corporatism.

5 Although in some countries (e.g. Germany and Austria) liberalism was meagre and short-lived.

6 The American corporatist experience being confined to the New Deal years and later on to a short-lived attempt by President Nixon to bring labour, business and government together in order to halt inflation. But these arrangements quickly disintegrated.

7 On the use of quasi-governmental organizations in policy-making see also Smith (1975).

8 These multi-national corporations figure prominently in neo-Marxist dependency theories. For a brief review of those, see Etzioni-Halevy (1981, ch. 3).

9 For a critical examination of the extent to which the corporatist model fits actual reality in one Western country, namely Australia, see Ballard (1980).

6 Modern theories: the Marxist view

1 Domhoff's ideas are akin to those of Marxists.

2 Here, Marxist ideas on bureaucracy only have been reviewed. For a general review of contemporary Marxism, see Etzioni-Halevy (1981).

3 That is, non-Marxist theories, such as structural functionalism or symbolic interactionism.

7 Bureaucratic power — a democratic dilemma

1   The recent literature is beset by a controversy over the most appropriate conception of power. Logically, the starting point for the discussion is Weber's definition of power as ability to carry out one's will despite resistance (see chapter 2). Many empirical studies have reached their conclusions on such ability by looking at actual decision-making. These studies have been criticized by Bachrach and Baratz (1962) who point out that power consists in non-decision-making as well, or in the capacity of suppressing issues and preventing them from coming up for decision. Beyond preventing grievances from surfacing, power has also been defined as the capacity to prevent grievances from developing by shaping perceptions and preferences (Lukes, 1974). To this some Marxists (notably Offe, 1974) have added that such power to shape perceptions is in fact built into the capitalist system. The definition of power adopted here, though simplistic, has the advantage of being in line with (or at least not out of line with) all of these conceptions, especially if resources are defined in a broad, not necessarily material, sense.

2   This definition is a modified version of some previous definitions such as, for instance, that by J. Schumpeter (1966, p. 269): 'The Democratic method is that institutional arrangement for arriving at political decisions in which individuals acquire the power to decide by means of a competitive struggle for the people's vote'.
Or that by Lipset (1965, p. 33):

> Democracy in a complex society may be defined as a political system which supplies regular constitutional opportunities for changing the governing officials, and a social mechanism which permits the largest possible part of the population to influence major decisions by choosing among contenders for a political office.

For similar definitions, see Dahl (1956); Eckstein (1966); Sartori (1962). The only addition in the definition suggested here is the clause on competing for office on the basis of policies and projected images. I suggest that this clause, however, is implicit in the other definitions as well, and the only reason for its not being spelled out is that it is considered self-evident.

For an alternative conception of democracy (based on the classical theories of J.-J. Rousseau and J.S. Mill), see Pateman (1970). According to this conception, elections, though part of democracy, are not sufficient; direct participation by the entire public in the decision-making process must take place as well before democracy can be said to exist. This, however, is basically a prescriptive rather than a descriptive theory, as Pateman herself specifies, and therefore not appropriate for the present discussion.

3   The argument is *not* that a modern bureaucracy cannot exist

without democracy. In the following chapter it will be seen that (in the West) the advent of democracy contributed to bureaucratic growth and development. But it was only one of several contributing factors. And we know, of course, of (non-Western) countries where modern bureaucracies exist and do quite well without democracy. The claim made here is rather the reverse, namely that a modern democracy cannot exist without a powerful and independent bureaucracy.

4 Policies are in any case guidelines for the allocation of resources from which some groups benefit more than others. However, such allocations may be ordered on a continuum from the macro (national) level, through the intermediate (interest groups or district level) down to the micro (local, family or individual) level. It is only on the macro and intermediate levels that one may talk of social policies as guidelines for resource allocation. And, indeed, using such policies to gain electoral support is a commonly engaged in and (by definition) legitimate device for gaining electoral support. But as one moves from the macro to the micro level the device turns into an explicit, personal exchange of material benefits for votes. It is *this* which runs counter to the requirements of democracy and has been outlawed in most democratic countries.

5 Quoted in Kellner and Crowther-Hunt (1980, p. 203).

6 Quoted in ibid. (pp. 12-13).

7 Whitehall is a street in London where many government offices are located. The name is frequently used as a synonym for the British bureaucracy.

8 In France, each incoming minister appoints a group of close political advisers, collectively named the ministerial cabinet.

8 The development of Western bureaucracy: overview and explanation

1 Main sources: Barker (1944); Gladden (1972); Jacobi (1973); Krygier (1979b); Rosenberg (1958); Sharp (1931).

2 The church as such was centralized to a much greater extent than other foci of power. But within the various political domains it initially served to countervail the power of secular rulers and feudals; it therefore had a decentralizing effect on each domain's internal structure.

3 I am grateful to Mr W.G. Craven of the Department of History, The Faculties, The Australian National University, for making this point.

4 Some countries with strong feudal traditions, and especially Germany, did not leave economic activity to individual initiative to the same extent as did Britain and the United States.

5 In 1934 it was transformed into the Federal Communications Commission.

6 Now the Federal Aviation Agency.

7 According to Schultze (1977, p. 7), there were other regulatory

activities − for instance food and drug regulation − but their impact on the economy was small.

8 GNP is the money value of all goods and services produced in a country's economy during a given period (usually a year).

9 On this, see chapter 2.

10 As is well known, there are several shortcomings to growth in GNP as a measure of economic growth: for instance the fact that economic development is a multivariate concept which also includes productive capacity and infrastructure. Nevertheless most studies and analyses employ this as a shorthand measure because it seems to be the best available.

11 Thus, between 1860 and 1965, GNP per capita grew by 17 per cent per decade in France, 20.2 per cent per decade in Denmark, 22.9 per cent in Italy, 28.9 per cent in Sweden, 13.4 per cent in the UK and 17.3 per cent in the US (Chirot, 1977, p. 157).

12 For the most recent developments, see the next chapter.

13 GDP is similar to GNP. It refers to the money value of all goods and services produced in a country's economy during a given period (usually a year), but excluding net income from abroad.

14 In non-Western countries, to be sure, bureaucracy has developed without democracy. But there, the dominant ideology was not that of individualism, and there was no popular suspicion and reluctance to accept state power to begin with. Hence such fears did not have to be allayed through the evolution of democracy.

15 It must be borne in mind, however, that prices fell at the time, so that in real terms GNP declined only to around three-quarters of what it was before.

16 More recent developments are analysed in the next chapter.

17 Some historians have even here emphasized the gains of the new working class − for example, working-class clubs, friendly societies, etc. − as against the 'idiocy of rural life'. It is doubtful, however, that these gains outweighed the slum conditions.

18 In Britain such occurrences are illustrated by Luddism and related riots and machine-breaking which took place from 1811 up until the 1840s. They are also illustrated by Chartism − a mass working-class movement for political reforms which instigated violent outbursts in 1839 and 1848. In the United States Dorr's rebellion (in Rhode Island in 1842) was the first of several violent disturbances instigated by workers.

19 Depending on whether direct taxes only, or indirect taxes, too, are taken into account. Lately it has been claimed that tax evasion schemes by the rich in effect render taxes more than mildly regressive. But for obvious reasons there are no hard-and-fast data to substantiate this claim. In any case, the welfare state is certainly important in counterbalancing this trend at least to some extent.

9 Recent developments: some apparent counter-trends

1 The *grands corps de l'État* include the upper civil administrative bodies dealing mainly with civil law, public monies and public administration. The technical *corps* include the upper administrative bodies concerned with technical matters. Informally and more importantly, they are breeding grounds for top position-holders in the French administration.

2 In France, each minister has a group of close political advisers, collectively named the ministerial cabinet.

3 For a discussion of these programs, see chapter 13.

4 Even though the follow-up proposition 9, calling for further tax-cuts, failed to get a majority in the 1980 referendum.

5 *Laissez-faire* liberalism (also known as Libertarianism) harks back to the nineteenth century. It is to be distinguished from twentieth-century liberalism (concerned mainly with the liberty of the disadvantaged as promoted by state intervention) and from conservatism (concerned mainly with the preservation of traditional institutions and values).

6 As cited in Sawer (1982, p. 5).

7 Except in South Australia.

8 In the 1977 Federal election it contested 44 seats for the House of Representatives, but only in six did it poll more than 3 per cent of the vote.

9 As noted before, GNP is the money value of all goods and services produced in a country's economy during a given period (usually a year). GDP is the money value of the same goods and services, but excluding net income from abroad.

10 The word 'movement' is used merely as a short-hand description. In fact, as was shown, the New Right is composed of various partly interlocking groups.

11 Alternatively, New Rightists have suggested that people should be enabled to pay for the services through a negative income tax system. This, however, has raised the problem of recipients' misusing the money, rather than spending it on the appropriate services.

12 Although a sizeable bureaucracy would still be needed to make decisions as to how the system should work and who should be entitled to obtain vouchers for which services, to allocate the vouchers, to distribute the money to the voucher-presenting enterprises, to institute and look after the proper accreditation of such enterprises and to supervise their performance, and finally, to institute proper methods of inspection and investigation so that the system was not abused.

13 For instance, the proportion of people aged 65 and over in Britain was 10.8 in 1951 and 15 in 1978; in the US it was 8.2 in 1950 and 11.2 in 1979; in France it was 11.5 in 1954 and 14 in 1979. Projections are for even greater proportions of the aged in the population towards the end of the century.

14 The end-of-1982 figure for Britain, for instance, is 13.2 per cent of
    the labour force, as against less than 3 per cent in the 1950s and
    1960s. The equivalent figure for the US is 10.4 per cent as against
    less than 5 per cent in the 1950s and 1960s; and the figure for West
    Germany is 8.7 per cent as against less than 3 per cent from 1955
    to 1974.
15 See, for instance, Mukherjee (1981, ch. 5).
16 The percentage of single-parent families (as defined in official
    statistics) grew in the US from 6.2 in 1970 to 10.4 in 1981 and in
    Australia from 5 in 1966 to 8.8 in 1975.

10 Bureaucratic development and the power of bureaucracy

1 As the corporatists have indicated, the first part of the nineteenth
   century may have been an exception from this point of view — see
   chapter 5.
2 One of the authors, Lord Crowther-Hunt, served on the Fulton
   Committee and subsequently was constitutional adviser to prime
   minister Harold Wilson, who was at the time dealing with the
   implementation of the committee's recommendations. The other
   author is a journalist.
3 Haines, it will be recalled, was prime minister Harold Wilson's Press
   Secretary and political adviser.
4 The details are not relevant in this context.
5 Tony Benn is an extreme left-wing Labour politician.
6 For a definition of *corps* see chapter 9 note 1.
7 See, for instance, Bruce-Gardyne and Lawson (1976); Kissinger
   (1979).
8 Richard Crossman was the British Minister for Housing and Local
   Government, 1964-6, and Secretary of State for Social Services in
   charge of the Department of Health and Social Security, 1968-70.

11 Bureaucracy and party politics

1 For an earlier version of the analysis of four of the seven countries
   included (Britain, Australia, US and Israel), see Etzioni-Halevy
   (1979).
2 Main sources: Birch (1973); Bridges (1971); Christoph (1975);
   Finer (1952); Ostrogorski (1902, vol. 1); Parris (1969); Sisson
   (1971); Wettenhall (1973).
3 Political patronage in the civil service may be defined as a system
   whereby the patron — a politician or a political party — provides
   appointments and promotions *in the civil service* for supporters
   who reciprocate by furthering the party's interests within the
   service. This is a more narrow phenomenon than political
   patronage in general, as defined in the next chapter.
4 The spoils system is commonly defined as consisting of two

elements. 1 political patronage in the civil service and 2 the substitution (following an election) of civil servants from the defeated party by appointees from the victorious party. This system was highly developed in nineteenth-century America (see below).

5   The role definition of British public servants thus hinges on the distinction between policies and party politics. For the problems created by this distinction, see, for instance, chapters 7 and 13.

6   On this reform, see also chapter 10.

7   Main sources: Bland (1932, 1944); Caiden (1967); Knight (1961); Spann (1972, 1973); Wettenhall (1973); Wiltshire (1974).

8   Main sources: Ferguson and McHenry (1950); Finer (1952); Fish (1900, 1905); Gosnell (1937); Ostrogorski (1902, vol. 2); Sorauf (1956, 1960); Van Riper (1958); White (1935, 1945, 1951, 1954, 1958).

9   Main sources: Akzin and Dror (1966); Eisenstadt (1967, 1974); Globerson (1970); Medding (1972); Shapiro (1975, 1977).

10   Literally: settlement. It is the name commonly used for the Jewish settlement in Palestine before independence.

11   At the beginning of modern Jewish colonization of Palestine at the turn of the century Palestine was under Turkish (Ottoman) rule. In 1918 the country became a British Mandate and it is mainly from that time onward that the Jewish community's political institutions developed.

12   Literally: Unity of Labour.

13   This authority was made up of two parts:
(1) The Zionist Executive (later the Jewish Agency Executive) was the local representative of the World Zionist Organization. Elected by the World Zionist Congress, it was in charge of finance (including the mobilization of capital from abroad), immigration, settlement, labour, industry and defence.
(2) The National Council was the executive of the (locally) elected assembly; it was concerned primarily with culture, education, health and welfare.

14   Literally: Land of Israel's Workers' Party.

15   Literally: Cohesion.

16   Literally: Movement for Israel's Tradition.

17   These recent developments have been widely reported in the Israeli press. See in particular Dan Margalit, 'The Lobby', *Ha'aretz*, 27 April 1978; Gad Lior, 'The Hottest Portfolio', *Yediot Ah'ronot*, 8 July 1981, p. 10; *Jerusalem Post*, 18 February 1981, p. 1. For further discussion of politicization in the Ministry for Religious Affairs, see chapter 13.

18   Main sources: Fried (1963); La Palombara (1964); Ledeem (1977); Zuckerman (1975).

19   Since shortly after the war the DC has been in power either by itself or as the dominant party in Italy's coalition governments. At the 1979 election the DC captured 38.3 per cent of the vote. In June 1981 it was obliged to surrender the prime ministership, for

the first time in 35 years, to the Republican party (PRI) but remained a major coalition partner.

20 More details on this in chapter 12.

21 This is an organization of laymen associated with the Catholic church.

22 Main sources: Duverger (1958); Langrod (1967); Meynaud (1964); Ridley and Blondel (1964); Sharp (1931); Suleiman (1974); Williams (1954, 1964).

23 Young university graduates could also compete in these examinations, but only a minority of those appointed to higher positions are not graduates of the ENA and they must have served at least ten years in a lower rank.

24 The SFIO, the Movement Republicain Populaire (MRP) and the radical party. The SFIO was the French Section of the International Workers' Union.

25 That is to say, the heads of divisions.

26 Main sources: Dogan (1975a); MacMullen (1979); Moulin (1975); Van Hassel (1975).

27 On ministerial cabinets, see above, chapter 9, note 2.

12 Bureaucracy and electoral manipulation

1 Political patronage or political clientelism may be defined as a system whereby the patron — a politician or a party — provides benefits for the client — who reciprocates by providing political support and/or certain political services. The political machine has been defined as a party organization that depends on such benefits. I prefer the more general term of exchange of material benefits for political support because the practice does not always involve the quasi-personal tie between a patron and a client which the terms patronage and clientelism imply, and because inducements are sometimes handed out by politicians rather than by party organizations. These points should become clearer throughout the subsequent discussion.

2 Graziano's theory, for instance, pertains to southern Italy and O'Connell's theory relates to Ireland (a country not included in the present analysis), and they may well serve to explain the phenomenon in those two societies.

3 This discussion is based mainly on Gwyn (1962); King (1970); O'Leary (1962); Ostrogorski (1902, vol. 1); Lloyd (1968).

4 On the characteristics of such machines, see the next section.

5 This is so because the use of electoral bribery is based largely on tying beneficiaries to the party or candidate by a bond of gratitude. Also, some material benefits to voters accrue only if the party or candidate comes to (or stays in) power — which makes their election a matter of self-interest to the voter.

6 Main sources: Loveday (1959); Loveday and Martin (1966); Martin (1958); Morrison (1950, 1951, 1952, 1953, 1960, 1960-1, 1966);

Nairn (1967); Parker (1960); Serle (1971).

7   From James Brunker to Henry Parkes (17 August 1864, pp. 35-6)
    (see also Brunker to Parkes, 3 August 1863, p. 34).
8   From Stephen Scholey to Henry Parkes (4 February 1872, p. 34).
9   Later, however, Perkins was charged with bribery and the election
    was voided.
10 I am grateful to Ms Eileen Price, Dr Bruce Mitchell and Professor
    John Nalson of the University of New England and Dr Colin
    Hughes of the Australian National University, for making these
    points.
11 Main sources: Fredman (1968); Greenstein (1966); Ostrogorski
    (1902, vol. 2); Reichley (1966); Rourke (1970); Speed (1970);
    Schlesinger (1975); Steinberg (1972). See also Gosnell (1937);
    Steffens (1904).
12 Especially, but by no means exclusively, on the State and local
    levels.
13 The Article was previously published in 1905.
14 Obviously these were not accurate measurements but rough
    estimates only.
15 According to Mladenka, this has been shown for Oakland by Levy
    et al. (1974); for San Antonio by Linebery (1977); for Detroit by
    Jones *et al.* (1978) and for Houston by Mladenka and Hill (1978).
16 Main sources: Deshen (1970, 1972); Eisenstadt (1967); Medding
    (1972); Shapiro (1977).
17 For an explanation of this and the subsequent terms – see previous
    chapter.
18 Although the *Histadrut* was set up in 1920 as a federation of
    labour unions it did not confine itself to traditional labour union
    activities. One of its chief functions was to provide employment
    for workers and for this purpose it did (among other things)
    establish its own numerous and increasingly powerful economic
    concerns.
19 Subsequent immigration was on a much smaller scale.
20 For more details see chapter 13.
21 See *Ha'aretz* (18 December 1981, p. 12; and 28 December 1981,
    p. 4).
22 Main sources: Fried (1963); La Palombara (1964); Parisi and
    Pasquino (1979); Pasquino (1979); Zuckerman (1975). See also
    Alberoni *et al.* (1967); Allum (1973); Bailey (1971); Sartori
    (1971); Stirling (1968).
23 Quoted by Zuckerman (1975, p. 16).
24 Quoted by La Palombara (1964, pp. 309-10).
25 Main sources: Duverger (1958); Sharp (1931); Suleiman (1974);
    Williams (1964).
26 Main sources: Covell (1981); Fox (1978); Moulin (1975).

13 Bureaucracy in a double bind — some case studies

1 *Congressional Digest* (March 1966, p. 67).
2 Ibid., p. 81 (both statements as cited by Marris and Rein, 1972, p. 250).
3 Voters had to affirm that they were indeed poor; so did the candidates, who could spend no money on their campaigns.
4 Some observers claim that the government also desired the loan to counteract possible blocking of supply by the Senate, and that Treasury also opposed the loan because it saw it as a threat to its own power. More on this below.
5 'Mr Williams' was the code name around Parliament House for a First Assistant Secretary in the Treasury (Kelly, 1976, p. 151).
6 On this see also chapter 9.
7 A special tax on high profits accruing from the utilization of resources.
8 This minister was later indicted on charges of bribery, fraud and larceny. He stood trial and was acquitted of bribery but subsequently stood trial and was convicted of fraud and larceny.
9 A few months later, Professor Yitzhak Zamir, the Attorney-General, instructed the police to begin investigation on this file.
10 Literally: 'The Country'. *Ha'aretz* is Israel's elite newspaper.

Bibliography

Aberbach, J.D., Putnam, R.D., and Rockman, B.A. (1981), *Bureaucrats and Politicians in Western Bureaucracies*, Cambridge, Mass., Harvard University Press.

Abrahamsson, B. (1977), *Bureaucracy or Participation*, London, Sage Publications.

Akzin, B., and Dror, Y. (1966), *National Planning in Israel*, Jerusalem, College for Administration (Hebrew).

Alberoni, F., Capecchi, V., Manoukian, A., Olivetti, F. and Tosi, A. (1967), *L'Attavisto di Partito*, Bologna, Il Mulino.

Albrow, M. (1970), *Bureaucracy*, London, Macmillan.

Allum, P.A. (1973), *Politics and Society in Post-War Naples*, Cambridge University Press.

Australian Bureau of Statistics (1981), *Australian Demographic Statistics Quarterly*, June, Canberra.

Australian Bureau of Statistics (1980), *Labour Statistics 1979*, Canberra.

Australian Financial Review (1981), 9 and 11 March.

Australian Government Publishing Service (1981), *Budget Statement 1981-82* (Budget Paper No. 1), Canberra.

Australian Public Service Board (1981), *Annual Reports 1976-1981*, Canberra.

Australian, The (1982), 16 January.

Bachrach, P., and Baratz, M.S. (1962), 'The two faces of power', *American Political Science Review*, 56, pp. 947-52.

Bailey, F.G. (1971), *Gifts and Poison*, Oxford, Basil Blackwell.

Ballard, J. (1980), 'The corpus of neo-corporatism', unpublished.

Bar, Y. (1981), 'Shafir lashes out at Burg over dismissal', *Jerusalem Post Weekly*, 7-10 January, p. 3.

Barker, E. (1944), *The Development of Public Services in Western Europe 1660-1930*, London, Oxford University Press.

Barnet, R.J. (1972), *Roots of War*, New York, Atheneum.

Beer, S. (1965), *British Politics in the Collectivist Age*, New York, Knopf.

Bell, D. (1973), *The Coming of the Post Industrial Society*, New York,

Basic Books.

Bell, D. (1975), 'The Revolution of Rising Entitlements', *Fortune*, April, pp. 98-103.

Bennis, W.G. (1968), 'The coming death of bureaucracy', in Athos, A.G., and Coffey, R.E. (eds), *Behavior in Organizations*, Englewood Cliffs, N.J. Prentice Hall, pp. 256-66.

Bennis, W.G. (1970), 'A funny thing happened on the way to the future', *American Psychologist*, 25, pp. 595-608.

Bennis, W.G., and Slater, P.E. (1968), *The Temporary Society*, New York, Harper & Row.

Bensman, J., and Rosenberg, B. (1969), 'The meaning of work in bureaucratic society', in Etzioni, A. (ed.), *Readings on Modern Organizations*, Englewood Cliffs, N.J., Prentice Hall, pp. 54-64.

Berger, B. (1971), *Societies in Change*, New York, Basic Books.

Billiet, J., Creyf, R., and Dobbelaere, K. (1978), 'Secularization and "pillarization" in Belgian political life', *Res Publica*, 20, pp. 407-31.

Birch, A.H. (1973), *The British system of Government* (rev. edn), London, Allen & Unwin.

Bland, F.A. (1932), 'The spoils system in the public service', *Australian Quarterly*, 4, pp. 34-43.

Bland, F.A. (ed.) (1944), *Government in Australia* (2nd edn), Sydney, Government Printer.

Bland, H. (1975), *Public Administration – Whither?*, Canberra, The Royal Institute of Public Administration.

Boissevain, J. (1970), 'Patronage in Sicily', in Heidenheimer, A.J. (ed.), *Political Corruption*, pp. 138-52.

Bridges, E. (1971), 'Portrait of a profession', in Chapman, R.A., and Dunsire, A. (eds), *Style in Administration*, London, Allen & Unwin, pp. 44-60.

Bruce-Gardyne, J., and Lawson, N. (1976), *The Power Game*, Hamden, Connecticut, Archon Books.

Burnham, J. (1942), *The Managerial Revolution*, London, Putnam.

Caciagli, M. (1977), *Democrazia Christiana e Potere nel Mezzogiorno*, Rimini, Florence, Guaraldi.

Caiden, G.E. (1967), *The Commonwealth Bureaucracy*, Melbourne University Press.

Canada Dominion Bureau of Statistics, *Canada Year Book* 1946, 1951, 1952, 1961, 1972, Ottawa.

Canada Dominion Bureau of Statistics (1954), *Vital Statistics 1952*, Ottawa.

Canberra Times (1982), 4 February.

Cawson, A. (1978), 'Pluralism, corporatism and the role of the state', *Government and Opposition*, 13, pp. 178-98.

Chapman, B. (1959), *The Profession of Government*, London, George Allen & Unwin.

Chapman, B. (1961), 'Facts of organized life', *Manchester Guardian Weekly*, 26 January.

Chirot, D. (1977), *Social Change in the Twentieth Century*, New York, Harcourt Brace Jovanovich.

Christoph, J.B. (1975), 'High civil servants and the politics of consensualism in Great Britain', in Dogan, M. (ed.), *The Mandarins of Western Europe*, pp. 25-62.

Cole, R.L. and Caputo, D.A. (1979), 'Presidential control of the senior civil service', *American Political Science Review*, 73, pp. 399-413.

Comparative Political Studies (1977), vol. 10, no. 1, April.

Conference Board (1981), *Statistical Bulletin*, New York.

Congressional Digest (1966), March.

Coombs, H.C., *et al.* (1977), *Report of the Royal Commission on Australian Government Administration*, Canberra, The Commonwealth Government Printer.

Courier Mail (1980), 7 October.

Covell, M. (1981), 'Ethnic conflict and elite bargaining', *West European Politics*, 4, pp. 197-218.

Crossman, R. (1972), *The Myths of Cabinet Government*, Cambridge, Mass., Harvard University Press.

Crouch, C. (1978), 'The changing role of the state in industrial relations in Western Europe', in Crouch, C., and Pizzorno, A. (eds), *The Resurgence of Class Conflict in Western Europe since 1968*, vol. 2, London, Macmillan, pp. 197-220.

Crouch, C. (1979), 'The state, capital and liberal democracy', in Crouch, C. (ed.), *State and Economy in Contemporary Capitalism*, London, Croom Helm, pp. 13-54.

Crozier, M. (1964), *The Bureaucratic Phenomenon*, University of Chicago Press.

Crozier, M., Huntington, S.P. and Watanuk, J. (1975), *The Crisis of Democracy*, New York University Press.

Dahl, R.A. (1956), *Preface to Democratic Theory*, University of Chicago Press.

Dahl, R.A. (1967), *Pluralist Democracy in the United States*, Chicago, Rand McNally.

Dahl, R.A. (1971), *Polyarchy*, New Haven, Yale University Press.

Dahl, R.A. (1976), *Democracy in the United States* (3rd edn), Chicago, Rand McNally.

Dahrendorf, R. (1959), *Class and Class Conflict in Industrial Society*, Stanford University Press.

Davis, M. (1981), 'The New Right's road to power', *New Left Review*, 128, pp. 28-49.

Debbasch, C. (1969), *L'Administration, Au Pouvoir*, Paris, Calmann-Lévy.

Deshen, S.A. (1970), *Immigrant Voters in Israel*, Manchester University Press.

Deshen, S.A. (1972), 'The business of ethnicity is finished?' in Arian, A. (ed.), *The Elections in Israel, 1969*, Jerusalem, Academic Press, pp. 278-302.

Diamant, A. (1981), 'Bureaucracy and public policy in neo corporatist settings', *Comparative Politics*, 14, pp. 101-24.

Dickey, B. (ed.) (1969), *Politics in New South Wales, 1856-1900*, Melbourne, Cassell.

DiPalma, G. (1979), 'The available state', *West European Politics*, 2, pp. 149-65.

Dogan, M. (1975a), 'The political power of the Western mandarins: introduction', in Dogan, M. (ed.), *The Mandarins of Western Europe*, pp. 3-24.

Dogan, M. (ed.) (1975b), *The Mandarins of Western Europe*, New York, John Wiley.

Domhoff, G. (1979), *The Powers That Be*, New York, Random House.

Downs, A. (1957), *An Economic Theory of Democracy*, New York, Harper & Row.

Downs, A. (1967), *Inside Bureaucracy*, Boston, Little Brown.

Duverger, M. (1958), *The French Political System*, University of Chicago Press.

Dye, T.R., and Zeigler, L.H. (1975), *The Irony of Democracy* (3rd edn), North Scituate, Mass., Duxbury Press.

Eckstein, H. (1966), 'A theory of stable democracy', Appendix B of *Division and Cohesion in Democracy*, Princeton University Press.

Economist, The, 1964-1982.

Edwards, J. (1974a), 'September 9, 1973',*National Times*, 11 November.

Edwards, J. (1974b), 'In seven momentous months Whitlam turned to refloating a sinking ship', *National Times*, 18 November.

Ehrmann, H.W. (1961), 'Les groupes d'intérêt et la bureaucratie dans les démocraties occidentales', *Revue Francaise de Science Politique*, 11, pp. 541-68.

Eisenstadt, S.N. (1967), *Israeli Society*, London, Weidenfeld & Nicolson.

Eisenstadt, S.N. (1974), *Change and Continuity in Israeli Society*, New York, Humanities Press, in collaboration with Am Oved of Tel-Aviv (Hebrew).

Eisenstadt, S.N., and Von Beyme, K. (1972), 'Bureaucracy', in Kernig, C.D. (ed.), *Marxism, Communism and Western Society – A Comparative Encyclopedia*, New York, Herder & Herder, pp. 327-37.

Eldar, A. (1981), 'The NRP – inspector general war', *Ha'aretz*, 2 January, p. 14.

Eldar, A. (1982), 'An inspector general who is not a leader', *Ha'aretz*, 1 January, p. 15.

Ellul, J. (1965), *The Technological Society* (tr. J. Wilkinson), London, Jonathan Cape.

Emy, H. (1974), *The Politics of Australian Democracy*, London, Macmillan.

Encel, S. (1970), *Equality and Authority*, Melbourne, Cheshire.

Epstein, L.D. (1967), *Political Parties in Western Democracies*, London, Pall Mall Press.

Etzioni, A., and Etzioni-Halevy, E. (eds) (1973), *Social Change: Sources, Patterns and Consequences*, New York, Basic Books.

Etzioni-Halevy, E. (1979), *Political Manipulation and Administrative Power*, London, Routledge & Kegan Paul.

Etzioni-Halevy, E. (1981), *Social Change: The Advent and Maturation of Modern Society*, London, Routledge & Kegan Paul.

Facts on File, New York, 1981.

Ferguson, J.H., and McHenry, D.E. (1950), *The American Federal Government*, New York, McGraw Hill.

Ferraresi, F. (1980), *Burocrazia e Politica in Italia*, Bologna, Il Mulino.

Field, G.L., and Higley, J. (1980), *Elitism*, London, Routledge & Kegan Paul.

Finer, S. (1952), 'Patronage and the public service', *Public Administration*, 30, pp. 329-60.

Fish, C.R. (1900), 'Removal of officials by the President of the United States', *Annual Report of the American Historical Association for the Year 1899*, Washington, D.C., Government Printing Office, vol. 1, pp. 67-86.

Fish, C.R. (1905), *The Civil Service and the Patronage*, New York, Longmans, Green & Co.

Fox, R. (1978), 'Why Belgium?', *Archives Européennes de Sociologie*, 19, pp. 205-28.

Fredman, L.E. (1968), *The Australian Ballot*, Michigan State University Press.

Freedman, J.O. (1978), *Crisis and Legitimacy*, Cambridge University Press.

Freudenberg, G. (1977), *A Certain Grandeur*, Melbourne, Macmillan.

Fried, R.C. (1963), *The Italian Prefects*, New Haven, Yale University Press.

Fried, R.C. (1976), *Performance in American Bureaucracy*, Boston, Little, Brown.

Friedrich, C.J. (1952), 'Some observations on Weber's analysis of bureaucracy' in Merton, R.K., Gray, A.P., Hockey, B. and Selvin, H.C. (eds), *Reader in Bureaucracy*, Chicago, Free Press, pp. 27-33.

Fulton (Lord) *et al.* (1968), *The Civil Service – Report of the Committee*, London, Her Majesty's Stationary Office, vol. 1.

Galbraith, J.K. (1952), *American Capitalism*, Boston, Houghton Mifflin.

Galbraith, J.K. (1967), *The New Industrial State*, Boston, Houghton Mifflin.

Gamble, A. (1979), 'The free economy and the strong state', in Miliband, R., and Saville, J. (eds), *The Socialist Register 1979*, London, The Merlin Press, pp. 1-25.

Gerth, H.H., and Mills, C.W. (1958), *From Max Weber: Essays in Sociology*, New York, Oxford University Press.

Giddens, A. (1973), *The Class Structure of Advanced Societies*, London, Hutchinson.

Gladden, E.N. (1972), *A History of Public Administration*, London, Frank Cass.

Globerson, A. (1970), *The Administrative Elite in the Government Civil Service in Israel*, Tel-Aviv, Hamidrasha Leminhal.

Goell, J. (1981), 'No job for political innocents', *Jerusalem Post Weekly*, 11-17 January, p. 8.

Gosnell, H.F. (1937), *Machine Politics*, University of Chicago Press.

Gouldner, A.W. (1954), *Patterns of Industrial Bureaucracy*, Chicago,

The Free Press.

Graziano, L. (1977), 'Patron client relationship in Southern Italy', in Schmidt, L.G., Landé, C., and Scott, J. (eds), *Friends, Followers and Factions*, Berkeley, University of California Press, pp. 360-78.

Great Britain Central Statistical Office (1981), *Annual Abstract of Statistics*, vol. 117.

Great Britain Central Statistical Office (1981), *Monthly Digest of Statistics*, no. 429, September.

Great Britain Department of Employment and Productivity (1971), *British Labour Statistics, Historical Abstract 1886-1968*, London.

Greenstein, F.I. (1966), 'The changing pattern of urban party-politics', in Herzberg, D.G., and Pomper, G.M. (eds), *American Party-Politics*, New York, Holt, Rinehart & Winston, pp. 253-63.

Grosser, A. (1964), 'The evolution of European parliaments', in Graubard, S.R. (ed.), *A New Europe?*, London, Oldbourne Press, pp. 219-44.

Gwyn, W.B. (1962), *Democracy and the Cost of Politics in Britain*, London, Athlone Press.

Ha'aretz, 1976-1982.

Haines, J. (1977), *The Politics of Power*, London, Jonathan Cape.

Hanley, D.L., Kerr, A.P., and Waites, N.H. (1979), *Contemporary France: Politics and Society*, London, Routledge & Kegan Paul.

Head, B. (1982), 'The New Right and welfare expenditures', in Sawer, M. (ed.), *Australia and the New Right*, pp. 100-19.

Heclo, H. (1978), 'Political executives and the Washington bureaucracy', in Caraley, D. and Epstein, M.A. (eds), *The Making of American Foreign and Domestic Policy*, New York, Dabor Social Science Publications, pp. 173-202.

Heidenheimer, A.J. (ed.) (1970), *Political Corruption*, New York, Holt, Rinehart & Winston.

Higley, J., Brofoss, K.E., and Groholt, K. (1975), 'Top civil servants and the National Budget in Norway', in Dogan, M. (ed.), *The Mandarins of Western Europe*, pp. 252-74.

Hobsbawm, E.J. (1962), *The Age of Revolution 1789-1848*, New York, Mentor Books.

Hoover, H. *et al.* (1955), *Commission on Organization of the Executive Branch of the Government – Task Force Report on Personnel and Civil Service*, Washington, D.C.

Howorth, J., and Cerny, P.G. (eds), *Elites in France*, London, Frances Pinter.

Huntington, S.P. (1968), *Political Order in Changing Societies*, Yale University Press.

Jacob, C.E. (1966), *Policy and Bureaucracy*, Princeton, N.J., D.D. Van Nostrand.

Jacobi, H. (1973), *The Bureaucratization of the World* (tr. E.L. Kanes), Berkeley, University of California Press.

Jerusalem Post, and *Jerusalem Post Weekly*, 1980-1982.

Jessop, B. (1977), 'Recent theories of the capitalist state', *Cambridge Journal of Economics*, 1, pp. 353-73.

Jessop, B. (1978), 'Capitalism and democracy', in Littlejohn, G., Smart, B., Wakeford, J., and Yuval-Davis, N. (eds), *Power and the State*, Croom Helm, London, pp. 10-51.

Jessop, B. (1979), 'Corporatism, parliamentarism and social democracy', in Schmitter, P.C. and Lehmbruch, G. (eds), *Trends Toward Corporatist Intermediation*, pp. 185-212.

Johnstone, M. (1979), 'Patrons and clients, jobs and machines', *American Political Science Review*, 73, pp. 385-98.

Jones, B.D., Greenberg, S.R., Kaufman, C., and Drew, J. (1978), 'Service delivery rules and the distribution of local government services', *Journal of Politics*, 40, pp. 334-68.

Jouvenel, B. de (1952), *Power* (rev. edn), London, Batchworth Press.

Kamenka, E., and Erh-Soon Tay, A. (1979), 'Freedom, law and the bureaucratic state', in Kamenka, E. and Krygier, M. (eds), *Bureaucracy: The Career of a Concept*, pp. 112-34.

Kamenka, E. and Krygier, M. (eds) (1979), *Bureaucracy: The Career of a Concept*, London, Edward Arnold.

Kasper, W., Blandy, R., Freebairn, J., Hocking, D., and O'Neill, R. (1980), *Australia at the Crossroads*, Sydney, Harcourt Brace Jovanovich.

Kaufman, H. (1981), 'Fear of Bureaucracy: A raging pandemic', *Public Administration Review*, 41, pp. 1-9.

Keller, S. (1963), *Beyond the Ruling Class*, New York, Random House.

Kellner, P., and Lord Crowther-Hunt (1980), *The Civil Servants*, London, Macdonald.

Kelly, P. (1976), *The Unmaking of Gough*, London, Angus & Robertson.

Key, V.O. Jr (1958), *Politics, Parties and Pressure Groups* (4th edn), New York, Crowell.

King, A. (1975), 'Overload: the problem of governing in the 1970s', *Political Studies*, 23, pp. 284-96.

King, J.P. (1970), 'Socioeconomic development and the incidence of English corrupt campaign practices', in Heidenheimer, A.J. (ed.), *Political Corruption*, pp. 379-90.

Kissinger, H. (1979), *The White House Years*, Sydney, Hodder & Stoughton.

Knight, K. (1961), 'Patronage and the 1894 Royal Commission of Inquiry into the N.S.W. Public Service', *Australian Journal of Politics and History*, 7, pp. 166-85.

Knoke, D. (1979), 'Power Structures' (mimeo), (For *Handbook of Political Behaviour*, Samuel Long, (ed.), Plenum) (second draft).

Krygier, M. (1979a), 'Marxism and Bureaucracy', PhD thesis, Australian National University.

Krygier, M. (1979b), 'State and bureaucracy in Europe', in Kamenka, E., and Krygier, M. (eds), *Bureaucracy: The Career of a Concept*, pp. 1-33.

Krygier, M. (1979c), 'Saint-Simon, Marx and the non-governed society', in Kamenka, E., and Krygier, M. (eds), *Bureaucracy: The Career of a Concept*, pp. 34-60.

Krygier, M. (1979d), 'Weber, Lenin and the reality of socialism', in Kamenka, E. and Krygier, M. (eds), *Bureaucracy: The Career of a Concept*, pp. 61-87.

Langrod, J.S. (1967), 'General problems of the French civil service', in Raphaeli, N. (ed.), *Readings in Comparative Public Administration*, Boston, Allyn & Bacon.

Lanouette, W.J. (1981), 'SES', *National Journal*, 18 July, pp. 1296-9.

La Palombara, J. (1964), *Interest Groups in Italian Politics*, Princeton University Press.

Ledeem, M.A. (1977), *Italy in Crisis*, Beverly Hills, Sage.

Lehmbruch, G. (1979a), 'Consociational democracy, class conflict and the new corporatism', in Schmitter, P.C., and Lehmbruch, G. (eds), *Trends Toward Corporatist Intermediation*, pp. 53-60.

Lehmbruch, G. (1979b), 'Liberal corporatism and party government', in Schmitter, P.C., and Lehmbruch, G. (eds), *Trends Toward Corporatist Intermediation*, pp. 147-83.

Levy, F.S., Meltsher, A.J., and Wildavsky, A. (1974), *Urban Outcomes*, Berkeley, University of California Press.

Lindblom, C.E. (1959), 'The science of muddling through', *Public Administration Review*, 19, pp. 79-88.

Lindblom, C.E. (1965), *The Intelligence of Democracy*, New York, The Free Press.

Lindblom, C.E. (1973), 'Rational policy through mutual adjustment', in Etzioni, A. and Etzioni-Halevy, E. (eds), *Social Change: Sources, Patterns and Consequences*, pp. 493-9.

Lindblom, C.E. (1977), *Politics and Markets*, New York, Basic Books.

Lindblom, C.E. (1979), 'Still muddling, not yet through', *Public Administration Review*, 39, pp. 517-26.

Linebery, R.L. (1977), *Equality and Urban Policy*, Beverly Hills, Sage.

Lior, G. (1981), 'The hottest portfolio', *Yediot Ah'ronot*, 8 July, p. 10.

Lipset, S.M. (1965), *Sociology of Democracy*, Neuwied, H. Luchterhand.

Lloyd, T. (1968), *The General Election of 1880*, Oxford University Press.

Long, N. (1966), 'Power and administration', in Woll, P. (ed.), *Public Administration and Policy*, New York, Harper & Row, pp. 42-57.

Loveday, P. (1959), 'Patronage and politics in New South Wales 1856-1870', *Public Administration* (Sydney), 18, pp. 341-58.

Loveday, P., and Martin, A.W. (1966), *Parliament, Factions and Parties*, Melbourne University Press.

Lowi, T.J. (1969), *The End of Liberalism*, New York, Norton.

Lukas, A.J. (1976), *Nightmare*, New York, Viking Press.

Lukes, S. (1974), *Power: A Radical View*, London, Macmillan.

McConnell, G. (1966), *Private Power and American Democracy*, New York, Alfred Knopf.

McCook, J.J. (1892), 'The alarming proportion of venal votes', *Forum*, 14.

Machin, H. (1977), *The Prefect in French Public Administration*, New York, St. Martin's Press.

MacMullen, A.L. (1979), 'Belgium', in Ridley, F.F. (ed.), *Government Administration in Western Europe*, Oxford, Martin Robertson, pp. 204-26.

MacNeil, N., and Metz, H.W. (1956), *The Hoover Report 1953-1955*, New York, Macmillan.

Mandel, E. (1975), *Late Capitalism* (trans. J. de Bres), London, New Left Books.

Margalit, D. (1978), 'The Lobby', *Ha'aretz*, 27 April.

Marris, P. and Rein, M. (1972), *Dilemmas of Social Reform* (2nd edn), London, Routledge & Kegan Paul.

Marris, R. (1972), 'Is the corporatist economy a corporate state?', *American Economic Review, Papers and Proceedings*, 62, pp. 103-15.

Martin, A.W. (1958), 'Henry Parkes and electoral manipulation, 1872-82', *Historical Studies ANZ*, 8, pp. 268-80.

Marx, K. (1969a), *The Civil War in France*, in Marx, K. and Engels, F., *Selected Works* (in 3 volumes), Moscow, Progress Publishers, vol. 2.

Marx, K. (1969b), *The Class Struggles in France*, in Marx, K. and Engels, F., *Selected Works* (in 3 volumes), vol. 1.

Marx, K. (1969c), *The German Ideology*, in Marx, K. and Engels, F., *Selected Works* (in 3 volumes), vol. 1.

Marx, K. (1969d), *The Eighteenth Brumaire of Louis Bonaparte*, in Marx, K. and Engels, F., *Selected Works* (in 3 volumes), vol. 1.

Marx, K. (1970), *Critique of Hegel's 'Philosophy of Right'*, Cambridge University Press.

Marx, K. and Engels, F. (1969), *Manifesto of the Communist Party*, in Marx, K. and Engels, F., *Selected works* (in 3 volumes), vol. 1.

Medding, P.Y. (1972), *Mapai in Israel*, Cambridge University Press.

Meier, K.I. (1979), *Politics and the Bureaucracy*, North Scituate, Mass., Duxbury Press.

Meltzer, A.H., and Richard, S.F. (1978), 'Why government grows (and grows) in a democracy', *The Public Interest*, 52, pp. 111-18.

Merton, R.K. (1957a), 'Manifest and latent functions', in *Social Theory and Social Structure* (rev. edn), New York, The Free Press, pp. 19-84.

Merton, R.K. (1957b), 'Bureaucratic structure and personality', in *Social Theory and Social Structure* (rev. edn), pp. 195-206.

Meynaud, J. (1964), *Technocracy* (tr. P. Barnes), London, Faber & Faber.

Michels, R. (1915), *Political Parties* (tr. E. and C. Paul), London, Jarrold & Sons.

Miliband, R. (1973), *The State in Capitalist Society*, London, Quartet Books.

Miliband, R. (1977), *Marxism and Politics*, Oxford University Press.

Miller, S. (1981), 'Right on', *Times Higher Education Supplement*, 3 July, pp. 11-13.

Mills, C.W. (1959), *The Power Elite*, New York, Oxford University Press.

Mills, C.W. (1973), 'The sources of societal power', in Etzioni, A., and

Etzioni-Halevy, E. (eds), *Social Change: Sources, Patterns and Consequences*, pp. 123-30.

Milne, E. (1976), *No Shining Armour*, London, John Calder.

Mladenka, K.R. (1980), 'The urban bureaucracy and the Chicago political machine', *American Political Science Review*, 74, pp. 991-8.

Mladenka, K.R., and Hill, K.Q. (1978), 'The distribution of urban police services', *Journal of Politics*, 40, pp. 112-33.

Morlan, R.L. (1949), 'City politics: free style', *National Municipal Review*, 38, pp. 485-90.

Morrison, A.A. (1950), 'Politics in early Queensland', *Royal Historical Society of Queensland Journal*, 4, pp. 293-312.

Morrison, A.A. (1951), 'Religion and politics in Queensland (to 1881)', *Royal Historical Society of Queensland Journal*, 4, pp. 455-70.

Morrison, A.A. (1952), 'The town "liberal" and the squatter', *Royal Historical Society of Queensland Journal*, 4, pp. 599-618.

Morrison, A.A. (1953), 'Liberal Party organization before 1900', *Royal Historical Society of Queensland Journal*, 5, pp. 752-70.

Morrison, A.A. (1960), 'The government of Queensland', in S.R. Davis (ed.), *The Government of the Australian States*, London, Longmans, pp. 249-332.

Morrison, A.A. (1960-1), 'Some lesser members of parliament in Queensland', *Royal Historical Society of Queensland Journal*, 6, pp. 557-79.

Morrison, A.A. (1966), 'Colonial society 1860-1890', *Queensland Heritage*, 1, pp. 21-30.

Mosca, G. (1939), *The Ruling Class* (tr. H.D. Kahn), New York, McGraw Hill.

Mosher, E.C., *et al.* (1974), *Watergate*, New York, Basic Books.

Moulin, L. (1975), 'The Politicization of the administration in Belgium', in Dogan, M. (ed.), *The Mandarins of Western Europe*, pp. 163-85.

Mouzelis, N.P. (1975), *Organization and Bureaucracy*, London, Routledge & Kegan Paul.

Moynihan, D.P. (1969), *Maximum Feasible Misunderstanding*, New York, The Free Press.

Moynihan, D.P. (1978), 'Imperial government', *Commentary*, 65, pp. 25-32.

Moynihan, D.P., and Wilson, J.O. (1966), 'Patronage in New York State 1955-1959', in Herzberg, D.G., and Pomper, G.M. (eds), *American Party Politics*, New York, Holt, Rinehart & Winston, pp. 213-31.

Mukherjee, S.K. (1981), *Crime Trends in Twentieth Century Australia*, Canberra, Australian Institute of Criminology & George Allen & Unwin, Australia.

Musgrave, R.A. (1969), *Fiscal Systems*, New Haven, Yale University Press.

Nachmias, D., and Rosenbloom, D.H. (1980), *Bureaucratic Government, U.S.A.*, New York, St. Martin's Press.

Nairn, N.B. (1967), 'The political mastery of Sir Henry Parkes', *Journal of the Royal Australian Historical Society*, 53, pp. 1-53.

Neal, L. (1978), 'Industrial democracy in the U.K., an employer's view', in *Proceedings of the International Conference on Industrial Democracy, Adelaide, South Australia*, Sydney, CCH Australia, ch. 9.

Nedelman, B., and Meier, K.G. (1979), 'Theories of contemporary corporatism — static or dynamic?', in Schmitter, P.C., and Lehmbruch, G. (eds), *Trends Toward Corporatist Intermediation*, pp. 95-118.

O'Connell, D. (1980), 'Clientelism and political culture in Ireland' (unpublished).

O'Connor, J. (1978), 'The democratic movement in the United States', *Kapitalistate*, 7, pp. 15-26.

OECD (1981a), *Economic Outlook*, no. 29, July, Paris.

OECD (1981b), *Long-Term Trends in Tax Revenues of OECD Member Countries 1955-1980*, Paris.

Offe, C. (1972), 'Political authority and class structures — an analysis of late capitalist societies', *International Journal of Sociology*, 2, pp. 73-108.

Offe, C. (1974), 'Structural problems of the capitalist state', in Von Beyme, K. (ed.), *German Political Studies*, vol. 1, London, Sage.

Offe, C. (1976), *Industrial Inequality* (tr. J. Wickham), London, Edward Arnold.

Office of Management and Budget (1982), *The United States Budget in Brief — Fiscal Year 1982*.

Official Yearbook of the Commonwealth of Australia, nos. 19-64, 1926-1980.

O'Leary, C. (1962), *The Elimination of Corrupt Practices in British Elections 1868-1911*, Oxford, Clarendon Press.

Ostrogorski, M. (1902), *Democracy and the Organization of Political Parties*, New York, Macmillan (in 2 volumes).

Page, C.H. (1946), 'Bureaucracy's other face', *Social Forces*, 25, pp. 89-91.

Pahl, R.E., and Winkler, J.T. (1974), 'The coming corporatism', *New Society*, 30, pp. 72-6.

Panitch, L. (1979), 'The development of corporatism in liberal democracies', in Schmitter, P.C., and Lehmbruch, G. (eds), *Trends Toward Corporatist Intermediation*, pp. 119-46.

Panitch, L. (1980), 'Recent theorizations of corporatism', *British Journal of Sociology*, 31, pp. 159-87.

Panitch, L. (1981), 'Trade unions and the capitalist state', *New Left Review*, 125, pp. 21-43.

Parisi, A., and Pasquino, G. (1979), 'Changes in Italian electoral behaviour', *West European Politics*, 2, pp. 6-30.

Parker, R.S. (1960), 'The government of New South Wales', in Davis, S.R. (ed.), *The Government of the Australian States*, London, Longmans, pp. 55-171.

Parker, S.R., Brown, R.K., Child, J., and Smith, M.A. (1972), *The Sociology of Industry* (2nd edn), London, George Allen & Unwin.

Parkinson, C.N. (1979), *The Law*, Melbourne, Schwartz.

Parris, H. (1969), *Constitutional Bureaucracy*, London, Allen & Unwin.
Pasquino, G. (1979), 'Italian Christian Democracy', *West European Politics*, 2, pp. 88-109.
Passigli, S. (1972), 'Proporzionalismo, frazionismo e crisi dei partiti: quid prior?', *Rivista Italiana di Scienza Politica*, 2, pp. 126-39.
Passigli, S. (1975), 'The ordinary and special bureaucracies in Italy', in Dogan, M. (ed.), *The Mandarins of Western Europe*, pp. 226-37.
Pateman, C. (1970), *Participation and Democratic Theory*, Cambridge University Press.
Patience, A., and Head, B. (1979), *From Whitlam to Fraser*, Melbourne, Oxford University Press.
Peled, M. (1981), 'When was Burg mistaken in his appraisal?', *Ha'aretz*, 8 January, p. 9.
Percival, B. (1974), 'Truffles and politics in Quercy', *Ethnos*, 39, pp. 1-4, 44-52.
Perrow, C. (1979), *Complex Organizations* (2nd edn), Glenview, Ill., Scott, Foresman.
Peters, B.G. (1978), *The Politics of Bureaucracy*, New York, Longman.
Philips, K.P. (1979), 'Political responses to the new class', in Bruce-Briggs, B. (ed.), *The New Class?*, New Brunswick, N.J., Transaction Books, pp. 139-45.
Polanyi, K. (1957), *The Great Transformation*, Boston, Beacon Press.
Polsby, N., and Wildavsky, A.B. (1968), *Presidential Elections* (2nd edn), New York, Charles Scribner's Sons.
Poulantzas, N. (1975), *Political Power and Social Classes*, London, New Left Books.
Poulantzas, N. (1978), *State, Power, Socialism* (tr. P. Camiller), London, New Left Books.
Putnam, R.D. (1975), 'The political attitudes of senior civil servants in Britain, Germany and Italy', in Dogan, M. (ed.), *The Mandarins of Western Europe*, pp. 87-127.
Putnam, R.D. (1976), *The Comparative Study of Political Elites*, Englewood Cliffs, N.J., Prentice Hall.
Randall, R. (1979), 'Presidential power versus bureaucratic intransigence', *American Political Science Review*, 73, pp. 795-810.
Redford, E.S. (1969), *Democracy in the Administrative State*, New York, Oxford University Press.
Rehfus, J. (1973), *Public Administration As Political Process*, New York, Charles Scribner's Sons.
Reichley, J. (1966), 'Reform and organization politics in Philadelphia', in Herzberg, D.G., and Pomper, G.M. (eds), *American Party Politics*, New York, Holt, Rinehart & Winston.
Reid, A. (1976), *The Whitlam Venture*, Melbourne, Hill of Content.
Richards, P.G. (1963), *Patronage in British Government*, London, Allen & Unwin.
Ridley, F., and Blondel, J. (1964), *Public Administration in France*, London, Routledge & Kegan Paul.
Riesman, D. (1961), *The Lonely Crowd*, New Haven, Yale University Press.

Rose, M. (1978), *Industrial Behaviour*, Harmondsworth, Penguin.

Rose, R. (1979), 'Ungovernability: is there fire behind the smoke?', *Political Studies*, 27, pp. 351-70.

Rose, R., and Peters, G. (1978), *Can Governments Go Bankrupt?*, New York, Basic Books.

Rosenberg, H. (1958), *Bureaucracy, Aristocracy and Autocracy*, Boston, Beacon Press.

Rosenbloom, D.H. (1971), *Federal Service and the Constitution*, Ithaca, N.Y., Cornell University Press.

Rourke, F.E. (1965), 'Bureaucracy and public opinion', in Rourke, F.E. (ed.), *Bureaucratic Power in National Politics*, pp. 187-99.

Rourke, F.E. (ed.) (1965), *Bureaucratic Power in National Politics*, Boston, Little Brown.

Rourke, F.E. (1970), 'Urbanism and the national party organizations', in Nelson, W.R. (ed.), *American Government and Political Change*, New York, Oxford University Press, pp. 182-95.

Rourke, F.E. (1976), *Bureaucracy, Politics and Public Policy* (2nd edn), Boston, Little Brown.

Russell, B. (1967), *The Impact of Science on Society*, London, Allen & Unwin.

Safran, W. (1977), *The French Polity*, New York, David McKay.

Salisbury, R.H. (1979), 'Why no corporatism in America?', in Schmitter, P.C., and Lehmbruch, G. (eds), *Trends Toward Corporatist Intermediation*, pp. 213-30.

Salter, J.T. (1935), *Boss Rule*, New York, McGraw Hill.

Sartori, G. (1962), *Democratic Theory*, Detroit, Wayne State University Press.

Sartori, G. (1971), 'Proportionalismo, frazionismo e crisi dei partiti', *Rivista Italiana di Scienza Politica*, pp. 629-55.

Sawer, M. (ed.) (1982), *Australia and the New Right*, Sydney, Allen & Unwin.

Sawer, M. (1982), 'Political Manifestations of Australian Libertarianism', in Sawer, M. (ed.), *Australia and the New Right*, pp. 1-19.

Scharpf, F. (1977), 'Public organizations and the waning of the welfare state', *European Journal of Political Research*, 5, pp. 339-62.

Schattschneider, E.E. (1960), *The Semi-Sovereign People*, New York, Holt Reinhart & Winston.

Schlesinger, J.A. (1975), 'The primary goals of political parties', *American Political Science Review*, 69, pp. 840-9.

Schmitter, P.C. (1979a), 'Still the century of corporatism?', in Schmitter, P.C., and Lehmbruch, G. (eds), *Trends Toward Corporatist Intermediation*, pp. 7-52.

Schmitter, P.C. (1979b), 'Models of interest intermediation and models of societal change in Western Europe', in Schmitter, P.C., and Lehmbruch, G. (eds), *Trends Toward Corporatist Intermediation*, pp. 63-94.

Schmitter, P.C., and Lehmbruch, G. (eds) (1979), *Trends Toward Corporatist Intermediation*, Beverly Hills, Sage Publications.

Schonfeld, W.R. (1981), 'The "closed" worlds of socialist and Gaullist elites', in Howorth, J., and Cerny, P.G. (eds), *Elites in France*, pp. 196-215.

Schultze, C.L. (1977), *The Public Use of Private Interest*, Washington D.C., The Brookings Institution.

Schumpeter, J. (1966), *Capitalism, Socialism and Democracy*, London, Unwin University Books.

Scott, J.C. (1973), *Comparative Political Corruption*, Englewood Cliffs, N.J., Prentice Hall.

Searls, E. (1981), 'Ministerial cabinets and elite theory', in Howorth, J., and Cerny, P.G. (eds), *Elites in France*, pp. 162-80.

Sedgemore, B. (1980), *The Secret Constitution*, London, Hodder & Stoughton.

Self, P. (1972), *Administrative Theories and Politics*, London, Allen & Unwin.

Serle, G. (1971), *The Rush to be Rich*, Melbourne, University Press.

Sexton, M. (1979), *Illusions of Power*, Sydney, Allen & Unwin.

Shapiro, Y. (1975), *The Organization of Power*, Tel-Aviv, Am Oved (Hebrew).

Shapiro, Y. (1977), *Democracy in Israel*, Ramat Gan, Massada (Hebrew).

Sharkansky, I., and Van Meter, D. (1975), *Policy and Politics in American Governments*, New York, McGraw Hill.

Sharp, W.R. (1931), *The French Civil Service*, New York, Macmillan.

Shonfield, A. (1965), *Modern Capitalism*, London, Oxford University Press.

Simon, H.A., Smithburg, D.W., and Thomson, V.A. (1965), 'The struggle for organizational survival', in Rourke, F.E. (ed.), *Bureaucratic Power in National Politics*, pp. 39-49.

Sisson, C.H. (1971), 'The politician as intruder', in Chapman, R.A., and Dunsire, F.J. (eds), *Style in Administration*, London, Allen & Unwin, pp. 448-56.

Smith, B.L.R. (ed.) (1975), *The New Political Economy*, London, Macmillan.

Sorauf, F.J. (1956), 'State patronage in a rural county', *American Political Science Review*, 50, pp. 1046-56.

Sorauf, F.J. (1960), 'The silent revolution in patronage', *Public Administration Review*, 20, pp. 28-34.

Spann, R.N. (1972), *The Public Bureaucracy in Australia*, AIPS Monographs, no. 8.

Spann, R.N. (1973), 'Bureaucracy and the public service', in Mayer, H., and Nelson, H. (eds), *Politics: a Third Reader*, Melbourne, Cheshire, pp. 579-612.

Speed, J.G. (1970), 'The purchase of votes in New York city', in Heidenheimer, A.J. (ed.), *Political Corruption*, pp. 422-6.

Steffens, J.L. (1904), *The Shame of the Cities* (republished 1948), New York, P. Smith.

Steinberg (1972), *The Bosses*, New York, New American Library.

Stevens, A. (1978), 'Politicisation and cohesion in the French administration', *West European Politics*, 1, pp. 68-80.

Stirling, P. (1968), 'Impartiality and personal morality (Italy)', in J.G. Peristiani (ed.), *Contributions to Mediterranean Sociology*, The Hague, Mouton.

Strauss, E. (1961), *The Ruling Servants*, London, Allen & Unwin.

Suleiman, E.N. (1974), *Politics, Power and Bureaucracy in France*, Princeton University Press.

Sydney Morning Herald (1976), 22 November.

Therborn, G. (1977), 'The rule of capital and the rise of democracy', *New Left Review*, 103, pp. 3-41.

Therborn, G. (1978), *What Does the Ruling Class Do When it Rules?*, London, New Left Books.

Thoenig, J.C. (1978), 'State bureaucracies and local government in France', in Hanf, K., and Sharpf, F.W. (eds), *Interorganizational Policy Making*, London, Sage Publications, pp. 167-97.

Thomson, D. (1966), *Europe Since Napoleon* (rev. edn), Harmondsworth, Pelican Books.

Thomson, V.A. (1965), 'Bureaucracy in a democratic society', in Martin, R.C. (ed.), *Public Administration and Democracy*, Syracuse University Press, pp. 205-26.

Times, The (1976), 15 November.

Toffler, A. (1970), *Future Shock*, New York, Random House.

U.S. Budget in Brief, Fiscal Year 1982.

U.S. Bureau of the Census, *Statistical Abstract of the United States, 1978, 1980, 1982*, Washington.

U.S. Financial Statement and Budget Report 1981-82.

[U.S.] Monthly Labor Review, August 1981.

Van Hassel, H. (1975), 'Belgian civil service and political decision making', in Dogan, M. (ed.), *The Mandarins of Western Europe*, pp. 187-95.

Van Riper, P.P. (1958), *History of the United States Civil Service*, Evanston, Ill., Row, Peterson.

Waldo, D. (1948), *The Administrative State*, New York, The Ronald Press Company.

Wallfish, A., and Bar, Y. (1981), 'Probe urged into sacking of police chief', *Jerusalem Post Weekly*, 4-10 January, p. 1.

Weber, M. (1924), 'Der sozialismus', in *Gesammelte Aufsätze zur Soziologie und Sozialpolitik*, Tübingen, J.C.B. Mohr.

Weber, M. (1947), *The Theory of Social and Economic Organization* (tr. A.M. Henderson), New York, The Free Press.

Weber, M. (1958), *The Protestant Ethic and the Spirit of Capitalism* (tr. T. Parsons), New York, Charles Scribner's Sons.

Weber, M. (1968), *Economy and Society*, vols 1-111, New York, Bedminster Press.

Weber, M. (1976), 'Some consequences of bureaucratization', in Coser, L.A., and Rosenberg, B. (eds), *Sociological Theory* (4th edn), New York, Macmillan, pp. 361-2.

Weingrod, A. (1968), 'Patrons, patronage and political parties', *Comparative Studies in Society and History*, 10, pp. 377-400.

Weller, P., and Grattan, M. (1981), *Can Ministers Cope?*, Hutchinson of Australia.

Wettenhall, R.L. (1973), 'The ministerial department', *Public Administration* (Sydney), 32, pp. 233-50.

White, C. (1980), *Patrons and Partisans*, New York, Cambridge University Press.

White, L.D. (1935), *Government Career Service*, University of Chicago Press.

White, L.D. (1945), 'Franklin Roosevelt and the public service', *Public Personnel Review*, 6, pp. 139-46.

White, L.D. (1951), *The Jeffersonians*, Macmillan, New York.

White, L.D. (1954), *The Jacksonians*, Macmillan, New York.

White, L.D. (1958), *The Republican Era*, Macmillan, New York.

Wildavsky, A. (1973), 'Government and the people', *Commentary*, 56, pp. 25-32.

Wilensky, H.L. (1975), *The Welfare State and Equality*, Berkeley, University of California Press.

Williams, P.M. (1954), *Politics in Post-War France*, London, Longmans, Green & Company.

Williams, P.M. (1964), *Crisis and Compromise* (3rd edn), London, Longmans, Green & Company.

Wilson, R.A., and Schultz, D.A. (1978), *Urban Sociology*, Englewood Cliffs, N.J., Prentice Hall.

Wiltshire, K. (1974), *An Introduction to Australian Public Administration*, Melbourne, Cassell.

Winkler, J.T. (1976), 'Corporatism', *European Journal of Sociology*, 17, pp. 100-36.

Winkler, J.T. (1977), 'The corporatist economy', in Scase, R. (ed.), *Industrial Society*, London, Allen & Unwin, pp. 43-58.

Wolfe, A. (1977), *The Limits of Legitimacy*, New York, The Free Press.

Woll, P.C. (1966), *Public Administration and Policy*, New York, Harper & Row.

World Almanac, The (1981), New York, Newspaper Enterprise Association.

Wright, E.O. (1978), *Class, Crisis and the State*, London, New Left Books.

Wright, V. (1978), *The Government and Politics of France*, Hutchinson of London.

Yediot Ah'ronot (1981), 8 July.

Zuckerman, A. (1975), *Political Clienteles in Power*, Beverly Hills, Sage Publications.

Index

absolutism, 29-30, 41, 53
Akzin, B. and Dror, Y., 169
Albrow, M., 52
anti-statist movements, 3, 131-6
Arendt, Hanna, 38
Armstrong, Lord, 151, 153
Australia, 199, 223; anti-statism
in, 133-4; breakdown between
Labor Party and Treasury,
215-16; bureaucracy, 123,
161-4; bureaucracy and
electoral manipulation in,
182-4; Committee of Review
of Administrative Functions,
136; controls on corruption,
184; Coombs Royal Commis-
sion of Enquiry, 94; economic
development in, 136, 137;
Gough Whitlam, 213, 214-15,
217, 224; government spending, 3, 213-19; Labor Party,
213-19; Liberal and National
Country Party, 140, 213;
Liberal Party, 135, 163, 217;
Libertarians, 134; loans,
214-15, 217; Malcolm Fraser,
135, 136, 213, 217; national
elections, 184; neutrality of
bureaucracy, 163-4; New
Right, 134; Northcote-
Trevelyan Report, 162; Prime
Minister's Department, 59;
Progress Party, 134-5; Public
Service Board, 162, 163; secret
ballot, 183; size of bureaucracy,

139; Treasury, 213-19, 223;
voucher system of education,
140
Austria, 65
authoritarian states, 77, 78, 84
authority, 27-8

Bailey, F.G , 193
Balogh, Lord, 150
Balzac, Honoré de, 9
Barker, E., 106
Belgium, 200; bureaucracy,
175-7; bureaucracy and
electoral manipulation, 198-9;
partisan selection system,
176-7; reforms in civil service,
176
Bell, D., 45, 113, 120, 141
Bennis, Warren, 1, 40
Bensman, J. and Rosenberg, B.,
35-6
Benziman, U., 191
Bland, F.A., 162
bureaucracy, 2, 40, 202, 203,
225-9; anti-statism, 3, 131-6;
ascendancy of, 60-1;
bureaucratic services, 145;
bureaucratic-technocratic
elites, 55; causes friction in
democracies, 97-8; corporatism
and, 69-71; curbing growth of,
136-8; definition of, 85;
democracy and, 2, 3, 32-5;
democracy: dilemma for b.,
87, 92-7; development of b.,

149-50; Lord Armstrong, 151, 153; Lord Balogh on, 150; overrode by politicians, 156-7; relationship with politicians, 60, 92, 148-9, 157-8; Report of the Hoover Commission, 95-6; *The Civil Servants*, 93; in United States, 165-8
Cole, R.L. and Caputo, D.A., 167
collectivism, 17-18
communism, 13, 17, 25, 34
Coombs Royal Commission of Enquiry on the Australian Government Administration (1977), 94-5
corporate organizations, 63
corporatism/corporatists, 63, 72-3, 146, 232; bourgeois-democratic c., 67; centralized trade union leadership, 73; church and, 72-3; compared with other schools of thought, 63-4; corporate organizations, 63; c. and bureaucracy, 69-71; c. and democracy, 68-9; definition of, 63; development of, 64-5; elitist theory and, 71-2; fascism and, 64-5, 66; importance of leadership, 63, 64; informality of, 69-70; need for centralization, 64; neo-Marxism and, 64, 66; public administration and, 70; reinforces the ruling class, 66-8; significance of, 71; societal c., 65; state c., 65; trade unions and, 67, 68, 72; types of, 65-6; in Western Europe, 64-5, 68
corruption, 47, 52, 91, 121, 178-9, 180, 181-2, 183-4, 186, 197, 200
Covell, M., 177
Crossman, Richard, 158
Crouch, C., 66, 67-8
Crozier, M., 40, 45, 48

Dahl, Robert, 42, 46, 47
Dahrendorf, R., 124

Debbasch, C., 60
democracies: Western, 4, 44, 49, 66, 72, 82-3; capitalist class in, 75; corporatism, 64-5, 67, 68, 69; development of bureaucracies in, 5, 89-90; development of democracy in, 89-90; economies of, 142-3; mandarins in, 71; militancy in, 67; relations with politics, 5; societal corporatism in, 66, 71; statements by participants in, 149-57
democracy, 41, 202, 203, 225-9, 233n., 234n.; bureaucracy and, 32-5, 78-81; bureaucracy: dilemma for, 87, 90-8; communism and, 13; corporatism and, 68-9; crisis situation, 1, 48; definition of, 86-7; evolution of, 120-1; Marxist view of, 76-8; Marx's view of, 13, 24, 83-4; Michel's views on, 19-20; Mosca's views on, 16-17, 24-5; pluralism and, 46-50; power struggles caused by bureaucracy, 87-8, 97-8; preservation of, 4-5; relationship with bureaucracy, 5; threatened by bureaucracy, 2, 3, 5, 33-4, 55-6, 60-1, 62, 78, 80, 89, 158, 159, 227; Weber's ideas on, 31
Diamant, A., 70-1, 73
Dickey, B., 183
DiPalma, G., 172
Dogan, M., 55, 60, 177
Domhoff, G., 51, 76
Downs, A., 86
Duverger, M., 173
Dye, T.R. and Zeigler, L.H., 4-5, 54

economic crises, 121-3
Edwards, J., 218
Ehrmann, H.W., 195
Eisenstadt, S.N., 189
Eisenstadt, S.N. and Von Beyme, K., 13, 107